INTERNATIONAL ACCLAIM FOR
AMERICAN ENGLISH FOR WORLD MEDIA

"A perfect book for the non-native English-speaker working in journalism. It reads like a breeze, packs in tips and interviews, and will raise your craft to the next level. Come to think of it, the native speaker has a lot to gain, too."
> —*John Darnton*, The New York Times; *Curator, Polk Awards*

"Diane Nottle combines a distinguished editing career with extensive experience teaching nonnative speakers. So it makes sense that this clear, concise and thorough guide hits just the right notes for international journalists aiming for English-language media. She anticipates their questions, fills in their cultural blanks and demystifies the idiom they never learned in school."
> —*Jack R. Hart, author,* Storycraft *and* A Writer's Coach: The Complete Guide to Writing Strategies That Work

"I wish such a book existed a quarter century ago when I first started out as a Chinese-born freelance journalist, writing in English for international publications. I could have benefited from both tips in writing proper English and some basic journalist techniques. And my copy editors at various newspapers would have had an easier time. I trust plenty of others in a similar position will find this compact book very useful!"
> —*Lijia Zhang, freelance journalist, author,* "Socialism Is Great!" A Worker's Memoir of the New China

"For those who aspire to work with English-language media, the ability to write in concise and engaging journalistic style is important. It is also a highly valued skill for those in China who want to take advantage of the opportunities presented by the country's development and opening-up. Diane Nottle's book is a step-by-step guidebook to learning professional media writing and thinking in English."

—*Ji Tao, Editor in Chief,* China Daily USA

"Diane Nottle's *American English for World Media* is not just a great language textbook for international media specialists. It is a well thought-out introduction to the world and culture of American journalism, written with both intimate insider knowledge and sensitivity to an international audience."

—*Dr. Hana Cervinkova, Director, International Institute for the Study of Culture and Education, University of Lower Silesia, Poland*

"A significant addition to the English for Specific Purposes field, *American English for World Media* is an essential guide for any international student of journalism working in the English language. Diane Nottle draws on her years as an accomplished journalist and trained teacher of English to non-native speakers, bringing rich experience and advice from a deeply informed community to the field of English-Language journalism. She has produced a text that is insightful, engaging, fine-grained and utterly pragmatic."

—*Caitlin Morgan, Director of English-Language Studies, The New School*

"*American English for World Media* is a much-needed resource for international journalists who want to understand and gain fluency in the many nuances of our language."

—*Ed Madison, Ph.D., University of Oregon School of Journalism; author,* Newsworthy

"Though *American English for World Media* is written for an international audience, it's a useful primer, refresher and reference book for anyone who works in today's crowded and confusing media world. From practical tips on how to approach sources to its succinct discussion of how journalism has changed, it's a survey of American journalism practices, pitfalls and platforms."

—*Merrill Perlman, former Managing Editor,*
New York Times News Service

"Finally! A must for journalists and aspiring journalists around the world who may need to work in English but for whom it is not their native language. Also a must for all those journalists who still struggle with *which* and *that* or *who* and *whom* and other pesky English-language oddities. From journalism jargon to idioms to pronunciation tips, and from antecedents to danglers, verb tenses and writing tightly, this indispensable volume includes it all—and more. I wish this had been around when I first started working with international journalists but am thrilled it's here now."

—*Michelle Betz, Project Administrator, Media Foundation*
360 and NearMedia LLC; former Director, UPI Next

"Diane Nottle has managed to squeeze the complexities encountered by journalists working with English as a foreign language into 200 pages abounding in problems that range from the simple choice of words to the macrostructure of a pitch and story, and from single sounds and their assimilation to questions of stress and intonation in oral language. *American English for World Media*, with its invaluable examples of improved versions of the same texts, is a must to be included in any course combining media studies and EFL."

—*Daniela Martino, Professor of English Language and Literature,*
Instituto Superior de Formación Docente y Técnica #8
(Technical and Teacher Training College #8), Radio
Broadcasting College of Buenos Aires

"CUNY's guide is a much-needed tool that promises to equip journalists, journalism and media teachers, and the ubiquitous citizen journalist. Today's one-man-army reporter who doesn't have the luxury of a copy editor will find this guide handy. The Arab world, believing that the accurate use of language has the power to unite diverse worlds, heartily welcomes this book."

—*Dr. Swapna Koshy, Associate Professor, University of Wollongong in Dubai*

"*American English for World Media* is a comprehensive book that touches upon the intricacies of the American branch of the English language. This book is perfect for novice journalists and experts alike. Diane Nottle discusses the problems faced by journalists while also providing viable solutions to hone their skills. She pushes all the right buttons; her experience and wisdom can be seen clearly as she engages the audience by using a minimalistic approach that makes the book entertaining to read, and easy to understand.

—*Mubasher Bukhari, Executive Editor, News Lens Pakistan; President, Media Foundation360*

AMERICAN ENGLISH FOR WORLD MEDIA

AMERICAN ENGLISH FOR WORLD MEDIA

The CUNY Journalism School Guide to Writing and Speaking for Professionals

Diane Nottle

TOW-KNIGHT CENTER FOR ENTREPRENEURIAL JOURNALISM

The City University of New York
CUNYJOURNALISM PRESS

CUNY JOURNALISM PRESS IS THE ACADEMIC IMPRINT OF THE CUNY GRADUATE
SCHOOL OF JOURNALISM, PART OF THE CITY UNIVERSITY OF NEW YORK
219 WEST 40TH STREET, NEW YORK, NY 10018
WWW.PRESS.JOURNALISM.CUNY.EDU

First printing 2016

Cataloging-in-Publication data is available from the Library of Congress.
A catalog record for this book is available from the British Library.

ISBN 978-1-68219-058-6 paperback
ISBN 978-1-68219-060-9 e-book

Typeset by AarkMany Media, Chennai, India. Printed by BookMobile in the
United States and CPI Books Ltd in the United Kingdom.

FOREWORD

Is news singular or plural? What's the correct way to ask a question in English? What does *beat around the bush* mean, or *strike while the iron is hot*? How can you be sure you're quoting sources accurately?

If you can't answer questions like these, your English-language skills may not match your ambitions for an international media career. But *American English for World Media* can help.

Language is a foundation of the journalist's craft. The four basic skills in any language are listening, speaking, reading and writing. As English becomes an increasingly global language, media professionals worldwide need them all: to do research, to conduct interviews, to write for an international audience, to make their audio and video marketable, to communicate with their peers.

This book was written for international journalists who have studied English but may not have used it professionally. Native speakers, too, will find it an invaluable guide, the missing link between what they learned in English class (if they were paying attention) and professional standards of usage.

Founded in 2006, on the cusp of the digital revolution, the City University of New York Graduate School of Journalism propels its graduates to careers in traditional and new media—*The New York Times*, Bloomberg, network television, Buzzfeed and their own startups, to name just a few. At CUNY, along with digital training for the 21st century, students master the foundations of their craft to produce clear, clean writing and speech for any medium.

In *American English for World Media*, you'll find:

- A guide to the professional jargon and forms you'll need to use from day one of working with English-language media.
- A review of the journalist's No. 1 task: asking questions.
- Tips on quoting accurately when interviewing in a language that is not your own (and may not be your source's).
- Advice on correcting and preventing the most common mistakes in writing and pronunciation.
- American idioms and how to use them wisely.
- A reader-friendly A-to-Z guide (searchable in the e-book) to English grammar and usage that lays down the rules and explains the reasoning behind them.

Throughout, you'll hear the voices of CUNY's professors—who are not only teachers, but also seasoned, working media professionals—along with journalists-in-training, who supply real-life illustrations of English in action.

American English for World Media is an up-to-the-minute guide and reference for media professionals and anyone else who needs to communicate in professional-level English.

Timothy Harper
Writing Coach
CUNY Graduate School of Journalism

ABOUT THE AUTHOR

DIANE NOTTLE coaches the international students at the City University of New York Graduate School of Journalism, where she founded the English for Journalists blog (www.englishforjournalists .journalism.cuny.edu).

As a journalist, she spent 35 years in daily newspapers, including 20 years as an editor at *The New York Times* specializing in arts and culture. Previously an editor at *The Boston Globe, The Rochester Democrat & Chronicle* and *The Roanoke Times,* she has published hundreds of articles in newspapers and magazines nationwide and abroad.

As an educator, she has taught journalism at Jinan University in Guangzhou, China; the University of British Columbia in Vancouver; Colorado State University, and Emerson College. Since earning a certificate in English language teaching from the New School in New York in 2008, she has taught English in Columbia University's American Language Program; at the University of Lower Silesia in Wroclaw, Poland, most recently as a Fulbright senior specialist; and at Hunan University of Science and Technology in Xiangtan, China. She is based in Manhattan.

CONTENTS

To Mrs. Adams

INTRODUCTION

There is no more underappreciated part of a news operation than the copy desk. (Just look at the number of copy editors who've been downsized out of their jobs in recent years.) And there is no better place to polish your English. Ask Camilo Gomez and Elena Popina.

In 2013, Gomez enrolled in the master's degree program at the City University of New York Graduate School of Journalism. He had already worked in the press office at the Ministry of Culture in his homeland, Colombia. His English was more than fluent, since he had started learning it at an early age. A core feature of the CUNY master's program is the mandatory summer internship between the second and final semesters, and Gomez landed a plum: an editing internship at the copy desk on *The Detroit News*, courtesy of financial help from the Dow Jones News Fund.

During a training program and the internship itself, he learned many lessons about English. "I learned about compound adjectives," he said, looking back. "I didn't know that there was a rule for hyphenating compound words that could be explained in the case of adjectives. I also improved my knowledge of punctuation—especially where to put commas." Writing headlines "forced me to expand my vocabulary," he added. Perhaps most important, "I became more curious about grammar and willing to look things up when I had doubts. Since most of the time the headline wouldn't fit, I had to use the dictionary and thesaurus quite often. Also, I would go to them whenever I had doubts about a word's exact meaning. Sometimes, I had to look up words or idiomatic expressions that I had never seen before and was glad to notice that many of them were either informal or exclusive to North America— which made me feel better about not knowing, as I had only been living here for a year." In short, looking things up became a good work habit: "I ended up learning them through having to look things up, again and again."

Elena Popina, a Russian in the CUNY class of 2013, planned but then had to skip a postgraduate semester when she became the first international student to win a coveted winter internship at Bloomberg, followed immediately by a job there as a staff writer. She had been polishing her English since she arrived at CUNY in 2012, rarely letting a week go by without a coaching session. From her editors first at *Crain's New York Business* and later at Bloomberg, she said, she learned many things about English: that the same verb can have radically different meanings when paired with adverbs in phrasals (*put off* versus *put aside*, for example); that words commonly used in speaking are less appropriate in writing (*a lot of* versus *many*); that "being concise made me friends with my editor." Perhaps her most eye-opening lesson came "after I saw four native-English editors disputing over whether the sentence one of them was editing needed *a, the* or nothing at all."

That's right: the experts don't always agree on what is correct English. Sometimes even they have to look it up.

Gomez and Popina are just two of the 600,000 journalists working in 134 countries, according to a 2013 estimate by the International Federation of Journalists. The British Council says more than a billion people worldwide are studying English. Where those two circles overlap are the readers of *American English for World Media*: journalists and other media professionals whose native language is not English, but who need to use English in their work.

Some may need English in their current jobs, others to fulfill their ambitions to publish beyond their homelands or to work in international media. They may dream of becoming foreign correspondents. They may want to work for international news bureaus in their homelands, like Dith Pran, the Cambodian translator for *The New York Times* immortalized in *The Killing Fields*—and by his later career as a *Times* photographer in New York. They may hope to freelance for international outlets. Or they may be preparing to start their own, like Mike Paterakis from Greece, class of 2013. His project in entrepreneurial journalism (see Chapter 1) was a website to report on how European Union policies affect ordinary citizens of member nations. In what language? English.

English is rapidly becoming the *lingua franca* of the 21st century, and international media professionals need to become both competent and comfortable in using it. But how? You may have studied it in school, but school English is not street English. Spellcheck will not catch every flaw, and grammar check may be more confusing than enlightening. In many parts of the world, contact with native speakers may be limited— or nonexistent. And you may not have the opportunity to study at a professional school like CUNY. This book brings CUNY's English-language coaching to you.

In fall 2012, after nearly four decades of daily newspaper editing, I began coaching the international students—officially defined as those who have come straight from their homelands—at the CUNY journalism school. Before long, I was also seeing U.S. citizens or longtime permanent residents who still had a few problems, a few refinements to make in their writing or speaking. For all of these students, the goal is to bring their English as close to a native speaker's as possible. Together we work on their writing assignments, sometimes draft after draft after draft. But coaching is by no means limited to writing. Students in programs such as entrepreneurial journalism, who make sophisticated pitches to venture capitalists, ask me to critique their proposals, their slideshows and their presentation skills. Those in broadcast bring me their scripts to improve and rehearse. One student, Natalia V. Osipova, asked for a fresh eye on the subtitles on her video capstone (the school's word for thesis), much of which consisted of interviews in Russian. That video was posted online by *The New York Times* (http://www.nytimes.com/video/nyregion/100000001996949/protesters-from-afar.html), where Osipova is now on staff.

Whenever I have taught journalism, international students and native speakers alike have been unanimous on what they consider the most valuable part of the experience: the opportunity to work with, and learn from, a professional editor. Any good editor is also a teacher and mentor, working closely with reporters to impart the reasoning behind the editing, in the hope that they will absorb it and get it right in the next story and beyond. That's what makes the copy desk such a good place to learn, whether the learner is editing like Camilo Gomez or being edited like Elena Popina and countless other journalists. It is the premise behind *American English for World Media*.

English is a difficult language to learn, a mongrel born of mixed ancestry. Being an island, Britain was long vulnerable to invasion from all sides. The origins of its language go back thousands of years, first to the tribes native to the British Isles, then to the Celts from the Continent who settled there. Two thousand or so years ago, the Romans invaded, bringing their language, Latin, which contributed the roots of so many English words that an English lesson with me often feels like Latin class. Five centuries later came the Germanic Anglo-Saxon tribes, who brought their own language into the mix; still later came the Vikings, adding Scandinavian influences. Finally, in 1066, came the Normans, whose French language was rooted in Latin but with a thousand years of evolution layered over it. The mixture of all those languages, plus a bit of Greek thrown in, form the basis of English as spoken today.

In the United States, the languages of indigenous American peoples add another layer, contributing words like *moccasin* and *succotash* and *skunk*, as well as place names like *Connecticut* and *Massachusetts*—each a mouthful for many non-native English-speakers. American English has since expanded with the continuing waves of immigration. Words have been lifted directly from Spanish (*guerrilla*), French (*detente, en route*), German (*Schadenfreude, gesundheit*), Italian (*graffiti, solo*) and, in New York, Yiddish (*shlep, bagel, mishegas, mensch*). As the nation and its population continue to evolve, words like *bonsai* and *feng shui* and *pho* have become part of everyday conversation.

In part because English is such a mongrel, it has more than one way to express just about anything. For example, its curse words—short, strong and frowned upon in polite company—tend to have Celtic or Anglo-Saxon roots, while euphemisms and elegant variations (see Chapter 10) come from Latin or French. Think of *posterior* (Latin) or *derrière* (French) versus just plain *ass* (Celtic). Which choice is best? That depends on the occasion and the impression you or your publication wants to make. So much in English is nuance that, in speaking or writing, saying precisely what you mean is often a matter of making the best choice.

Many English language-learners outside the United States are taught British English rather than American. The idea that "England and America are two countries divided by a common language" has been variously attributed to Oscar Wilde, George Bernard Shaw and Winston Churchill, but whoever said it, the idea is clear: British and American English are two different animals. The differences fall roughly into three categories: pronunciation, spelling and usage. An American television audience will understand you if you say *to-mah-to* instead of *to-may-to, die-rect instead of duh-rect*; an American copy editor will quietly change your *labour* to *labor, organise* to *organize, programme* to *program*. But if you report that "observers said they were *gobsmacked* by how *knackered* the president appeared as he began his *holiday*," your American audience may not know what you're talking about. (Translation: observers were *amazed* by how *exhausted* the president appeared as he began his *vacation*.) At CUNY we work in American English, hence the focus of this book. But important British variations (and their Canadian and Australian offshoots) are noted.

At CUNY, I have worked with graduate students and professionals from more than a dozen countries, and the list keeps growing with each year's new admissions: Argentina, Austria, Belarus, Belgium, Brazil, China, Colombia, Denmark, Ecuador, France, Greece, India, Italy, Japan, Morocco, Nepal, Portugal, Russia, Spain, Taiwan, Thailand, Uruguay, Vietnam. They speak nearly as many native languages, and each brings its own problems to their work, be they different sentence structures, English sounds that don't exist in their languages, or concepts for which English has no word. Still, the international students' work shares many common flaws.

A few weeks after I arrived at CUNY, the school's IT director, Dan Reshef, made an offhand remark while setting me up in the system: "If you find the students are making a lot of the same mistakes, you might want to blog about it." That was the genesis of English for Journalists (www.englishforjournalists.journalism.cuny.edu), which now regularly draws up to 1,500 hits a month and was read in 138 countries in 2015. As I write, there have been nearly 60 blog posts, on subjects from articles to wordiness; this book covers many more points. Though based on the blog, it is not merely a reprint.

Nor is this a stylebook, a guide to usage adopted by a particular news organization. (The journalism school follows Associated Press style.) While this book lays down the rules, it also explains the reasoning behind them. When teaching English, I always stress how important it is to understand—to put it in journalistic terms—not just the "what," but the "why." (See 5W's, p. 31.) When learners understand the "why" behind a grammar point, they are far more likely to absorb it. With luck and repeated use, it should eventually become automatic.

The examples cited are drawn largely from the reporting-based coursework of CUNY's journalists-in-training. While Dan Reshef phrased his suggestion in terms of "mistakes," I encourage students to think in terms of "improvements"; so often, an edit isn't a matter of being wrong, but being not quite right, or idiomatic. These are, in fact, the same kinds of improvements a professional copy desk would make on reporters' copy. Novice or veteran, native speaker or not, every writer needs editing.

Newspaper people used to joke that "broadcast journalism" was an oxymoron—a contradiction in terms—but in the 21st century, journalism isn't just about writing anymore, especially as news "papers" shift to the Internet and incorporate more and more video and interactive features. The principles of English expressed in this book apply to all forms of communication: print, television, radio, online, social media, app or some other medium not yet invented. Who among the language-conscious hasn't groaned at hearing a TV reporter use garbled grammar, been befuddled by a poorly constructed sentence on a website, or shaken her head at spellings clearly derived from text messages? This book's mission is to apply the high standards of editing for print to the news media of the early 21st century and beyond. Speed, convenience and conversation may be the goals, but in communicating clearly with the widest possible audience, good English still beats all.

FIRST, A REFRESHER

Maybe you studied English in school, or at a university as part of your journalism training. Maybe your study was less formal if you were, for example, an immigrant learning survival English. Maybe you practice with books, movies, travel or conversation with English-speakers. In any of these cases, you probably have a working proficiency.

This book was written with media professionals at the high-intermediate and advanced levels in mind. It frequently uses basic grammatical terms that may be unfamiliar to those who learned English outside the classroom. Whether as an introduction or a review, here are brief definitions of key terms used throughout the book.

PARTS OF SPEECH

Each word in a sentence has a particular function, technically termed *part of speech*. English has eight or nine of them, depending on who's counting. Here are the mostly widely recognized parts of speech.

noun As American schoolchildren learn to recite in singsong, "a noun is the name of a person, place or thing." That pretty much sums it up. Nouns may be used as *subjects* (performing the action in a sentence) or *objects* (receiving the action). Nouns do not have gender in English, as they do in many other languages, but they do have *number*—singular or plural. Adjectives do not have number and do not change form.

verb A verb denotes an action (*report, edit, interview, verify, corroborate*) or a state of being (forms of *be*). The verb indicates whether a sentence is in *active voice* (the subject acts) or *passive* (the subject is acted upon), with active voice preferred in journalism whenever possible. (See page 191.) English verbs must agree with their subjects in number; a singular subject takes the singular verb, while plural subjects take plural verbs. The *base verb* of a regular verb is the simple present tense in first person singular (I). The *infinitive*, a verb form used as a noun, is *to* + *base*. (See page 210.) In English as in many other languages, verbs have *tense*—that is, different forms indicating whether the action takes place in the past, present or future. Depending on the tense, the verb may include an *auxiliary*, or helper verb, like *is, do* or *have*.

adjective A word that modifies, or describes, a noun.

adverb A word that modifies a verb.

pronoun A substitute for a noun, often to avoid repetition. The most common pronouns are *I, me, you* (singular or plural), *he, him, she, her, it, we* and *they*. (Those whose native language, like Chinese, doesn't distinguish between masculine and feminine in pronouns need to be especially careful with the third person singular: *he* and *she*.) Possessive pronouns are *my, your, his, her, its, our* and *their*. Relative pronouns, which "relate" one part of sentence to another, include *who, whose, which* and *that*. Reflexive pronouns are the ones containing *-self: myself, yourself, ourselves, themselves*, etc. (See page 261.)

preposition Often short words—in, *for, of, on, to, with, up, down, like* and dozens of others—that indicate the relationship between one part of speech and another. Prepositions always appear in *prepositional phrases*, with nouns as their objects: *down the hill, on the road, to the lighthouse*. Entire prepositional phrases may function as adjectives (*the fool on the hill*) or adverbs (*he ran like the wind*). If a word you recognize as a preposition appears without an object, it is probably functioning as an adverb (*he looked up*) or as part of *phrasal verb*, a verb plus adverb that has a specific meaning (*If you don't know a word, look it up in the dictionary*).

article Those three little words—*a, an, the*—whose size belies their importance in English. (See page 198.) *A* and *an* indicate any (noun): *a newspaper, an aggregator. The* indicates a specific (noun): *the paper, the website. The* may be singular or plural, but *a* and *an* are always singular.

conjunction A word that connects other words or parts of sentences. The word *conjunction* is derived from the Latin roots *con-* (together) and *junct-* (join). The most common conjunctions are *and, but* and *or.*

interjection A word or phrase *parenthetical* to the sentence (that is, easily removed without the danger of not making sense) and often used to express surprise or shock: *Oh, no! Gee whiz! Holy cow!*

SENTENCE, CLAUSE, PHRASE

A sentence is a sequence of words that expresses a complete thought. It typically consists of a *subject* (noun) and a *predicate* (verb plus object, adjective or noun, or none of those). The smallest unit that expresses a complete thought is a *clause*; two or more clauses may be joined in a single sentence. (See below.) A *phrase* is any group of a few words, generally not expressing a complete thought.

COMPOUND AND COMPLEX SENTENCES

A *compound sentence* consists of more than one clause of equal weight connected by a conjunction: *It's raining, but I don't have an umbrella.* A *complex sentence* consists of a main clause and one or more *subordinate* clauses of lesser importance, which may be *essential* to the meaning of the sentence or *nonessential*. (See page 233.)

CONTRACTIONS

Shortened versions of verbs, with an apostrophe (') in place of what has been removed. Common contractions include *I'm* for *I am*, *you're* for *you are*, *he's* for *he is*, *isn't* for *is not*, *aren't* for *are not*, *don't* for *do not*, *can't* for *cannot*, *haven't* for *have not*, etc. Contractions are generally used in less formal speech and writing. *Ain't* is an old form of *are not;* in standard modern English, it is considered poor grammar and sounds uneducated. As Americans learned in elementary school, " *'ain't' ain't a word and you ain't supposed to use it.*"

PARTICIPLES

Verb forms used with an *auxiliary,* or helper, to indicate an action in progress or completed: *am going, have gone,* etc. The *present participle* is the *-ing* form; the past participle of a regular verb is the *-ed* form. For irregular verbs, past participles vary widely (*gone, thrown, sung,* etc.); check a list in a good grammar book or online. Participles may also be used as adjectives: *singing sands, "Gone Girl."*

POSSESSIVE

A form of a noun or pronoun that shows it possesses another noun. It is generally formed by adding *'s* to a noun. Pronouns have their own possessive forms: *my, your, his, her, its* (not *it's,* the contraction for *it is), our, their* (not *they're), whose* (not *who's).*

CHAPTER 1

PRINCIPLES AND FORMS
OF AMERICAN JOURNALISM

As a working or aspiring journalist, you may be well versed in the way the media operate in your country. But practices around the world vary along with the cultures, traditions and political climates in which they are rooted—as the CUNY journalism school's international students quickly become aware. During one coaching session, Qingqing Chen, class of 2014, said Chinese journalists organize their facts differently from the American way: the Chinese, she said, present background information first and then draw a conclusion, telling what the facts add up to. Americans do the opposite, first stating the conclusion—what we see as the news value—and then filling in the background, as in the traditional *inverted pyramid* format. (See page 35.) After half a year at CUNY, Miyuki Inoue—an experienced reporter for Asahi Shimbun in Japan, which had sent her to New York to study entrepreneurial journalism—pointed out that Americans in general (and New Yorkers in particular) are more direct than the Japanese. Her culture prizes politeness over saying exactly what you mean, and the resulting indirectness carries over into its journalism. If you want to work in or with English-language media, you will need to understand their values and expectations.

The press has been an integral part of American society since the colonial era in the 17th and 18th centuries. Freedom of expression is one of the basic freedoms guaranteed in the First Amendment to the

Constitution: "Congress shall make no law respecting an establishment of religion, or prohibiting the free exercise thereof; *or abridging the freedom of speech, or of the press*; or the right of the people peaceably to assemble, and to petition the Government for a redress of grievances." Basically, that means Americans are free to say or publish whatever they want, even if it isn't true, without fear of prior restraint or censorship. (Anyone who feels damaged by false reports, however, may seek compensation through the court system.) The reasons for the First Amendment go back to the British colonial government's attempts to control the flow of information through censorship, taxation and harassment of publishers like John Peter Zenger.

Partly in reaction to these early tensions, American journalists came to view their role in society as *adversarial*. They do not work for the government or any of the organizations they cover; rather, they position themselves as *adversaries*—not necessarily opponents, as the dictionary definition of the word implies, but as independent observers whose first loyalty is to the facts and the truth. Nor do journalists much care for being treated like publicists—for example, when sources demand positive coverage. (See Chapter 13.) Instead, they tend to subscribe to the *watchdog* theory of journalism: like the dog guarding a home, the journalist stands as a guardian of the public, calling attention to corruption, inefficiency, incompetence and assorted other wrongs by government, business, organizations and newsmakers.

In the American view, the journalist's mission is to gather the facts and present them, in the words of the legendary *New York Times* publisher Adolph S. Ochs, "without fear or favor" so that citizens may make their own informed decisions on the issues. American journalists have traditionally strived for *objectivity*, or neutrality, in their reporting. They do not want to be seen as taking sides, either for or against the people and institutions they cover. They avoid *conflicts of interest*—the appearance that they have a vested interest in the effects of their journalism—that might compromise the credibility of their reporting. To avoid compromising their objectivity, a few go so far as to refuse to register with political parties or vote in elections.

Although most American news organizations are profit-making enterprises, journalists have traditionally not allowed themselves to be influenced, at least in principle, by the business side of the operation. A *firewall*—a complete separation of operations—has existed between the newsroom and the departments that sell advertising or try to raise *circulation,* the number of copies sold. (The equivalent in television is *ratings,* on the Internet *hits.*) Contrary to popular belief, responsible journalists do not cover stories merely to sell more papers or get more hits. Nor do they owe their advertisers positive coverage, although the firewall has started to crumble in the changed economic climate of the 21st century, when the news side feels more pressure to help generate revenue and keep the business afloat. Even so, American journalists above all value accuracy, fairness and *balance,* presenting as many legitimate sides as possible in every story.

In the past, journalists functioned as *gatekeepers* who wielded a great deal of power. It was they who decided what news passed through the "gate" of publication and what did not, what was important to the audience, and therefore what to report and publish. To some extent, they still do. But in the early 21st century, new media have brought new models. Today, instead of one-way communication—journalist to reader, with letters to the editor the primary way of talking back—the buzzwords are *conversation* and *community engagement.* The daily news meeting may start with a discussion not of the day's stories, but of the previous day's *metrics*—the statistics showing how many readers clicked on each story, and how much of it they read or viewed or listened to—as a basis for deciding what they'll want to read today. News outlets and their audiences now routinely communicate with each other through online comments, social media and other means. In *citizen journalism,* ordinary people untrained in journalism play an active role in news-gathering, contributing their reporting, photos or video to existing media—or creating their own media outlets. In an era of easy-to-use online platforms, anyone can declare himself a journalist, for better or for worse. Citizen journalism takes a number of forms, from breaking news on a blog to tweeting from news events like the Arab Spring. Traditional journalists may be uncomfortable with competition from "reporters" unversed in professional techniques and ethics, but citizen journalism seems unlikely to go away, and is increasingly important and influential.

As this digital age has disrupted older media, journalism has had to reinvent itself over and over again with new forms. *Social media*—digital platforms like Facebook, Twitter, Tumblr and Instagram—are no longer just popular ways of sharing your life with your friends, but tools for reporting news to the world. Creative journalists, teamed with videographers, web producers, graphic artists and technical support, have ventured far beyond the printed page. Some have produced multimedia online reports like *The New York Times*'s groundbreaking "Snow Fall: The Avalanche at Tunnel Creek" in 2012 (http://www.nytimes.com/projects/2012/snow-fall/#/?part=tunnel-creek); others specialize in *interactive* features in which audience participation helps determine how it is told the story. *Mobile* platforms for presenting news on phones and tablets are a growing part of the industry. While most journalists consider themselves more skilled at words or images than numbers, *data-driven journalism* has taught them how to read beyond the myriad forms of data available today to find the story those numbers tell. Some journalists cover *hyperlocal* beats on websites devoted to intensive coverage of very small areas, neighborhoods or just a few blocks. As the traditional firewall between the news and business sides slowly crumbles, nearly all journalists are under pressure to think like business people and, along with Miyuki Inoue, explore *entrepreneurial journalism,* which essentially means creating new businesses (and revenue) out of the journalism they already practice. Whatever the medium, these are all valid forms of journalism for the 21st century.

While the media have changed and the genres have expanded, today's journalists continue to tell stories, across a variety of platforms, using many of the same forms practiced in the days when "the media" meant newspapers.

As any journalist will tell you, *news* is the lifeblood of the media. News is what's happening right now (or what has happened in the very recent past) and how it will affect people's lives. News runs the gamut of human experience: it can be an attack on a school in Gaza, the mysterious disappearance of a plane from the sky, a water main break that floods a college campus, the discovery of body parts in a suburban trash can, a beloved actor's suicide or any other occurrence that demands attention and sometimes action. We tend to think of news as serious, but lighter matters, too, can make news. In the United States, "spot" or "hard" news articles still tend to be written in inverted pyramid format, but that is changing as the media evolve.

A *news analysis* is essentially what the label implies: a piece that looks closely at a topic in the news and analyzes what it means to its audience. This form tends to be assigned to more seasoned reporters whose experience gives them the background and context to put the news into perspective. An analysis may take the form of an *explainer*, which directly explains developments and their likely impact.

In contrast, *features* are the "soft" counterpart of "hard" or breaking news. If a "spot" news story's value is its immediacy, the feature's is often its timelessness, the fact that it is not directly related to a current news development but is nevertheless worthy of attention. Like their colleagues on the news desks, feature reporters cover an infinite variety of stories; they produce interviews and *profiles* (in-depth, well-rounded, not-always-flattering portraits of people in the news), travel essays, advice on home design and cooking, fashion coverage, society gossip and many other topics. Features tend to present a more human side of the news, and in fact non-journalists often refer to features as *human interest* stories. Magazine editors call them *back of the book,* a term derived from their position in the back of the printed magazine, behind the major stories. *News features* are features written "off the news"—that is, in response to it, and riding on its timeliness.

As mentioned above, journalists strive for objectivity, but that doesn't mean the media are devoid of opinion. An American newspaper, and its website, generally have at least one clearly marked page devoted to opinion, known as the *editorial* page. An *editorial* is an essay on that page expressing an opinion on a topic in the news, generally unsigned because it represents the position of the publication, not necessarily the opinion of the writer. The editorial page usually includes *letters to the editor*, many of them readers' responses to news coverage. Many newspapers also have an *op-ed* page, named for its customary position opposite the editorial page. On the op-ed page, staff members and outsiders alike may express their own points of view in *columns,* named for their original length—one column of type, today about 1,000 words. Columns may appear in other sections as well. The local news section may have its own *columnist*; a feature section may have a humor columnist; sports columnists have produced some of the best writing in journalism. Having your own column is a highly desirable job, and while many young journalists dream of being columnists, they are likely to achieve their goal only after many years of solid news reporting. So are those who specialize in the arts and aspire to produce *reviews* or *criticism,* informed assessments of books, films, television, music, dance, visual art, etc.

In newspapers, opinion pieces are clearly designated as such, even when they appear on the news pages, with different typography, writers' photos or labels like "Film Review." Newer forms of expression, especially online *blogs,* have sometimes blurred the distinction between facts and opinion. *Blog* is short for *weblog,* the original term for a website where the writer periodically posts, or "logs," essays or updates on the news, their personal lives or any subject they want. While many blogs have developed into serious news operations, the smart reader—and the smart journalist—will heed an old English adage: "Consider the source." Blogs on the website of a major news organization may be expected to adhere to that organization's professional standards, while personal blogs are rarely subject to any standards or editing at all. A blog often reflects the writer's agenda, even when breaking legitimate news; to cite just one example, political motivations were suggested when the conservative Drudge Report exposed President Bill Clinton's affair with Monica Lewinsky in 1998. While even professional bloggers have been afforded more leeway than traditional journalists, they too bear the burden of accuracy and thorough reporting.

Web-surfing and digital media seem to have shortened attention spans, encouraging users to jump from one web page to another to another without fully digesting any of them. That change, plus the economics of smaller and smaller *news holes* (see page 36), have led editors to give reporters shorter and shorter word counts for their stories. And it's the rare print journalist who has escaped being assigned to compile *briefs*, a column of one- or two-paragraph news items of lesser interest to the publication's readers. That said, *long-form* journalism running 3,000 words or more continues to thrive in publications as venerable as *The New Yorker* and *The Atlantic* (and their websites), and as up-to-date as Amazon's Kindle Singles.

When I mentored Pakistani journalists for UPI Next, the media development division of United Press International, I noticed a common weakness in many first drafts: the reporters tended to open their stories with long passages of facts and background, burying the news under several paragraphs. This may be the way news is reported in Pakistan, but not in the United States. In the British press, *obituaries* of prominent people—articles announcing their deaths and telling why their lives mattered—tend to read like essays, with details like age and date of death supplied in display type, while American obits tend to be written as news stories beginning with *the 5W's*. (See page 32.) It cannot be said too often: conventions vary. This book is written from the American journalist's point of view, based on American language, writing styles and standards. Those working for international media bear the burden of becoming familiar with their formats and standards, and following them. When in doubt, ask your editor—who won't be shy about letting you know when you're wrong.

CHAPTER 2

MEDIA JARGON

It's your first day *stringing* from your hometown for a major international news organization. So far you've only *pitched* a few story ideas to your assigning editor, but early this morning she got you *on the horn* to contribute reporting on a *hard news* story expected to *break* within 24 hours. She's flying in a staff reporter to be there when it happens, but in the meantime she wants you to *file* as much *B-matter* as possible so that the reporter needs to write only the *lede* and maybe a *kicker* for the first *post.* "Give me plenty of *color,*" she said, "and make sure all the quotes are *on the record.* I don't know what kind of *news hole* I'll have tonight, so keep it *tight. Slug* it JABBERWOCKY. Oh, and can you *shoot* video? We'll need some *B-roll* for the web."

Translation, please!

Every profession has its own insider language, or *jargon.* Its roots often go deep in history, and part of the fun in journalism is keeping tradition alive by using the words and knowing where they came from. Maybe no one shouts "Stop the presses!" anymore; it's much faster and quieter to push the "update" button. But digital-age journalists do continue to use terminology that dates back to the *hot-type* era (when newspaper type was literally set in hot metal, as opposed to *cold,* or photographic, typesetting).

Here are some widely used terms specific to the media, many of which are used throughout this book. Jargon varies from one newsroom or medium to another, and some use terms heard nowhere else. At *The New York Times*, for example, assigning/content/story editors are called *the backfield*, a term that comes from American football. Before the digital age, *The Boston Globe* used to assign story lengths in *twls* (pronounced *twills*) for *typewritten lines*. Expect variations.

the 5W's The five most important facts in any news story: *who, what, when, where, why.* (*How* is sometimes considered *the sixth W*.) In a classic *inverted pyramid* story, the 5W's should all be in or near the *lede* without overloading it.

advertisement, advertising Two related terms often confused by non-native English-speakers. *Advertising* refers to the field ("*Mad Men*" *is set in the world of advertising in the 1960s*) or the part of a media enterprise that generates revenue (*Revenue from online advertising has yet to make up for print losses*). An *advertisement*, or *ad* for short, is a single piece of advertising. (Noun: *Have you seen the ad for the latest iPhone?* Adjective: *It's quite a clever ad campaign.*) Print ads come in two forms: *display* advertising, which takes up multiple column inches in various shapes and designs, and *classifieds*, those tiny ads that were once a major source of revenue for newspapers but have now been rendered almost extinct by the Internet. In addition, *house ads* are ads prepared by the publication for itself, its products or its causes, used in print to fill awkward or unneeded space, or occasionally to punish a reporter who misses deadline by taking the place of the copy. (Editor: "If you don't file in five minutes, I'm going to *house-ad* you for the first edition.") Pronunciation note: AD-vertising is standard usage in both British and American English. But *advertisement*? In American, *ad-ver-TIZE-ment*; in British, *ad-VER-tiz-ment* (*AD-vert* for short).

art Visual elements that accompany a story and break up long passages of text, such as photos, illustrations, map, graphics, GIFs, etc.

attribute, attribution Identify the source of a fact, a quotation, a song lyric, etc., using phrases like *he said* and *according to.* In Western journalism, nearly every fact needs to be properly attributed. (See *plagiarism* below.) The verb is pronounced *at-TRIB-ute*; the noun pronounced *AT-tri-bute* means trait, quality or characteristic.

B-matter Background material prepared in advance for a breaking news story to save time on deadline. An experienced reporter who knows a story is about to break will do as much research and writing as possible beforehand to minimize work on deadline—with luck, only a *lede* needs to be written and details (*TKs*) filled in. Not to be confused with:

B-roll In film or video, secondary footage used to supplement the main footage—for example, a cutaway shot in an interview to show what the source is talking about.

beat The topic or area a reporter is assigned to cover. A beat may be geographical, like the New York City neighborhoods to which CUNY journalism students are assigned in their introductory reporting course. Or it may be a topic like city government, police and public safety, science, classical music or the super-rich. Police reporters, please note: officers also patrol a *beat*, the area for which they are responsible.

breaking news News that is happening right now and being reported live. Breaking news makes up a large proportion of *hard news* (see below).

budget A list of stories in the works for a given *news cycle* (see below), circulated within departments and at news meetings to help determine play and avoid duplication. Some publications call it a *digest*, while at others the *digest* is a column of news briefs.

bureau An outpost of a publication distant from its headquarters. Large media companies have bureaus around the country or in foreign capitals around the world (though many have closed in recent years for economic reasons); New York City publications based in Manhattan have bureaus in the other boroughs. A bureau may be a newsroom in itself, with reporters, editors and support staff, like the Washington bureau of a major publication, or it may consist of a single reporter working from home.

color The details and perspective that humanize a story and make it more interesting. Color may include descriptions of people or places; quotations from interesting or offbeat characters; relevant background or history; or the reporter's personal observations (while avoiding opinion or editorializing).

copy The stories reporters write, or any text written for publication.

CQ A note in copy meaning the writer or editor has checked, triple-checked and stands by the accuracy of what is marked CQ. Often used with unusual spellings of names (*William Paterson CQ University, the ballerina Jenifer CQ Ringer*), places (*Llanfairpwllgwyngyllgogerychwyr CQ*), facts, etc. Variously believed to be an abbreviation for the Latin phrase *cadit quaestio* (the question falls, or is settled) or "correct as quoted."

daybook A list of events scheduled for a particular day that may warrant coverage, such as the AP Daybook. At CUNY, a daybook story is often the first-semester student's first reporting assignment: she chooses or is assigned an event from the list; attends, takes notes and conducts appropriate follow-up interviews; and files a story on deadline.

file Turn in *copy* to the editors, as in "Has Harper filed yet?"

graf Short for *paragraph*.

hard news Serious news of widespread importance, often involving government, public affairs, breaking stories, etc. The opposite is *soft news*, often used to refer to features or sections on lifestyles and culture, to name just two.

H & J *Hyphenate and justify*—that is, align copy onscreen to the column width it will fill in print, often to determine if a story will fit its assigned space. In *justified* type, the lines are filled out from left to right, and words that don't fit on a line are broken with hyphens; careful copy editors will check each hyphenation to avoid bad breaks (incorrect, funny or embarrassing ones, such as *mans-laughter* for *manslaughter*). Some publications or sections have adopted a *flush left/ragged right* design, in which type is *flush*, or aligned, only on the left. The opposite is *flush right*.

inverted pyramid The traditional structure of a hard news story, with the most important facts—*the 5W's*—high in the story and details in descending order of importance. Think of an Egyptian pyramid turned upside down, or inverted, with its wide base at the top and its point at the bottom. The inverted pyramid format dates back to the days when newspaper pages were composed by hand, as opposed to computer, in the composing room. If a story set in type was too long for its allotted space, the fastest, easiest solution was to cut it from the bottom, so smart reporters put the least important information there. (This process was called *cutting on the stone*.) But see *kicker*.

kicker A strong finish to a story, meant to leave an impression on the reader. In the pre-computer era, stories written in inverted-pyramid style were not intended to have strong endings so that they could be cut quickly from the bottom. Now that editing and page composition are done electronically, it's easier to condense a story rather than chop it, and even news stories may have kickers. Features often have them, and opinion pieces almost always. (Another meaning: a *kicker* can also mean a small headline above the main one, which it supplements. Some publications call this an *eyebrow*.)

kill Cancel publication of a story. When a story is killed, the copy itself will probably be *spiked* or, in computer-age terminology, *deleted* from the system. (Old-time newsrooms had metal spikes on which paper copy was impaled when the editors were finished with it.) To *hold* a story means to delay publication for another time, not to kill it entirely.

lede The opening of a story, written in such a way as to grab readers' attention and pull them into the story. News ledes tend to take a straightforward approach, packing in *the* 5W's; features and opinion pieces may begin with anecdotes or other more roundabout ways to begin the story before getting to the *nut graf* (see below). The spelling *lede* is a holdover from the days of hot type, when type was set as individual letters made of metal, some of which was lead (the element Pb, pronounced *led*). (To make a too-short story fill out its space, lead slugs were placed between the lines; today the process is still called *ledding,* even though a computer inserts the white space.) To avoid confusion, the beginning of a story came to be spelled *lede.* Nowadays, some people spell it *lead*; purists stick with *lede.*

masthead The list of a publication's top editors, usually published on the editorial page of a newspaper or near the front of a magazine.

news hole The amount of space in print available for news/editorial copy, determined by the *ad hole,* the space sold to advertisers. Since advertising brings in revenue, the ads are placed first, with the news hole consisting of the space left around them, usually to an approximate predetermined ratio.

news peg What makes a story timely or important—the reason to do it *right now.* Think of a peg on the wall on which you might hang your coat. The news peg is the event or current issue on which you "hang" your story. Since *news holes* are limited, stories with strong news pegs are generally published faster and given more prominent display, or *play,* so when *pitching,* always keep any possible news peg in mind.

nut graf The paragraph early in a story, especially one not written in inverted pyramid format, that spells out for the reader exactly what the story is about.

on/off the record Whether information, interview material or quotations may be used and attributed for publication. American journalists work under the assumption that all the research they do is *on the record* unless the source specifies in advance that it is *off the record*— not to be quoted. Sometimes a source will speak off the record but *on background,* meaning the material is not to be quoted but the information may be used, or even *on deep background,* meaning it is for the reporter's information only; if used, it must be confirmed and attributed to other sources.

pitch A query or story proposal to an editor, producer or publication in hope of getting the assignment. If you know baseball, think of the pitcher who throws the ball to the batter. Professionals in all media pitch their ideas in hopes of getting desired results. Staff reporters and freelancers seeking assignments pitch story ideas to editors. Publicists pitch ideas to reporters and editors alike in hopes of getting coverage for their clients. In Hollywood or television, writers, directors and sometimes actors pitch film concepts to producers. In advertising, *pitch* means an idea for promoting or selling a product. (A suggestion for a story you don't plan or hope to do yourself is called a *tip.*)

plagiarism The mortal sin of presenting words taken from another source as your own. While such borrowing is considered perfectly acceptable in some cultures, in the West it is most emphatically not. Journalists have been dismissed from their jobs for plagiarism; elected officials have been publicly embarrassed and sometimes forced to resign over plagiarism in their distant past; students have been expelled from schools and universities. Journalism consists largely of material gathered from sources other than the reporter's firsthand observations, but almost every fact needs to be *attributed,* or credited to the source. If you need to lift someone else's words, present them as a quotation, properly attributed.

quotation (quote for short) The exact words of a speaker, document, text, etc., set off in quotation marks (" ").

shoot To take photographs, film or video.

slug A name for a story, equivalent to a filename in word-processing software, by which the story is consistently identified throughout the process of budgeting, reporting, editing and production.

story An article being reported, for print or broadcast. (Also casually called *piece,* as in *I did a piece on that last year.*) While *story* is universal in the newsroom, some publications also use *article.*

style In journalism, there's style and then there's style. As in other forms of writing, style can refer to the individual stamp a writer puts on copy; many are proud of, even vain about their style. It also means the conventions chosen by a particular publication to give its writing consistency, conciseness and clarity. Every professional publication follows a particular style that is likely to cover usage, punctuation, typography and many other things. It lays down rules on things like how to render dates, which states or months may be abbreviated and which may not, whether to use courtesy titles like Mr. and Ms., etc. Large newspapers such as *The New York Times* may issue their own stylebooks (or, increasingly, put their style guides online for quick reference and easy updating); most smaller American papers follow Associated Press style, available online by subscription (www.apstylebook.com). Too many reporters feel they don't need to learn style—"the copy desk will fix it"—but in fact knowing style can make writing, especially on deadline, more efficient. For journalists whose native language is not English, a good style guide offers a bonus: insights into the language and how it works.

tight Using as few words as possible to say what you mean. Since print space and airtime are limited, journalists place a premium on *writing tight,* and editors spend a large part of their time *tightening* reporters' copy. Most journalists start their careers as verbose, or wordy, writers— using more words than necessary—and some never break the habit. But tightening is a useful skill to develop. If you're assigned 1,000 words for a story but your first draft is 1,100, you can often cut those 100 words and even more by tightening rather than cutting facts or ideas. If your story has been H&J'ed, you can tighten visually by trimming *widows*—lines of one or two words at the end of a paragraph. Cutting a widow is as good as cutting 10 words if it saves a line.

TK A notation in copy that a piece of information is missing and will be added later. Some seasoned journalists use *TKs* liberally to avoid interrupting the flow of their writing as they look up or verify facts. *TK* is a shorter version of *HTK*, for *hed to kum,* which used to be rubber-stamped on paper copy to indicate that a story was ready to be typeset but the *hed,* or headline, would be coming later.

typo Short for *typographical error,* generally a small error such as a misspelling.

NEWSROOM POSITIONS

Job titles vary from country to country, from medium to medium, from newsroom to newsroom, even within newsrooms. They may also give little idea of the work the holders actually do. (In book publishing, for example, an *editor* often mostly acquires new titles and authors, leaving the editing to *copy editors* or *line editors,* who edit line by line.) These are some of the most common terms for positions in American newsrooms in various media.

anchor The star of TV news; the host or main news reader on a newscast, who holds the program together from a desk on a studio set but may travel to the sites of major breaking news or special events. (The term comes from a ship's anchor, which allows the ship to stop and stay in place.) In U.S. media, the anchor seat is the most visible, most prestigious and best-paying position in TV news; prominent anchors on American networks have included Walter Cronkite, Dan Rather, Diane

Sawyer and Tom Brokaw. Anchors sometimes carry the title *managing editor* of their programs.

director In television, the *news director* is responsible for the overall operation of the news department. See *producer* below. (In American film and theater, the director is in overall artistic charge of the production.)

editor In text media, one of the many people, at various levels of hierarchy, who assign stories to reporters and prepare them for publication. Levels in newsrooms of varying sizes include, from the top down:

> *editor in chief* or *executive editor*: Usually the top editor in the newsroom, responsible for all phases of its operation and its long-term strategy.
>
> *managing editor*: Responsible for day-to-day operation of the newsroom, both content and administration.
>
> *department* or *section editors:* The heads of various departments, such as city editor, sports editor, features editor, lifestyle editor, editorial or opinion editor, etc.
>
> *assigning, content* or *story editors:* Those who directly supervise reporters. These editors assign stories to staffers and freelancers; they are the first readers, looking mainly for big-picture aspects like content, accuracy, fairness and organization. They also coordinate with designers and production editors to produce the finished product.
>
> *copy editors:* The detail-oriented editors who perform the final stage of copy preparation after the assigning editors have finished their edits. They polish spelling, punctuation, sentence structure, word choice, accuracy, etc. They also backstop the assigning editors; write headlines, captions and other typographical elements; and generally make the bylined reporters, and the publication, look good. In the Internet age, the copy

desk bears increasing responsibility for fact-checking. (Once upon a time, reporters were held responsible for their own accuracy.)

In pre-computer days when stories were typed and edited on paper, the copy chief sat in the center, or *slot*, of a horseshoe-shaped desk and handed copy to the editors sitting around the *rim*. These terms are still in use. A typical newsroom dialogue: "I need to make a change in my story. Has it been slotted yet? "No, it's still on the rim."

In television or film, an editor takes the many pieces of footage shot for a report and edits them into a smooth, coherent story.

producer In television news, a producer's work includes assigning reporters, deciding on the running order of stories, and managing the newscast minute by minute from the control room as it is in progress. As in a print newsroom, there are various levels of producers, including *executive producer*, reporting to the news director, and *show producers*, described above. Producers may be responsible for as little as a single segment or as much as an entire series.

In online media, almost anyone who produces *content* (see page 275) for the web is called a producer, rather than a reporter, editor, etc.

publisher The head of the business and financial operation of a publication, just as the *executive editor* or *editor in chief* heads the news operation. At a small publication, the publisher may also be the owner; in large media corporations, the publisher is an executive appointed by the parent company.

reporter A journalist who reports the news, gathering information and producing an accurate, coherent story. Text reporters collaborate with editors in shaping their stories and write the drafts, which may change significantly over the editing process. (Some publications use the term *writers* instead, but since actual writing is only part of a journalist's job, *reporter* seems more accurate.) TV reporters also gather information but make their reports on camera.

researcher A support-staff journalist, especially at a news magazine or website, who does research for stories that will eventually be written by reporters. In the past, researchers at news magazines were almost all women, while reporters—with their higher prestige, visibility and salaries—were exclusively men. The feminist movement of the 1960s and '70s brought that discrimination to an end; today researchers are also more likely to be credited for their contributions.

stringer A freelancer who does reporting for a publication on a recurring basis. News organizations often use *stringers* to get stories from places where they have no bureaus; to give young journalists a chance to prove themselves; or, especially nowadays, to save money on staff salaries and benefits. That said, many prominent journalists began their careers as stringers.

DEAN SARAH BARTLETT

PERPETUAL ANTICIPATION

Sarah Bartlett has been with the CUNY Graduate School of Journalism since its inception and, in 2014, became its second dean (after founding dean Stephen B. Shepard). She has helped shape its programs as a member of its founding curriculum committee; as creator of both the Urban Reporting and the Business and Economics concentrations; and as a founder of the school's Center for Community and Ethnic Media. Having begun her career in documentary films, she became a researcher, reporter and editor for the magazines *Fortune* and *Business Week*. Later she covered urban affairs, business and financial issues for *The New York Times* and was editor in chief of Oxygen Media. She is the author of *The Money Machine: How KKR Manufactured Power and Profits* (Warner Books, 1991) and *Schools of Ground Zero: Early Lessons Learned in Children's Environmental Health* (American Public Health Association, 2002).

What makes good writing? Or good communication?

For me, clarity is really important. A lot of times, people focus on being flowery, or trying to sound very poetic, and I feel being clear and concise and to the point is always preferable. Making a story compelling by weaving in those old tools—anecdotes and scene-setting and telling even small stories within a larger story. Building in little storytelling arcs, mini-arcs, if you will, within a larger piece. Having a thread that runs through an entire story. I always used to think about this as making an argument: I'm trying to construct an argument. I'm trying to teach my students: what question are you trying to answer? And then: in what ways are you answering it?

How do you make your writing clear? Students assume that, just because they know what they're talking about, it automatically comes through in their writing.

To me, it's putting yourself in the shoes of whoever is reading it—trying to imagine that someone is coming to this cold and knows nothing about the story or the subject. I always try to anticipate what their questions might be, and then at what point during the storytelling that question might arise, and then answer it. People often would say when they read my writing that, just when they're beginning to be curious about something, there's a paragraph that explains it. Being able to anticipate where you're going to lose people or where there might be confusion setting in.

I also rewrite a lot, so I'm constantly reviewing my own work to say, "Is that clear? Is there a sort of disconnect between this idea and that idea, and if so, how can I bridge that?" So it's that revision process that's just so critical. I rewrite e-mails. It's just my form of expression.

You spent a long time in business journalism. What's the difference between doing general journalism and a specialty? Or *is* there a difference? Are the goals the same?

I think the goals are the same—at least, they always were for me. The language is what's different. So in the case of business journalism, there are more technical terms. In some ways, that raises the ante in being a clear writer because you don't want to lose people who might not be familiar with a term. Not trying to dumb things down or be patronizing, but trying to make sure you're writing in a way that's inclusive, that you're not losing a lot of people. The terminology—just being aware that what's second nature to you may not be terms that are second nature to everybody else.

What do the international students at CUNY need to learn about the way they use language?
Obviously it depends what format they're going to be specializing in. The demands on written English for a print piece are different from, maybe, more colloquial English that might be in a radio or a video piece. So I guess I would focus a lot on the written English. And that was where I found there were idiomatic issues—getting comfortable with language. Also, maybe interviewing: they may be lacking self-confidence in their interviews, so they're not necessarily eliciting the same level of detail, or the same nuance, that you might get in an interview. And then it's even harder for them to translate that into writing because they didn't get it in the interview stage. You can't really manufacture that to compensate in the writing.

If you had to give one piece of advice to international journalists about working with English-language media, what might it be?
Work with an English-language coach. . . . People often say, "Read, and it will help you write better." That may be true for style; I don't think it's necessarily true for grammar and for learning a new language that you're not familiar with. To me it's more taking classes, going online and using online resources. Grammar, grammar, grammar! Take quizzes, interactive quizzes that start to really challenge you so that you're making progress on your writing. Those are the things that I would be doing.

It's very hard for a journalism professor in an English-language school to ignore grammatical errors that creep in because of language issues. It's not that those students aren't smart; it's not that they're not trying. It's that they don't necessarily have the preparation. Being able to address that problem, trying to fill that need with this additional, extra-curricular language instruction, I think, could be really helpful.

CHAPTER 3

WORKING IN ENGLISH

You may already be working as a journalist in your own language. You may be reasonably fluent in English. You may think, "I should be writing for English-language media!" But it may not be such a simple matter.

International applicants to the CUNY journalism school strike me as incredibly brave; those who are admitted and actually enroll are even braver, going through a graduate professional school, with its nonstop demands, in a foreign language while living in a foreign culture. Like the school, professional media are a fast-paced, high-pressure, deadline-driven work environment, and never more so than in the digital era, when it's vital to be first with the news. Anyone who is not fully bilingual tends to be far slower writing and speaking in a second language.

"You know you're fluent when you dream in French," my high school French teacher used to say. It's not necessary to dream in English to work in it productively, but thinking in English is an important step. When interviewing international applicants, I often ask about their writing samples: "Are these translations, or were they originally written in English?" The answer tells me a great deal about a writer's comfort level and confidence. English originals, especially on breaking news, indicate the writer's ability to think, organize and write on his feet. (*Think on your feet* is an idiom that means being able to react quickly to new circumstances.) Translations—presumably done at greater leisure than an original story on deadline—may indicate problem areas. One applicant for the class of 2016 submitted an impressive magazine cover profile, well written and beautifully translated—except for repeated errors in subject/verb agreement (see page 227), showing that his grasp of that particular grammar point was weak.

When we think in our native language, we're thinking not only in its words, but also in its structures and concepts. Translation is a slow process—something like writing a story in longhand on a yellow legal pad and then typing it into a computer. On my college newspaper, I had to make a transition—a big one—from writing in longhand, as I had throughout high school, to composing at a typewriter. Learning to think in English is a similar transition.

Suppose you're a Japanese journalist stringing for an American news outlet. A tsunami hits the coast of Honshu, and your American editor wants a full story to post on the website as soon as possible. Do you write it in longhand before sitting down at your screen? Of course not; that would add a middle step and waste valuable time. Thinking—and writing—in English from the start brings you up to speed with the rest of the news operation.

People from different cultures think and structure their storytelling in different ways. For example, "the Chinese start out writing in a spiral," says Donna Drewes, a former television journalist who is now an adjunct associate professor at New York University, where she teaches communication and coaches students on writing. "They talk around and around and get to the main point in the middle." So do people from African, Latin American and Arab cultures, as well as African-Americans and Native Americans, according to Milton J. Bennett in *Basic Concepts of Intercultural Communication* (Intercultural Press, 1998). Intercultural communications scholars like Bennett would call that a *contextual* style: the writer first presents the context, then draws a conclusion. English-speaking cultures tend to be more linear; their storytelling proceeds in a straight line from Point A to Point B. So, to tell a story effectively for an English-language medium and its audience, you need to think, write and rewrite in a more linear style—as those Pakistani journalists I mentored for UPI Next (see page 29) did to achieve their goal of global publication. While English-language writers do think of stories in terms of a beginning, a middle and an end—what is often called the *narrative arc*—in the media the beginning generally carries more weight to grab the reader's attention with the 5W's, and the end may have less.

Thus working in English isn't just a matter of language. It also involves the forms and processes of journalism: pitching a story and getting the assignment; reporting it; structuring the story, and working with your editors once you've completed a draft. Through each crucial step, the trick is thinking in English rather than translating language or form, from the page or what's in your head.

THE PITCH

Civilians—that's what I call people not involved with the media—tend to think that getting the news to them is a relatively simple matter: reporters go out and find stories, get the facts and write them up; editors correct the spelling, add a few commas and publish. In fact, the process is more complex. Editors, especially assigning editors, are often involved with a story from the very beginning, given that they decide what will be assigned, to whom; how it will be *played*, or presented to readers and viewers; story lengths, in words or screen time; and balance with all the other stories competing for that space or time. Even if you're a staff writer with a track record and a certain rapport with your assigning editor, you'll probably start by making a *pitch*.

Refresher: a pitch is a query proposing a story to an editor. It's rare for a writer to get an assignment, as I did in 1987, by calling an editor and saying, "Hey, Harry, need a piece on windows?" (He did. The story, an essay headlined "If the windows are open, it must be spring," ran on the cover of *The Boston Globe* Home section a few weeks later.) Like a creative director in advertising working on a campaign to sell a client's product, a reporter needs to sell a story—to the assigning editor. To do that, she needs to explain, concisely but convincingly, what makes her idea a *story*; what makes it a story for that particular publication;

often, how she plans to report it; and—especially if she is a freelancer approaching a new editor—why she is the right, best or only possible person for the job. Even if you're writing just a pitch and not a draft of the story, an editor is unlikely to consider it seriously unless it is well thought out and executed. It should contain every piece of information the editor needs to know to make an intelligent decision, with at least a preliminary set of 5W's.

Pitching is an art in itself. Case study: one CUNY international student's progress in pitch-writing. Early in her first Craft of Journalism course, she wrote:

> *Fresh Direct. This name is synonym of pollution and traffic for a majority of Mott Haven's inhabitants. As Climate March is approaching September 21st, residents and community organizations are striving to make their voices heard. They don't agree with the Court's decision allowing the online grocer to build a new facility in their neighborhood in front of the waterfront. Company's plans as well as jobs opportunities might topple down.*
>
> *The relocation would create jobs in the South Bronx especially in Mott Haven. At a time of high unemployment rate the web-based retailer's move, which has been offered $1,3 million, could be a solution to cut down the number of unemployed people. Therefore, generating some 1 000 jobs. The issue had been discussed in court from 2012 until late March 2014.*
>
> *Will it be the end of a possible economic change in the South Bronx?*
>
> *The stake here is either environmental or economic for Mott Haven people.*

This pitch is clearly not the work of a seasoned professional. Details are sketchy even for a pitch, which is not intended to be a finished story. What court decision? And what does "discussed in court" mean? (In the United States, court cases are not "discussions"; they are presentations of evidence leading to a judgment or settlement.) What $1.3 million offer? Who has offered the money to whom, and why? What is the unemployment rate in Mott Haven? None of these questions—all fundamental to the strength of the proposal—are addressed in the pitch; worse, the sketchiness suggests the writer doesn't even know the answers. She also seems to be pegging this local environmental issue to the broader People's Climate March without making the connection clear.

The pitch also contains a number of problems with English, many related to constructions in the writer's native French. Climate March was not approaching Sept. 21; the Climate March on Sept. 21 was approaching. Articles are missing, and a number of phrases are not idiomatic. Some sentences are not complete thoughts, but fragments. FreshDirect is a trade name, and one word.

If I were an editor receiving this pitch riddled with problems in both basic journalism and English, I would not even consider giving this writer the assignment; if you can't write the pitch, you probably can't do the story successfully. But I might consider a version that read more like this:

> *In Mott Haven, the name of the online grocer FreshDirect is synonymous with pollution and traffic. Now residents and community organizations are protesting a court decision allowing FreshDirect to build a new facility on the waterfront in their neighborhood.*
>
> *FreshDirect says the $1.3 million facility would create 1,000 jobs in the South Bronx. In Mott Haven, where the unemployment rate is 9 percent, it could put people back to work. But economic gains could bring environmental losses.*

As edited, the pitch still lacks certain specifics, like description of the court case and the nature of the protests. Since the relevance of the Climate March is unclear, except as a coincidence of timing, it can be dropped from the pitch and should be used in the story only if the writer can establish a connection to the Mott Haven protests. While no pitch is expected to tell the whole story, it needs to be as specific as possible.

A few months later, the same student, having completed her first semester, was pitching another story:

Fatal police shootout in Paris: A small part of France, Martinique, is mourning

Only 1 900 miles away from New York City, Martinique is mourning a child lost on duty. In the wake of Charlie Hebdo's terror attack on Wednesday that killed 12 people, the murder of a policewoman in a suburb of Paris, 24 hours later has paralyzed with fear the inhabitants of the island.

The 27 policewoman, Clarissa Jean-Phillippe, was still an apprentice and had just spent the holidays in her native town of Sainte Marie, northern Martinique. She went back to France to finish her internship at the municipal police station of Montrouge, and was gunned down by Amedy Coulibali, a jihadist killed yesterday Friday 10th January, by the GIGN (Groupe d'Intervention de la Gendarmerie Nationale). After highjacking a kosher supermarket in Viennes murdering 4 hostages, the then-jihadist claimed himself as an associate of the murderers of the Charlie Hebdo's massacre. He shot her many times in the back, fatally hitting her in the throat.

Jean-Phillippe died shortly after on the scene though wearing a bulletproof jacket.

The shootout has now been linked to the Charlie Hebdo's disaster. In Martinique people can't help but worry as 200 000 Martinicans live in Paris, some even compare the situation with 9/11 terror attack.

Clearly the student had learned something about making a pitch. This is much clearer than the previous one, with more—and more specific—information. But in fact it's too much information, with more details than the editor needs to make a yes-or-no decision on the assignment. (Those details, among them the exact location of the policewoman's hometown, the GIGN reference and Coulibabi's connection to the Charlie Hebdo attack, which had been reported elsewhere, could be saved for the story.) And the pitch is missing one crucial piece of information: why this reporter is uniquely qualified to do the story. Among the errors in language, this was not "Charlie Hebdo's terror attack" but an attack on Charlie Hebdo; the word is *hijacking* (and that's probably the wrong word for taking over a supermarket); the policewoman was more likely wearing a bulletproof *vest* than a jacket; if she was shot in the back, the bullet probably hit her *neck* rather than her *throat*; and the last sentence is a run-on (see page 225). Here's an edited version:

> *Martinique mourns a daughter killed in France*
>
> *The murder of a policewoman from Martinique in a Paris suburb, 24 hours after the Charlie Hebdo terror attack on Wednesday, has paralyzed the inhabitants of her island home with fear.*
>
> *The policewoman, Clarissa Jean-Phillippe, 27, had just spent the holidays on Martinique. Still an apprentice, she had just returned to the Montrouge police station outside Paris when she was gunned down by Amedy Coulibali, a jihadist killed in the shootout at a kosher supermarket in Viennes. Shot in the neck, Jean-Phillippe died shortly after. She had worn a bulletproof vest.*
>
> *In Martinique people can't help worrying, as 200,000 Martinicans live in Paris. In man-on-the-street interviews, some are even comparing the situation with 9/11. I am on the scene in Martinique and have been granted an exclusive interview with Jean-Phillippe's aunt, speaking for her family.*

Note the addition of the last sentence, which makes clear why this reporter is the one to do the story. She sent the pitch to *The New York Daily News*, which bought the story—her first professional clip in English.

Once an editor approves an assignment, it's time to jump on the story. To write the pitch, you've already done some preliminary reporting to get a reasonably clear idea of just what the story is. But any story idea is subject to change as the facts emerge from further research and interviews. More than one reporter has found that a story isn't quite what he thought it was. Think of a pitch the way scientists think of a hypothesis: as a supposition to be tested through experiments. Good scientists base their conclusions on the results of their experiments, which may or may not support their initial hypotheses. And journalists report the stories they find, not the ones they hoped or expected to find.

Much of a journalist's research consists of going out and talking to people, or *sources*. Chapters 4 and 5 will focus on such mechanics of interviewing as asking questions in English and quoting sources effectively. Some general advice, especially for journalists working outside their own cultures and native languages:

Be prepared. No professional reporter would go into an interview without thoroughly checking out the source and the background of the story. It's not enough to interview someone because "So-and-So told me I should talk to you"; be very clear in your own mind about who the source is, what his relevance is to the story, what qualifies him to speak on the subject and what makes him credible. In addition to formulating your questions in advance, you may want to practice them (ideally with a native English speaker, if you know one) to resolve any problems with pronunciation, phrasing or word choices.

Make appointments. To Western journalists, this may sound like a *no-brainer.* (That's an idiom meaning something so obvious you don't have to think about it.) But just as different cultures have their own storytelling styles, they have different attitudes toward time and access. In Japan, an experienced Japanese reporter told me, it is common for journalists to wait outside officials' homes early in the morning or late at night in hopes of getting exclusives—a practice that Americans would normally consider an invasion of privacy. Americans live by schedules and timetables; the Chinese do not. (After a year in New York, one Chinese professor, previously mystified by Americans in China who were constantly pulling out their calendars, said, "*Now* I understand.") To Westerners, the Chinese seem to live in a here-and-now culture and come across as pushy and presumptuous when they demand our attention *right now*. In the West, whenever possible it is standard professional practice to set up an appointment for an interview, whether in person, by phone or on Skype, at a specific date and time, to be confirmed as the time approaches.

Appointments may be made by phone or, increasingly, e-mail, which allows the reporter to introduce herself, present her credentials and describe in writing exactly what she is hoping to accomplish. Such an e-mail can be concise but relatively detailed, giving the source the information he needs to prepare for the interview (as well as think about what information he doesn't want to reveal). For an example, see page 121.

Granted, there may be times when a reporter needs to camp out on a source's doorstep to get the needed information. Otherwise, making an appointment, and arriving punctually and prepared, demonstrates respect for the source's time.

Talk to strangers. American children are warned not to talk to strangers, for fear they will be kidnapped or molested. Some grow up to be journalists despite a residual shyness that, at least early in their careers, makes them uncomfortable approaching sources and asking questions. Imagine, then, the discomfort of reporters, especially women, from cultures that stress modesty, self-restraint and minding your own business in a field that requires sticking your nose into other people's. For such reporters, approaching strangers to ask questions is a major challenge—especially if the assignment is a *man-on-the-street* interview, in which the reporter goes up to total strangers on the street to ask for details of a news event they've witnessed or their opinions on a current issue. Even a veteran foreign correspondent who had reported from a dozen countries once confided, "Aw, I always hated man-on-the-street stories."

As CUNY students learn each fall, it's often counterproductive to go up to a stranger, notebook in hand, and immediately start firing questions. People tend to freeze up when approached by "the media," so instead, approach them as a human being. Start out with *small talk,* those small, all but meaningless phrases that help kindle a conversation:

> *"Is this seat taken?"*
> *"Nice day, isn't it?"*
> *"Do you come here often?"*
> *"I see you're reading (name of publication). Have you seen the article about . . ."*

Using phrases like these and sticking to safe subjects like the weather or sports, you can build a casual conversation to the point where you can identify yourself as a reporter without necessarily making potential sources uncomfortable. Small talk also gives you time to tune your ear to their accents and let them get over any discomfort with yours, or your nationality. Once you've made the connection, ease into the subject on which you need information, and ease into your questions:

> *"You know, I've noticed a lot of new high-rises going up in the neighborhood. I was thinking that might make a story. What are people in the neighborhood saying?"*
> *"I hear there was a big crowd on the street the night that kid was shot. Do you know anybody who was there? . . . Oh, you were! That must have been really scary. Would you be willing to tell me about it?"*

Of course, get your source's names and identifying information, even if she demands anonymity. (See page 103.) As you finish, end with phrases like *"It was nice meeting you"* and *"I really appreciate your help."*

The point is to build your source's trust in you, especially when you are assigned a beat. Any beat is something of a closed society, whether it's a close-knit ethnic neighborhood, the U.S. Department of Defense or the New York dance world. A newly assigned journalist arrives as an outsider, as a Chinese student became all too aware when she was reporting from an African immigrant neighborhood in the Bronx. When she tried to interview customers at a market there, she e-mailed me that she had been "banned by the African store owner's wife to ever come to their store again." Why? The woman said it made the customers nervous, though more likely it made *her* nervous. It takes time and effort to develop contacts and relationships with sources you will need again and again. So don't start investigating an exposé the first day; instead, attend community meetings, explore neighborhood hangouts and engage people in conversations rather than interviews. Once you've stopped being a stranger, they will open up.

Take notes in English. The more you practice a foreign language, the more proficient and confident you can expect to become. If you are interviewing sources in English and producing a story in English, why not start the process early and write down your notes in English? Notetaking not only gives you practice in listening and transcribing, but also improves the odds that what you reproduce—especially quotes—will be accurate. An occasional lapse is understandable; in the heat of the interview, you may encounter a word you don't exactly know, or a concept may come to mind that you cannot yet express in any language but your own. Otherwise, use English. Even when using a recorder (see page 87), jot down key points in English to remind you of the flow of the interview.

Meet deadlines. Journalists from cultures with a different sense of time from the West's may not realize the importance of deadlines. In my first semester at CUNY, a Craft of Journalism professor consulted me about a Chinese student who was routinely missing deadlines. "When she is in our classroom, and we say file by 3 p.m., she files by 3 p.m.," he said. "But when she is working on her own and knows weeks in advance that a deadline exists, she misses it." Once again: to Westerners, the Chinese seem to live in the moment but are rather vague about any point in the future. So this particular student did fine with an assignment that was right in front of her while missing future deadlines—presumably easier ones.

Deadlines exist for good reasons, above all for delivering the news to its audience on schedule. Newspaper deadlines were traditionally dictated by production and delivery schedules, with time factored in to print the paper and drop it on subscribers' doorsteps on time. On a 24-hour online news cycle, journalists may feel they are under constant pressure, if not rigid deadlines, to break and update news. In broadcasting, a newscast's time slot dictates its deadlines.

Most English-language media are deadline-oriented, for reporters and editors alike, and that part of the work culture must be respected. If you don't meet the deadline for one assignment, you may not get another one. Once you have an assignment, start locating potential sources and setting up appointments in a way that fits into your time frame yet leaves enough time to construct the story. And if you really can't meet a deadline, tell the assigning editors so they can adjust their plans.

THE WRITING

Judith Watson, now an associate professor at the journalism school after serving as associate dean (see page 65), recalls one student who was an investigative journalist in Nairobi before enrolling at CUNY. "He didn't take a single investigative course," she said. "He already knew how to do all that." What he did need to learn was how to present his material to an international audience—and that meant an English-speaking one.

Think back to the differences in various cultures' communication styles. When you're putting together journalism, you're writing in the style of yet another "culture," and you need to master its conventions. For Beimeng Fu, a member of CUNY's Class of 2015 from Shanghai, thinking in English isn't always a matter of language. "Sometimes if you have to think about complicated topics, like for my feature writing class, it's really a structural matter," she said. She's right. You may have a lede that grabs the reader and won't let go; you may have the facts and figures to back it up; you may have quotes that lets readers hear the speakers' voices. But there's more to journalism than finding facts; they need to be organized in a way that holds readers' interest so they'll stick with the story.

Curiously, the classic newswriting format in English is based on the assumption that the reader may *not* read a story from beginning to end. There are really just two basic ideas you need to understand to write a professional news story or release: *the 5W's* and the *inverted pyramid*. The 5W's are the most important facts in any news story: *who, what, when, where* and *why*. (Sometimes *how* is considered the "sixth W.") They should be in, or close to, the lede, or opening, of the story. The *inverted pyramid* is the basic format of a news story. The pyramid is like the ones in Egypt; "inverted" means it's upside down. The most important facts should be at the top, followed by somewhat less important, and ending with the least important. As that reader's attention tapers off, so does the information, until only the least important details remain. And then the story ends.

That's really all you need to know to write a news story. The tricky part is gathering your information and figuring out which facts are the most important and which are least. You'll spend the rest of your life trying to figure that out, story by story.

The inverted pyramid is by no means the only way of structuring a story, and it tends to work better for hard news than features. A variation is the *martini glass*: a story with a news lede in inverted pyramid form (the bowl of the glass), followed by a step-by-step process like a chronology (the stem) introduced by a phrase like "Police gave this account," and finally a concluding point (the base). Here is a brief but classic example by Lewis Kamb from *The Seattle Times* on April 12, 2015:

> *Seattle police arrested a naked man Saturday night after he allegedly broke into a University District apartment building and struggled with officers who responded to confront him.*
>
> *Seattle police gave this account of the incident in a press statement issued early Sunday:*
>
> *Officers responded to the apartment building in the 4200 Block of Brooklyn Avenue Northeast shortly after the building's manager called to complain a suspicious person had entered the locked building and made his way into a storage area. The manager told police nobody was allowed into the unit, and that he had the only key.*

Officers responded and found the man completely naked inside the small storage unit. After the man refused the officers' orders to exit, police took him into custody after a brief struggle. The man bit one officer's gloved thumb, but didn't break the skin.

The suspect was later booked into the King County Jail for investigation of burglary, assault, drug possession and possession of stolen property. Police said the man had a small amount of methamphetamine. Police didn't provide an explanation about why the man wasn't wearing clothes.

In this story, first paragraph is the "bowl" of the martini glass, the next three are the "stem" and the last is the "base."

The format that some at CUNY call *the kebab* (which I have long taught as *the boxes*) begins with a lede and a nut graf and ends with a kicker. Think of them as cherry tomatoes on the ends of a kebab skewer, with chunks of meat, or information, in between, separated by a slice of onion here, a mushroom there—the transitions. The kebab works best for features in which the goal is not to make sure the reader gets the basic facts, but rather to hold her interest from beginning to end.

Now, think back to your culture's storytelling style and the ways it differs from these three possible English-language formats. Your success may depend on how well you adapt your thinking and storytelling.

Whatever the form, it is crucial to maintain focus. From the basic news writing of Craft, Beimeng Fu moved on in her second semester to feature writing, which she found more challenging. Features usually involve more time, more space, more interviews and more angles; the amount of information can be overwhelming, especially in a long-form piece. (See Tim Harper, page 81.) As Judith Watson says, "The longer the story, the easier it is to lose the thread."

Fu was working on 1,200-word feature on the Chinese luxury travel industry. The night before it was due, she learned that one of her sources had quit his job because of what she described as "scandals" involving his company. Was the story now a feature about luxury travel, or an investigative piece on the scandals? Suddenly she was running the risk of *split focus* if her story was not clearly about one theme or the other. Since she was too close to deadline to do an adequate job on the investigative piece, I suggested she might do two stories: the feature now, the investigation later, perhaps as a larger project such as her capstone, or thesis project. That's one of the beauties of journalism: your work is never complete, just complete for that one day of publication. There will always be another chance to advance the story.

Fu was also working on another story with a potential split-focus problem, on private garbage collection companies in New York City. Some were using scare tactics against new competitors; some were driving their trucks too fast to make as many collections—and money— as possible. Now, Fu said, trade organizations were working to improve both situations. Should the story be about the problems, she asked, or the organizations? In this case, I suggested, it could be about both if she led by presenting the problems and later offered the potential solution. In this way, she could move from A to B without losing focus.

Bear in mind that there is rarely a single "right" way to structure almost any story. Occasionally the news is so clear-cut that the lede all but writes itself. But these are rarities. Each new assignment is an opportunity—within the confines of media conventions—to tell a story in your own way.

Above all, when you write, write in English. Many international students have told me it is actually harder, not to mention slower, to write in their native languages and then translate into English. If you don't feel confident in your ability to write in English from the very first draft, you are simply not ready to report breaking news on deadline. Instead, start with features with looser deadlines, and work your way into news.

This is not to say you must never fall back on your native language if it helps speed your work. "Sometimes when I find it really hard, I will outline a little in Chinese, and it makes me much clearer," Fu said. "If I have to figure out something complicated, the structure, maybe it's better in Chinese." But she does the actual writing in English. "Basically, Chinese knowledge is a tool," she added. "You prefer to be thinking English; it's easier, more direct. It's only when some term is so much more familiar to you in Chinese than in English—something kind of complicated—you'll write it down because you don't have to check the dictionary."

That dictionary, by the way, should be an all-English one, not your native language to English, so that you're not just translating words, but seeing the definitions and vocabulary-building synonyms in English. Start with a learner's dictionary like those published, in print and online, by Longman and Merriam-Webster; then graduate to regular dictionaries or their free, word-by-word online versions.

BEING EDITED

This is your big chance to learn, and to polish your English. Editors at all levels are experts in not only the forms of media writing, but also on the English language. They are also the final decision-makers on whether a particular story fits their publication's needs and specifications. In print, that student reporter's story from Martinique for *The Daily News* bore little resemblance to what she had turned in; it had been given a new lede, reorganized and polished by the copy desk. Yet it was still her reporting and her story.

Editors perform many tasks, but they exist for one reason: to make the publication look good. By extension, then, they also exist to make you, the writer, look good.

Media work is a collaboration. Unless you're self-publishing your own blog, your copy will (or should) never go straight from laptop to publication. Instead, editors—possibly a series of them—will read it for structure, accuracy, coherence, objectivity, balance, fairness and potential libel, as well as language issues like spelling, grammar, usage and word choice. They will ask questions at every stage of the process and expect you to be able to supply the answers. They will seek out the details you didn't know were missing. Editors rarely get bylines, although even that is changing; the Associated Press now often lists editors' names at the bottom of stories, giving them both credit and accountability. But from beginning to end they can be instrumental in shaping a story.

So take advantage of their expertise. First, understand that their work improves yours. Let go of your ego. Don't feel threatened or fight back against editing (as did one just-out-of-Harvard reporter at *The Boston Globe* in the 1980s who would go back into the computer after his stories were edited and undo the editing). Editors have a stereotypical image as burned-out or frustrated writers, but the fact is, they have different skill sets and, often, different temperaments from reporters. Any publication needs both.

All but the smallest publications have more than one level of editing. The editors variously called *assigning, story* or *content* editors begin the process, often directing teams of reporters, making their assignments and being the first readers to work out the general shape of the stories. *Copy editors* polish the stories, and the *copy chief* or *slot* reads them one last time before pushing the button that sets them in type or publishes them instantly online. A smart reporter will make friends with editors, especially the copy desk.

While reporters cannot always be in the newsroom when their work is being edited, they can use the times they *are* present as lessons in both journalism and English. Unless you're on a tight deadline or your editor is the type who doesn't like to be watched while working, ask to sit next to him as he works; look at the changes and ask him to explain them. As I've said before, any good editor is also a teacher, and this is a prime opportunity for both sides.

You can learn from editing even if you cannot be present when it happens. If you are, say, freelancing from abroad for a U.S.-based publication, cultivate relationships with your editors that will make them want to help you learn. If you sense they have the time and the inclination, ask them to e-mail you their markups so that you can easily see exactly what changes they made. Failing that, take the time to compare the draft you filed with the published work.

JUDITH WATSON

CAPTURING THE LEDE

As associate dean of the journalism school from its founding until 2014, Judith Watson has had an overview of the school's growth and growing influence. Now an associate professor of Craft of Journalism, the school's core reporting program, she brings to the classroom her 25 years of experience as a reporter, columnist and editor for print and broadcast. In 15 years at United Press International, she was New York bureau chief, New York State editor and Albany capitol bureau chief. A past president of the New York State Society of Newspaper Editors, she has been honored for her work by the Albany Legislative Correspondents and the Women's Press Club of New York State.

What makes good writing?

Good writing is good thinking. It's taking the 10 pounds of information and figuring out, "What does it all add up to?" You figure out what it adds up to and what the lede is—what is the most interesting thing about it, or the newest thing—and how you can tell that story in a compelling way, and in as brief a form as possible so you're not wasting anybody's time, or at least you're giving them a great story to read. You should take as long as it takes, but no longer.

How do you figure out what's the most important thing, or the most interesting thing?

If your mother calls you tonight, and you're talking to her on the phone, and she says, "What did you do today?" "Well, I covered a story about XYZ." Hopefully you would not say, "I covered a story about homeless people." You would say, "I covered a story where we discovered that homeless people are living on 10 cents a day." You would almost instinctively capture the lede right there. I sometimes say to students, "Read through your notes, put them away, and then write down one sentence, or two maximum, what your story's about.

The hardest thing that we teach here is not just "What is the story about?" but more important, "What is it *not* about?" Because that's the stuff—weeding out all that crap so the story doesn't wander around; it stays focused on "Here is *this* story." It's not *that* story—you could go write that story somewhere else—but *this* story has to be about *this*. And it can't be about 10 things. And it can't be about this broad thing. It's *one* thing.

Even from early on in Craft I, after they get through daybooks (see page 34) about "this and that happened today," *this* happened; that's what the story is. And then which details to fill in is a matter of choice. That's training wheels. But once they start focusing on stories that they've dug out, like for their community districts, it becomes a lot more difficult. What *is* this story about? And it can't be a topic. It's got to be a story.

What's the difference between a topic and a story?

A topic can read like a term paper. It's about everything—you throw in the kitchen sink[1]—and it's about this and that. A story follows a storyline. It's much more focused about one or two things that you're trying to say—painting a picture.

A story that says, "The Irish-American parade went down Fifth Avenue today, and 20,000 people attended, and these people attended, and then there were some floats that did this," etc., etc. It happens every

---

1 *Throw in (everything but) the kitchen sink* is an idiom meaning to use or mention almost everything available, which is usually too much.

year. This is not news. A narrower story might be, "The mayor led the parade and walked with the head of the gays and lesbians for the first time. Or: "Before that happened, the parade occurred, but marred by protest from blah-blah-blah." That is a story. That is something happening that's new, as opposed to something that happens every year.

In class, early on, we start telling students they must write pitches for any story they want to do, before they start going out and dredging up fact after fact after fact—interview 20 people—and they still don't know what they've got. It's like they think, "Maybe I'll try to make a story out of this," and the answer is no, no, no, no, no. You have to have done enough pre-reporting to know, "This is what looks like the story," and now do a pitch that really makes you focus—makes you declare, commit to "This is the story I'm going to tell you." And how am I going to go about it? Who do I need to interview? So you have to do the pre-planning. This is particularly important when you're out there shooting video, trying to do a TV story, because now you've got equipment and you're shooting scenes. You can spend two days shooting and editing, and end up having to completely reshoot the story because you didn't have the story.

You've been talking in terms of students. Would your advice to professional journalists around the world be any different?

Not much. Figure out what the story is—and isn't—and try to figure out how to tell it in a compelling way where you're not wasting the audience's time. And know the audience that you're writing for or shooting for, because it makes a tremendous difference in how you approach the story. You need to be able to sell it if you're freelancing it, or even inside a publication, you've got to sell an editor on this, and so you really need to be quite clear in your own mind and quite confident you can deliver. And you need to show how you're going to deliver.

CHAPTER 4

ASKING QUESTIONS

What's the single most important part of any journalist's job?

It's not gathering facts, although it's a big part of that process. It's not writing them up, or standing in front of a camera and reporting them. It's not spelling the words right, or pronouncing them properly. It's not even deciding what stories will go on the front page, the home page or the evening news.

It's asking questions.

Reporters gather information by asking questions—of themselves ("What's happening on my beat?"), of their editors ("Do you think this is a story?" meaning "Is it worth pursuing?") and most certainly of their sources in the countless interviews they will do in their careers. But it's not just reporters who ask questions. Editors constantly question their reporters, from the very beginnings of the reporting process ("What's happening out there?") to the work in progress ("Are you 100 percent sure this is accurate?" and "Can you really trust your source?") to the final polishing on the copy desk ("When you say *youngsters* here, do you mean children, which is what the word means, or young people?"). They ask one another, "Is this a page one story? How many words is it worth?" They ask about the possibilities for visuals ("Can we get art with that?"). In a newsroom, the questions never end. If you're not inquisitive, you need to consider another line of work. If you are, but English isn't your native language, you need to master the grammar of forming questions before asking them professionally.

Question formation is one of the many ways English differs from other languages. In some languages, a question is a declarative sentence with a single word or a phrase added at the beginning (like *est-ce que* in French or *czy* in Polish), or at the end (like *ma* in Chinese or *ka* in Japanese). In writing, a question may be punctuated differently from a statement; in Spanish, for example, a question is framed by an upside-down question mark at the start of the sentence and a right-side-up one at the end. In speaking, a change in vocal intonation may indicate a question—like the upswing in pitch at the end of a question in English. Phrasing and speaking questions properly is especially important if you are doing on-camera interviews or audio; you want to sound good not only to your sources, but to your audience as well.

In English, a *declarative sentence*—one that states, or declares, a fact or opinion—consists of a subject, a verb, and sometimes an object, a predicate nominative (noun) or predicate adjective. Some simple examples:

> *Dogs bite.* (Subject + verb.)
> *The man bit the dog.* (Subject + verb + direct object. An old saying from journalism: "Dog Bites Man" is not news; "Man Bites Dog" is.)
> *Dogs are animals.* (Subject + verb + predicate nominative.)
> *Cats are cuter than dogs.* (Subject + verb + predicate adjective.)

To make a question out of any of those sentences, you need to add an *auxiliary,* or helper, verb and *invert* the word order—that is, turn it around—by placing the subject between the two parts of the verb phrase:

question =
auxiliary + subject + base verb (+ optional predicate)

For a negative:

question =
auxiliary + subject + not + base verb (+ optional predicate)

or , using contractions:

question =
auxiliary + -n't + subject + base verb (+ optional predicate)

So:

Do dogs bite?
Did the man bite the dog? (Notice that the past tense takes the base verb, i.e., the present tense, not the past participle. So it's not *"Did the man bit?"*)
Are dogs animals?
Aren't cats cute?

Somewhat more sophisticated examples:

What do you do? (I call this "the American question." Americans tend to define themselves, and others, by their jobs, which also suggest education, income and social class. When you meet Americans for the first time, it's often the first question they ask.)
Do you work in the media? or *Are you in the media?*

Other kinds of questions start with *question words*. In journalism, we use question words all the time: they're our 5W's:

Who's in charge here?
What's your circulation?
When's my deadline?

Where were you on 9/11?
Why did you lie to the police?
How did the accident happen?

Non-native speakers who have not mastered thinking in English tend to fall back on their native sentence structures and translate directly. Spanish-speakers often try to construct a negative by simply by adding *no,* as they would in Spanish: *Yo no vendre hoy* translates literally as *I no come today.* That sounds uneducated to English-speakers, whose grammar demands *I'm not coming today* or *I won't come today.* The same applies to questions. A CUNY student from Spain wrote:

Why the most contagious ideas are not always the best or the most noble ones?

And one from Italy wrote:

Why the police should be interested in making up an official version?

Those questions don't work in English because the word order has not been inverted. They should have read:

Why are the most contagious ideas not always the best or the noblest ones?

And:

Why should the police be interested in making up an official version?

To work with English-speaking media, you will need to form questions properly for any number of tasks: interviewing native speakers;

using English as an intermediary language between you and sources who are not native speakers; translating quotes from interviews in your own language; writing in Q&A format; setting up polls and interactive features. An extreme but effective case: in 2012, *The New York Times* restaurant critic Pete Wells wrote a review entirely in questions ("As Not Seen on TV," http://www.nytimes.com/2012/11/14/dining/reviews/restaurant-review-guys-american-kitchen-bar-in-times-square.html). It went viral, partly because the restaurant was owned by Guy Fieri, a TV celebrity chef, partly because it was so negative and partly because of its all-question format. The lede:

> *GUY FIERI, have you eaten at your new restaurant in Times Square? Have you pulled up one of the 500 seats at Guy's American Kitchen & Bar and ordered a meal? Did you eat the food? Did it live up to your expectations?*

By continuing in this vein throughout the review, Wells made his point.

BASIC INTERVIEW QUESTIONS

It's often said that in the media, we don't report the truth; we report what people tell us. The basic tool for getting information from sources is the one-on-one interview. You ask questions; your source responds. "Never go into an interview without at least 10 questions," I was advised in my college newspaper days. "More like 30," a *New York Times* reporter said decades later.

The quality of the questions you ask will ultimately determine the quality of your story. To draw the best information, the most revealing quotes out of your sources, your questions need to be the best they can be, in both grammar and content. Your questions can also help you steer an interview—that is, determine the course it takes and what information, both expected and not, it produces.

Each month, *Vanity Fair* magazine devotes its back page to a feature called the "Proust Questionnaire," named for the French novelist

Marcel Proust, who used such questionnaires to reveal subjects' personalities. The modern-day magazine uses the questionnaire as a tool for celebrity interviews, to make the subjects talk candidly about themselves. The questions vary from month to month, but they regularly include:

What is your current state of mind?
What is your greatest fear?
What living person do you most admire?
When and where were you happiest?
What is the trait you most deplore (hate) in yourself? In others?
What is your greatest extravagance?
What do you most dislike about your appearance?
On what occasion do you lie?
Where would you like to live?
How would you like to die?

In addition to the simplicity and directness, note the structure of these questions: they are open-ended, encouraging the subject to talk rather than answer with a terse yes or no. Use them as templates for your own.

Vanity Fair presents Proust questionnaires in straight question-and-answer format, with no interpretation or writer's voice. Q&As can be an effective format for telling a story in the subject's own words, and sometimes editors specifically ask for that format. Lena Masri, CUNY class of 2015, successfully published her interview with a survivor of a terrorist attack in Denmark (http://www.poynter.org/news/mediawire/330439/danish-terrorist-attack-survivor-its-a-fight-that-we-cant-ignore/) during her second semester at CUNY. An excerpt:

What were you thinking at the time?
A billion thoughts go through your mind. Most of them are about fleeing. The worst thing was that I couldn't see how I could get out of there. I had heard someone yell something in a non-European language that sounded like Arabic. I thought

about the Charlie Hebdo attack, and I was thinking, "In a minute he is going to come in here and shoot us."

We were all defenseless. People were lying on the ground and were completely exposed.

When writing Q&As, you may reword questions to improve clarity and focus. But, as in any quotation (see Chapter 5), the speaker's words must be presented exactly as spoken. For eight years, Deborah Solomon wrote the weekly "Questions for . . ." column for *The New York Times Magazine*. Readers assumed that the interviews were printed as they happened—until one of the subjects complained. The line "Interview has been condensed and edited" was then added to the bottom. Solomon eventually left the column.

In a more traditional, "written" interview, the reporter organizes all the information and interweaves facts and observations with direct quotations throughout the story. (See page 92.)

FOLLOWING UP

Each fall, first-semester students at CUNY seek help with their Craft assignments. Since I coach them on their journalism as well as their English, I ask them the kinds of questions about their copy that any decent editor would:

"How old are his kids? Why are they relevant to this story?"
"When did she arrive in the United States? Has she become a citizen?"
"Are these really condos, or coops, or rentals?" (see page 256.)

From the *deer-in-the-headlights* looks in the students' eyes (that's an idiom, meaning "so frightened or surprised that you cannot move or think," according to Cambridge Dictionaries Online), I always know the answer before they say it: "I didn't ask."

They may have gone into the interview with their lists of 10 or 30 or however many questions, and moved straight down the list. The mistake they made was not asking follow-up questions. In fact, many beginners don't seem to know they *can* ask follow-ups. They don't realize it's not just all right to depart from the interview "scripts" they've written for themselves; it's mandatory.

Here's how simple follow-ups during a hypothetical interview with an immigrant might have drawn more information (and headed off questions from editors) in one of the examples above:

Reporter: *"Since you came to the U.S., have you always been working?"*
Source: *"When I first came here, I couldn't find a job at all because I didn't have a work visa."*
Follow-up: *"How long have you been here?"*
"Thirteen years."
Follow-up: *"And you have the visa now?"*
"I don't need one anymore. Now I'm a citizen."

And you can write: *Ms. Source, who didn't even have a work visa when she arrived in New York, is now a U.S. citizen.*

As part of pre-arrival coaching, a student from Italy translated a Q&A he had published in Italian into English. It concerned the murders of three Italian nuns in Burundi, and his source was the director of a radio station there. His questions included:

You strongly oppose the official version given by the police about the murder of three missionaries. Why?

Why should the police be interested in making up an official version?

What is the political context in which the crime took place?

What has this to do with the missionaries? (A very British phrasing. Americans would say: *What does this have to do with the missionaries?*)

You broadcast an interview with a person claiming to be one of the perpetrators of the crime. Who is this person, and why did he decide to speak out?

Maybe these questions were all on his original list; maybe not. Some may have come to mind as his source answered others. The interview may have proceeded more like this:

Question: *You strongly oppose the official version given by the police about the murder of three missionaries. Why?*
Follow-up: *Why should the police be interested in making up an official version?*
Question: *What is happening in Burundi? What is the political context in which the crime took place?*
Follow-up: *What does this have to do with the missionaries?*

Follow-up questions tend to be spontaneous, developing in the reporter's mind from what the source has said. That means you need to be flexible and unafraid to depart from your "script" for the interview. You need to *go with the flow*—an idiom meaning to react and respond to what is actually happening, not what you might want to happen.

Follow-ups can also be used to check what you think you've heard—especially important if you're not a native English-speaker. Student reporters often feel shy about asking sources to repeat what they've just said. They shouldn't. Accurate reporting is more important than momentary damage to the ego.

Imagine yourself traveling in a foreign country whose language you may know just a little. On the street you ask a passerby for directions, and you don't quite catch the answer. Would you smile, thank him and go on your way, just as lost as before? Or would you ask, "Could you please repeat that more slowly?" Of course you would. Then why wouldn't you ask the same of a source? There is no shame in asking for repetition or clarification when inaccurate reporting could have serious professional consequences. You don't want to amass a track record of corrections of your stories just because you were too shy to ask.

By asking follow-up questions, you can fact-check on the spot and avoid embarrassing questions later from editors.

> **Editor:** *"This guy's name is Shuman? Are you sure it's not S-C-H-U-M-A-N-N?"*
> **Reporter:** *"Uh . . . I didn't ask. I just assumed it was Shuman."*

Editor shakes head in dismay. You slink back to try to track down the source and check the spelling.

Such a scene can easily be prevented with a simple follow-up question during the interview, in this case a man-on-the-street:

> **Reporter:** *"Could please I get your name?"*
> **Source:** *"Sure, Don (you hear Shuman)."*
> **Reporter:** *"Is that S-h-u-m-a-n?"*
> **Source:** *"No, it's S-c-h-o-e-m-a-n."*
> **Reporter:** *"And do you go by Don or Donald?"*
> **Source:** *"Actually, I was christened Donn. D-O-N-N."*
> **Reporter:** *"Thanks."*

And on to the next question.

(In the United States, a nation of immigrants and their descendants, it is crucial to check and triple-check names, which vary widely in spelling. Even a name as common as Smith can be spelled Smyth; Murdoch can just as easily be Murdock. Never assume any name is spelled the way you hear it.)

The information obtained from such simple follow-ups will help make a story as specific as possible. So if a source mentions having two children, ask their names and ages, just in case they turn out to be relevant to the story. If a tourist in Times Square mentions being from California, ask where in California; it could be a major city like Los Angeles or a small town in the Napa Valley, and that perspective may shape his perceptions. If a subject you are profiling says his family left Germany in 1936, don't assume they fled the Nazis; ask. It is much easier to ask follow-ups on the spot than to track down your source later.

In class a student's question often leads to a better lesson than the one on the professor's plan. Similarly, an unexpected remark from a source can change the direction of an interview—and a story. Here's where it's vital for reporters to be able to think on their feet. Instead of pursuing your original list of questions (which you may postpone or drop entirely), it may become necessary to improvise an entirely new line of questioning.

The better you master asking questions in English, the easier it will become to think on your feet. Remember that asking a question is a matter of not only the order of the words, but also the way you say them. English-speakers' voices tend to rise in pitch at the end of a question; if yours does not, a source may think you are making a statement rather than asking a question, and ignore it. Listen to the way native speakers sound when they ask questions in the movies, or in real life, if you have access to any. Follow their lead, and practice.

TIMOTHY HARPER

MAKING A PLAN

An adjunct professor and coach, Tim Harper is the CUNY journalism school's guru of long-form writing. It's a subject he knows well, from both sides. In addition to having written a dozen books, on subjects ranging from the United States Constitution to freelance writing to beer, he serves as the editor of CUNY Journalism Press. He has published hundreds of articles in major newspapers and magazines and has also taught at schools including New York University and Columbia Graduate School of Journalism.

What makes good writing?

Good writing is good communication—being concise and clear, and getting the message across that you want to deliver.

How is that different in long-form?

The big thing about long-form is the misconception that you just write long, and that by writing something long, that gives you a lot more room and you can show a lot more of your writing chops, and you can be a better writer and tell more of the story. In fact, good long-form depends very much on the same rigor and discipline and conciseness as shorter writing—as spot stories, as a story that you might read about a fire, or an auto accident, or Congress passing a law.

Long-form depends not on the diversions and the beautiful language, but on moving the story forward all the time. Every sentence, every paragraph, has to keep the story moving, going someplace, going from point A to point B. We look for narrative a lot in long-form. We want to tell a story, and typically there are several stories, several narratives within the story, and keeping track of all those and keeping the reader interested and with you is the real challenge. It can be very difficult, and it's something that all of us who write long-form are learning about all the time. The more long-form you write, the more you realize you have to learn.

What about organization? Is there one "best" way to organize a long-form story?

The best way *is* to organize. Most people don't spend enough time on the organizing part of it. I spend the most time on the reporting; I spend the next most time on the organizing. The least part of the time that I spend on a story or a book is the writing, when you're actually sitting down and doing the work.

One key to being efficient and productive is to organize before you do anything else. You figure out what you're going to do, what you're going to say, what are going to be the main parts of this story. Then you look at how you might get those, what you need to do. You make a plan; you go after it. The plan changes; you focus; your structure changes. But you're always re-evaluating what you're going to be doing, where you're going, so it's not a surprise when you sit down with all the stacks of material and think, what do I need to do? Where? How do I do this? You're working on this all along, and even sometimes in the writing, often your story structure will change as you see how transitions work together and what makes more sense. But the main thing is to be thinking about this all the time. To many students, the big hang-up is that they do lots of reporting without thinking of the story structure. Start at the beginning.

You said something very important: "the plan changes." I would guess that in long-form, there's more time for it to change.

More time and opportunity; more sources, typically. You're covering broader ranges. It's not unusual in long-form for somebody to spend a lot of time—weeks, months—on a piece and get it done and look at it and realize, "That just didn't work. I need to start over. I need to reorganize. I need to tell this with a different voice, different shadings, different perspectives, different rhythms." And oftentimes those first drafts are part of the process of getting to where you need to be to make the piece a lot better.

You teach and coach many international students. What specific problems do you see in their adjustment to working in English?

Beyond the technical parts of language . . . there is sometimes a misunderstanding of journalism in America and how we look at stories and how we look at journalism, how we read and how we consume news. But when it gets right down to it, once international students understand the common aspects of news and communication, and the universal aspects of storytelling, the "once upon a time," then they get it.

CHAPTER 5

QUOTING ACCURATELY AND EFFECTIVELY

Quotations bring journalism to life. Even when reading text, the audience wants to hear human voices. In audio and video, sources speak for themselves, with no middleman transcribing their words, though of course editors do choose what goes in and what ends up *on the cutting-room floor.* (That's an idiom meaning left out, from the days when film or videotape was spliced together physically rather than digitally.) All journalists must be able to render their sources' words, and their intentions, quickly and accurately to the best possible effect.

For international journalists working in English, the task has an added layer: accurately hearing and reproducing speech in a foreign language. Every reporter needs to be able to take trustworthy notes, fast. In the past some learned shorthand, the system of rapid note-taking once used by secretaries to take dictation from their bosses. Some have devised their own personal shorthand. Some jot down what they can and let memory serve for the rest. Some take minimal notes on the scene—for example, when a source is clearly uncomfortable having his words recorded in front in him—and then write down everything they can remember the minute they're out the door. And some reporters, though far from all, use recorders to do their note-taking for them.

Relying on memory is fine for scene-setting and general description, but rarely for quotations—*quotes* for short. (*Quote* can also be a verb:

reporters quote their sources.) In American print media, what appears within quotation marks is assumed to be the exact words of the speaker. That's why it is so important that quotes be 100 percent accurate. They tell readers not only *what* a source said, but also *how.* So quotes need to be accurate in terms of fact and the speaker's manner of expression.

To report quotes accurately, you need to hear them accurately, and here your listening comprehension skills matter most. Case in point: a Fulbright scholar from Vietnam in CUNY's class of 2014—fluent in Vietnamese, French and English—was assigned to cover a Brooklyn neighborhood as her Craft beat. The residents were largely Italian- and Irish-Americans, plus some recent immigrants. "I can't understand them!" she moaned. To develop her listening comprehension, I gave her some homework: watching YouTube videos of people with those particular accents. "Give me 10 good quotes from each, as if you were writing a story," I told her, "and mark the parts you can't understand." A week later, she came back with the quotes, and together we listened to the videos to check her accuracy. I filled in the gaps (though, to be frank, there were parts even I couldn't understand). Anyone with an Internet connection can do the same exercise. If no native English-speaker is available to check the quotes, you can check them yourself by turning on the captions. (Captioning, though, like most voice-recognition software, is notoriously and sometimes hilariously inaccurate. For an extreme example, watch this video of former Australian Prime Minster Julia Gillard with the captions on: https://www.youtube.com/watch?v=hCJ_aavenyo.) Another good way to test your comprehension is to watch movies or TV shows with English captions instead of translations to see how the words you hear are written. (See page 306.)

Telephone interviews can pose a particular challenge: without the visual cues of speaking face to face, you may find it harder to understand what a source is saying. Recording may not be the answer; in many American states, it is illegal to record a phone conversation without the other party's consent. So you, as a reporter, face a double task: not only understanding what your source is saying, but also using follow-up questions (see Chapter 4) to confirm that you are hearing accurately.

USING A RECORDER

Whether a smartphone app, a digital mini or a Skype accessory, a recorder can be a valuable tool for any reporter. For journalists working outside their native language, it is a godsend. You can listen to a difficult passage over and over again—or play it for a native speaker—until you get the quote exactly right. If an editor questions a quote because it sounds awkward or unidiomatic, the recording stands as evidence. "Did he really say it this way?" is a comment I frequently make on international students' work—for example, in this sentence from a Catalan student's report on a talk by the Dominican-American writer Junot Diaz:

Of his community-oriented action and activism, Diaz said, "We will not going to survive what we have to survive without art."

As written the quote is unidiomatic. It's possible, though unlikely, that Diaz said it as written; he probably said either "we will not survive" or "we are not going to survive." A recording would have let the student go back and check.

Recordings are especially useful when English is neither your native language nor your source's, and you may not have fully understood on first hearing. But they must be used efficiently. A student from India apologized for being behind schedule in bringing me a story for review. "It took a long time to transcribe the interviews," she explained. I smiled because she reminded me of a writer I had edited back in the 1980s, a nutritionist—not a trained journalist—who was working on a major article for *The Boston Globe* Food section on school lunches. Both had made the same mistake: wasting time transcribing entire interviews before sitting down to write.

Most people talk much faster than they can write, or even type. The eight-minute interview with Carrie Brown on page 285 turned out to yield, unedited, more than 1,000 words—a full column of newspaper type—that took me nearly two hours to transcribe and check. (I do not type 125 words a minute.) Multiply that by the number of sources needed for a well-rounded, fully reported story. Unless you're a superb typist capable of taking dictation, transcription *is* going to take a long time—and add to normal deadline pressure.

Instead of transcribing interviews, conduct them mindfully. By all means, record if you feel you have good reason, like a language barrier or a long-term project. (In 35 years as a journalist, I never used a recorder until I started doing interviews for a book whose final draft was years away, when the interview would have faded from memory. In those 35 years, I was accused of misquoting exactly once. Many professionals never use recorders at all.) Once you press the "record" button, make sure the device is working reliably, and then let it do its job. At the same time, take notes by hand—not necessarily the entire interview, unless you don't trust your recorder to function properly, but as a sketch or outline of which topics were discussed at what point. When you sit down to write, figure out the shape of the story: the 5W's, the lede, the major points to cover. Block out the story. *Then* go back to the recording and, working from your notes, fast-forward to the key points, typing only the quotes you need. Transferring the recording to the laptop, or whatever you use to write, makes it easier; instead of juggling two devices, you need only switch back and forth between windows. Some transcription software, like InqScribe, lets you do both on the same window.

Some journalists have used voice recognition software to dictate their stories to a computer, and some have experimented with using it to transcribe interviews. If you feel you *must* have a complete transcript or think it would be the most efficient way to produce a story—a Q&A, for example—you might give it a try. Once again, such software tends to be far from accurate, so carefully check the finished text against the recording. Better yet, try an online transcription service like Rev.com.

Don't turn off the recorder too soon. You may think you've come to the end of an interview, but often, when you're saying thank-you and goodbye, the source will make a comment that turns out to be the most important, most relevant quote of the session—the one you really need. Make sure to get it.

CLEANING UP QUOTES

Earlier in this chapter, I said, "What appears within a pair of quotation marks are assumed to be the exact words of the speaker." Well, no, I didn't say exactly that; go back and look it up. What I said there was grammatically correct; what I said in this paragraph is not, if you want to *split hairs.* (That's an idiom meaning to make small distinctions, often in unimportant matters.) The subject of the full sentence is the clause *what appears within quotation marks,* which can be assumed to be singular from *appears,* the verb's singular form. But then I violate singular/plural agreement with the plural verb *are assumed.*

The fact is, people—even native English-speakers, even very well-educated ones—do not ordinarily speak in perfect English. (One CUNY journalism professor interviewed for this book repeatedly started sentences with *there's* and then followed it with a plural subject, which means she should have started with *there are.*) Writing tends to be more formal, and therefore more correct. Speech is more spontaneous and therefore more likely to include errors as our minds wander, we don't think the grammar through or—let's be honest—we simply don't know what is correct. (Witness the many highly educated people who say *whom* when they mean *who,* or *between you and I.*) If, while being interviewed, I said that sentence in the last paragraph as written there, should you quote it as is or clean it up? What if you are quoting a member of New York City's—indeed, America's—large immigrant population whose English is still a work in progress? What about African-Americans who may not speak in "standard" English?

Schools of thought on those questions vary. Major print media discourage rendering quotes in dialect, which may make sources sound uneducated. When in doubt, check with your editor or follow the publication's rules, which may be detailed in its stylebook. Associated Press style, which the CUNY journalism school follows, states:

> *Never alter quotations even to correct minor grammatical errors or word usage. Casual minor tongue slips may be*

*removed by using ellipses but even that should be done with
extreme caution.*

*Use sic, the Latin word meaning thus or so, to show that
quoted material or person's words include a misspelling,
incorrect grammar or peculiar usage. Place (sic) in the text
directly after the problem to show that the passage is precisely
reproduced. . . .*

*If there is a question about a quote, either don't use it
or ask the speaker to clarify.* (In other words, ask a follow-up
question.)

While those are generally sound guidelines, other authorities give
writers more leeway. Greg David, director of CUNY's business and economics reporting program (see page 187), is one of them. "This is a very
controversial issue, and I wouldn't say I'm in the mainstream," he said. "I
think that people—by that I mean sources—want their quotes to convey
what they mean, not necessarily the way they talk in an interview."

For his second-semester course Covering the Economy, he said,
"students interview these economists, and they get these truncated, not
very good quotes, and then the same economists appear in *The New
York Times* or *The Wall Street Journal* with these wonderful quotes. And
I say to my students, 'Do you think they talk differently to the reporters
at *The Times*? And the answer is no, probably not. So I think that's what
reporters at the best places do. Now it's also possible that reporters at
those places are more aggressive in asking questions, so they massage
the quote to where they want it."

As both reporter and editor, David admits, he has often changed
the order of quotes. "I've never had anyone call me up to say, 'That's not
the order I said those sentences in,' " he said. "I frequently change the
order of the quotes that are presented to me so that the impact statement
is first and the explanation statement is second because that's how the
story reads better. And I don't see that as a fundamental problem."

Most style guides discourage rendering quotes in dialect or
other nonstandard English to avoid making sources appear stupid or

uneducated. Sportswriters routinely clean up quotes from athletes, who are not generally known for their grammar and diction. David cited a story on the Dominican baseball player Sammy Sosa when he was competing for a home run title. "One person didn't clean his Spanish one day, and it caused a storm because it was regarded as a racist," David said. "So I think that's another example of how cleaning up makes sense. And cleaning up quotes can be as simple as fixing the grammar. Why *wouldn't* you fix the grammar? Sometimes people say things that aren't exactly true and didn't mean it that way; sometimes they are confused. You sometimes have to check, but sometimes it's so self-evident you can just fix it. So I don't believe that the way someone says it is absolutely the way it should appear in a text piece."

Broadcast reporters, he noted, "are much better because they can't do that. I've been interviewed many times by broadcast reporters. The best of them just ask me the same question over and over and over and over again 'til I give them what they want. Print reporters can do that in some regard, but . . . sometimes you just do it in the rush of things, or you'll go back. Is there a line to watch? Of course there's a line to watch. You never want someone to call you up and say, 'That's not what I said, and that's not what I meant.' But I've never had someone call me up and say, 'That's exactly what I meant, but you took three words out.' . . . Frankly, I don't think they remember how they said it.

"As long as you do the right thing, which is say what they mean, say it in a way close to what they said, and you're just making them appear a little better by fixing the grammar, fixing the order, inserting the word—I mean, are you expected to put the *ummm*'s in?" (Full disclosure: the *ummm*'s have been excised from this interview.) "In my view," David concluded, "quotes are not sacrosanct."

Many journalists writing for international media will interview sources in their shared native language, then translate the quotes into English for publication. When translating, it is perfectly acceptable to rework quotes as long as they remain true to the speaker's intentions, and especially if there is no direct equivalent in words or concepts. A student from Spain wrote: *One historian has continued in office without pay for the mere determination "to not give up."* An American would be more likely to say *not to give up,* and wording the quote that way would not change its meaning. Writing on high oil prices at home, a Brazilian student quoted a source as saying, "Stay home, take the bus, but don't fill up! Let them have more gasoline *in their stocks!*" Idiomatic English would be *in stock,* and it's all right to change the quote.

USING QUOTES TO TELL THE STORY

It is not enough to hear and render quotes accurately. Journalists need to use them effectively to humanize stories and move them along. Of course they want to write in their own voices and put their narrative stamp on stories, but readers and viewers want to hear other voices, too. Each quote needs to be part of a balanced whole. Quotes should never be the whole story; even in a one-source story, you don't want your work to read like a transcript—a string of quotes, one after another, without direction or interpretation from the writer. The best journalists weave quotations throughout the narrative as a whole like bright threads in a tapestry, making it more colorful and, at the same time, strengthening it.

Beginning reporters, especially those who have previously done mostly academic writing, make a common mistake: they write large blocks of descriptive text without any quotes. In early 2015 a student from India was working on her first *profile*—a well-rounded examination of a person in the news, *warts and all.* (That's an idiom meaning not entirely complimentary, showing the person's flaws and weaknesses as well as virtues and strengths.) Grammatical and other problems aside, her first draft had one major flaw: it presented little or no information in direct quotes. Consider this passage:

> *Born in Youngstown Ohio, an old steel town of the northeast, Meghan Louttit grew up in Middletown that had a population of only around fifteen hundred people. With cousins and grandparents living in the town, she never felt that the town was small or that she needed to move out of the small town.*

But the person who influenced Louttit to pursue her dream of becoming a journalist and move to a big town where she would meet people was her mom, Ms. Cheri. She supported Louttit in whatever she wanted to do and that freedom of going to school wherever she wanted helped her look for journalism schools across the country.

From a very young age Louttit had interest in writing. When she had first learnt to write at a very young age, she would use the scraps of paper, which her mother cut out to take notes, and write stories on them. Sharing her childhood memory, she recollects writing three pages long books on small things like a bicycle or a bunny. Her interest to draw and illustrate her own book, dates back to the time when she had first learnt to read and write. Meghan Louttit still nurtures that idea of illustrating or designing books but now her interest has shifted to designing a web page for The New York Times.

A graduate from the E.W. Scripps School of Journalism, Meghan Louttit fell in love with the campus and the colonial style buildings once she walked into the campus. Only two months into the journalism program, Louttit attended a conference on the influence of digital media on elections. It was 2004, just after the elections and one of the speakers at the conference was Joe Trippi, Howard Dean's campaign manager. His speech and the discussions in the conference made her realize that online media was very interesting and maybe that was what she wanted to do once she graduated.

This passage is written entirely in the reporter/narrator's voice, and not at all in the subject's—which the reader is longing to hear. Yet from the wording I could practically hear Louttit speaking. I returned the copy to the student with those sentences marked, "This would be stronger as a direct quote." Did she, in fact, have direct quotes on any or all of those topics? Now was the time to go back to her recording, transcribed or preferably not, and look for Louttit's exact words. Even if she had good, expressive quotes on just a few of those ideas, they would make her story much livelier.

Here's the second draft:

Born in Youngstown, Ohio, an old steel town, Louttit grew up in nearby New Middletown, population 1,500. Daughter of a high-school mathematics teacher and an elevator technician, Louttit grew up with her younger brother and cousins.

"My mom was very influential. She put the idea early on if I go to college I could leave," she said. Louttit wears a black bracelet on her left hand that has her mother's name on it, Cheri. It is a sign to commemorate her mother's victory as a cancer survivor.

Only two months into the freshman year at the E.W. Scripps School of Journalism at the University of Ohio, Louttit attended a conference on the influence of digital media on elections. It was 2004, just after the presidential elections and one of the speakers at the conference was Joe Trippi, Howard Dean's campaign manager.

"I had no idea what I was doing. But at the conference I realized this was so cool and interesting," said Louttit.

The panelists at the conference created a strong impact on her; she gained much knowledge about the importance of the media and what impact it had on readers. So Louttit got hold of Joe Trippi's book, "The Revolution Could Not Be Televised: Democracy, the Internet, and the Overthrow of Everything" and read it. "It was one of the first media books I read," she said.

After attending the media conference, she and seven other students realized there was no online media outlet at the school. So, they came up with the idea of an online magazine. While working on the online magazine, she learned HTML, CSS and JavaScript, all coding languages required to make the webpage. There were no coding classes at that time in the

*school, so she learned coding in her work-study programs and
also from students who knew it.*

*By the time Louttit finished the homepage for the online
magazine, she had failed more times than she succeeded.*

*"But the learning process was the most important thing
because you have to fail to know what doesn't work and how
to figure out an issue and make it better," she said.*

Though still not ready for publication, this draft is a big step forward. By adding quotes, the reporter let her subject help tell the story, in the process engaging readers more directly than before.

This passage from a Spanish student, in a story about victims still missing from the Spanish Civil War of the 1930s, cries out to be told in a direct quote:

> *ARMH was founded when Emilio Silva, a 40-year-old journalist, started looking for his grandfather, a disappeared victim of the political repression. He knew that a group of Phalangist gunmen had executed him in October 1936 and that his remains were in a mass grave in northwestern Spain. With the help of a team of volunteers, he unearthed the body of his grandfather along with twelve other Republicans. The exhumation was widely covered, and many other Spaniards then went to Silva with a desire to recover their own family members.*

Imagine how much stronger the passage would be if the reporter could supply quotes like these:

> *"I knew that a group of Phalangist gunmen had executed him in October 1936 and that his remains were in a mass grave in northwestern Spain," Silva said. With the help of a team of volunteers, he unearthed the body of his grandfather along with twelve other Republicans. The exhumation was widely*

covered, and afterwards, "many other people came to me wanting to recover their own family members," he said.

Of course, such quotes should be used only if the source actually said them.

Not everything a source says is so fascinating that it cries out to be a direct quote—for example: *"The festival will be held Saturday and Sunday, 10 a.m. to 6 p.m., rain or shine," Mr. Source said.* Reserve quotes for the most expressive, the most telling, the quirkiest speech—in short, the ones that give the flavor of the speaker's personality: *"I don't care if the heavens burst open and Zeus himself throws down thunderbolts at us," Mr. Source said. "The festival will go on."* Routine information may be *paraphrased*—that is, reported in fewer or better words than the source said, and outside quotation marks: *Mr. Source said the festival would go on rain or shine.* And never waste words repeating in a quote what you've already said in narrative: *Mr. Source said the festival would go on rain or shine. "It will go on rain or shine," he said.*

An Italian student wrote:

Grace Akello underlined the importance of an event like RAFF to raise awareness on Africa among Italians beyond the limited representations provided by the media. "I want to thank all of you and, more generally, the population and the Italian Government for the way they were accepting the people who land on your shores in search of a better future in Europe."

Thirteen words shorter and more interesting:

Grace Akello underlined the importance of an event like the RAFF in raising awareness of Africa among Italians beyond the limited representations provided by the media. She thanked Italians and their government for "accepting the people who land on your shores in search of a better future in Europe."

Like a translation, any paraphrase must accurately reflect the speaker's words and intention.

ATTRIBUTION

"Who says?" is another of my frequent comments on student work. Like most facts reported in the media, quotes need to be *attributed* to their sources. It's not enough to report a piece of information; what gives it credibility is where it came from. That means identifying the source by full name whenever possible and a few words of identification—a title, for example, or whatever qualifies him to be speaking, and quoted, on the subject:

> *"You have a bunch of new types of serious games," said Eric Greenbaum, a virtual reality developer and founder of the New York City Virtual Reality Meetup.*

> *"The stronger dollar has reduced earnings from abroad," said Scott J. Brown, senior vice president and chief economist of Raymond James.*

> *Serena Liguori, associate director at Herstory Writers Workshop, said this law was put in practice without much forethought.*

Note that the verb most commonly used in attributing quotes is *said.* Beginning journalists, having been told to avoid repetition in their copy, often reach for synonyms like *stated, declared, explained, opined, joked, quipped* and *according to.* In doing so, they fall into the trap of elegant variations (see page 205):

> *One of the issues he tackled was patriarchy. "All it does is to create victims," he assured.*

Monteiro affirms Santa Cruz was conscious when he arrived to the hospital.

"I came here for love," Elena underlines with a sly smile and a sudden light in her eyes.

In journalism the convention is *said*. It's simple, it says what it means, and there is rarely any need to replace it. Reserve *according to* for information that can be verified against documents, data, official statements and other sources, not for spoken words: *Almost 20,000 children are reported missing in New York State, and nearly all of them—96 percent—are suspected runaways, according to the 2014 Missing Persons Clearinghouse Annual Report.* When in doubt, stick with *said*.

In multi-sentence quotes, the attribution should generally follow the first complete sentence or thought, to help break up the long quote and make the paragraph read smoothly and end strongly. One student wrote:

"I am lucky to be healthy. There's nothing I would rather do with my time," said Jane O'Brien, 35, a volunteer.

Instead, place the attribution in the middle:

"I am lucky to be healthy," said Jane O'Brien, 35, a volunteer. "There's nothing I would rather do with my time."

Similarly:

"It started out definitely helping our trade balance as well as Petrobras, at least until the dollar went up," ~~explains~~ *said Adriano Pires, founder and director of the energy consultancy CBIE. "In the long haul, it should hurt our investments in deep-sea drilling."* ~~explains Adriano Pires, founder and director of energy consultancy CBIE.~~

If the first sentence in a quote is very long or complex, the attribution may be placed after the first cohesive phrase, where the speaker might have paused to take a breath:

Cabrera moved back home, but not for long. "I was kicked out again because I met a boy," he said, "and he was so disrespectful, so my mother told me to leave with him."

A quote itself is nearly always stronger than its attribution—another good reason to tuck the attribution into the quote rather than end with it, especially at the end of a story. If your story isn't an inverted pyramid, a strong quote often makes a good *kicker,* or ending. Don't sabotage a kicker quote by ending with the attribution. Instead, follow the example of that story about oil prices in Brazil. It ended:

She has a faint understanding about why the prices had to go up in the last few months. "I have a friend who works in Petrobras and explained that they had to do it—that the government was holding up the price and it was outdated," she said by phone. "But it doesn't feel to me that gasoline was ever cheap, was it?"

QUOTES AS LEDES

While quotes are often among the strongest parts of a story and make powerful endings, they tend to be weaker as ledes. Reporters are often tempted to lead with quotes, only to find them moved down by editors or slashed altogether. But without an established context—who is speaking? What is the setting or occasion?—a quote doesn't tell the reader much. Consider this lede from a first-semester student:

"I stand here today to inform you of the tortures, and I am begging you to use your First Amendment right to bring the truth on these stories," Victoria Phillips, a JAC (Jails Action

Coalition) community activist shouted. "Don't sugar-coat it when you speak about the unspoken voices behind walls," she added, making a vigorous demand to the press, urging us to speak about the unspeakable reality of New York City's convicts.

What tortures? What stories? The writer used up more than 60 words before coming out and telling the reader what the story was about: *"the unspeakable reality of New York City's convicts."* And it wasn't until the third paragraph that she mentioned the occasion:

On the steps of the City Hall this morning, heartbreaking/ powerful stories of convicts' daily lives of Riker's Island, were being unveiled. Many committees, including the Jail Association Coalition and Incarcerated Nation Campaign, gathered to speak up on behalf of the currently incarcerated people of the New York City's jails. Formerly incarcerated but also employees such as Phillips, brought light on the so-called cruel living conditions of the detainees.

By first setting the scene, the writer could have given readers the facts of the report and used the quote later to support and humanize them. Here's an alternative lede:

Advocates for inmates at New York City jails took their cause to the steps of City Hall this morning, telling powerful stories of what they described as cruel living conditions.

"I stand here today to inform you of the tortures, and I am begging you to use your First Amendment right to bring the truth on these stories," shouted Victoria Phillips, a community activist with the Jails Action Coalition. "Don't sugar-coat it when you speak about the unspoken voices behind walls."

This rewrite is by no means the only possible way to approach the story. (There is no one "right" way to tell almost any story, and no two editors see the same story exactly the same way.) But it does have the advantage of starting the reader off with the who (*advocates for inmates*), the what (*took their cause*), the when (*this morning*), the where (*the steps of City Hall*) and the why (*cruel living conditions*). Now the reader is up to speed on what the story is about, and more receptive to Phillips's plea.

MULTI-PARAGRAPH QUOTES

Long passages of quoted speech may be broken into paragraphs, each opening with quotation marks, but with no closing quotes until the very end of the passage, and with no need to repeat the attribution. A short example:

> "*I saw him die,*" *Cabrera said.* "*Then I ran home crying. I tried to do the best I could to be there for him.*
>
> "*I wish he was here with me so we could spend the rest of our lives together because we were so close.*"

Since, once again, the words within quotation marks are assumed to be the speaker's exact words, only continuous quotes should be rendered this way. Any omission should be indicated by an *ellipsis*, or three periods: . . . Then, if the publication's policy is not to indicate ellipses, at least the editor will know that material has been left out. An ellipsis should not be used to indicate a pause, an interruption or a thought trailing off; a full break in speech is indicated by a dash (–).

PARTIAL QUOTES

Quotes do not necessarily have to be full sentences. Partial quotes may be used when only some of the speaker's words are relevant; when the speech is unclear or the reporter is not sure of the entire quote; or when the exact words create a grammatical problem.

This previously quoted sentence on oil prices in Brazil contained an unclear antecedent (see page 194):

"It started out definitely helping our trade balance as well as Petrobras, at least until the dollar went up," said Adriano Pires, founder and director of energy consultancy CBIE.

What is "it"? An unclear antecedent, that's what it is. Instead:

The plunge in prices "started out definitely helping our trade balance as well as Petrobras, at least until the dollar went up," said . . .

(Notice how I used ellipsis to avoid retyping the rest of the sentence.)

In academic writing, brackets—those square parentheses, [ ] —are often used to add words that will clarify a quotation. Journalism prefers not to use brackets, since they insert words the speaker didn't say and interrupt the flow of a quote. One student's story about a charity run included this quote:

"I love my job," said Rosa Amelia Perez, 52, manager at the Children's Tumor Foundation who oversees the events. "Whatever it takes to make [the event] work. I don't care. I am here for the cure."

Perez actually said, "Whatever it takes to make *it* work." In the interview, it would have been clear to the reporter that *it* meant the run, but in print the antecedent would have been unclear. The reporter chose to clarify in brackets. Instead, she could have taken the unclear part of the sentence out of quotation marks, reworded it, then returned to Perez's exact words:

Whatever it takes to make the event work, she added, "I don't care. I am here for the cure."

Greg David, the business reporting professor, notes that prestigious publications like *The New York Times* and *The Wall Street Journal* use very few partial quotes. "Yet people who are stuck on trying to replicate the way things were absolutely, actually said have all these partial quotes," he said. "Similarly, I don't see that many parens in *The Times* or *The Journal*," he said, referring to material within parentheses or brackets. "In my view, they just fix up the quotes."

ANONYMOUS QUOTES

Some sources, especially those speaking on sensitive topics, ask or demand not to be identified publicly. Such requests should be allowed only rarely. The *anonymous pejorative*—a negative statement expressing criticism or disapproval—is to be avoided at all costs, since it allows a source to attack without being held accountable.

In general, all information gathered for the media is assumed to be *on the record*—eligible for publication—unless there is a clear advance agreement that it is *off the record*. Some sources may agree to speak on the record if, and only if, they are not identified, either by name or by a description that will make them recognizable. In some cases, journalists must agree to anonymity to get the information they need. In such cases, make sure granting anonymity does not violate the standards of your publication, and obtain authorization from your editor to quote anonymously in specific cases. Perhaps most important, explain to your audience why anonymity was granted. It's not enough to say a source *asked not to be identified;* the source needs to speak *on condition of anonymity.* Whenever possible, you should also give a good reason for granting it. Some examples:

> From Reuters: "*We are deeply concerned by yet another mass death sentence handed down by an Egyptian court to more than 100 defendants, including former President Morsi,*" *the State Department official said, speaking on condition of anonymity.*

From the Associated Press: *The official said one drone strike was on Jan. 14 and the other on Jan. 19. The official was not authorized to discuss details of the attacks and spoke on condition of anonymity.* (Note the repetition of "the official" to avoid identifying the source by sex using "he" or "she.")

Most reputable publications resist using false names except under special circumstances. But sometimes sources will protect themselves by refusing to identify themselves or giving only part of their names, as in this passage from a *New York Times* story on a police plan to get anonymous tips on crimes via text messages:

"*It's still a snitch,*" *said a 16-year-old who would give his name only as Brian.*

One of the points of using quotations is to give your reporting added credibility. Allowing too many anonymous sources undermines that credibility, making readers wonder just who the sources are, why they aren't identified or—as many suspect—whether you're just making it all up. Earn their trust by naming your sources unless it would keep you from getting the information. And above all, quote them accurately.

WAYNE SVOBODA

ON DEADLINE

As director of reporting and writing, Wayne Svoboda supervised Craft of Journalism, the core of the master's degree program. He has been a correspondent or editor for publications including *Time, The Economist* and *The Des Moines Register*, as well as freelancing for such publications as *The Wall Street Journal*. A Fulbright scholar, he has taught journalism and American studies in Russia and the Czech Republic. He has also directed the journalism program at Queens College and was an assistant professor at Columbia Graduate School of Journalism.

What makes good writing?

Good writing is clear. Clarity is the most important thing—clarity and the confidence to believe that you can write with a clear tone, I suppose.

A lot of people are wordy. . . . I was talking to somebody yesterday—I think the line someone was using was "Easy writing makes hard reading, and hard writing makes easy reading." And maybe that's to your question. It's just difficult. To write in a clear way, that's a difficult task. Without being glib about it, if it were easy, then more people would do it well. But just look at the evidence. Most people don't do it well. That tells me it's not easy. It's difficult. And people, I think, are foolish, because they think, somehow, it ought to be easy. I don't know why people think that.

What advice do you give students about making it clear, making it clean?

The first obvious thing that students fail to do is to write in advance of the deadline. When you write hot—when you write in a way that allows you to write the final word and hit "send" a minute before it's due, that's just guaranteed to be a disaster. That's what I've observed and learned over the years, and I tell students not to do it that way. A few of them do, but most of them choose to write until the last moment. That's a pity, I think, because it almost guarantees that your writing will be unclear.

If you don't write up until the last moment, how do you use that time between when you stop and the deadline?

Maybe two things right away come to my mind. One, you walk away, and then come back to it with fresh eyes, cold eyes. But the other thing you do is try to find a mate. Try to find someone who can look at it and read it, and have that person tell you, is this clear?

Typically, anytime you write something, you think it's clear because you've been wrestling with it forever. And so you think, how could anybody not understand? Students need to learn to let someone else have a look, and they need to have faith. When people say it's not clear, they need to not argue with them and say it *is* clear. They need to say, "Thank you very much."

How do you find, or make, the time for that on deadline? Do you cut yourself off half an hour before the deadline so you have time?

Half an hour is almost a failure because, yes, you have a little time to walk away and come back and look, depending on how long the story is. But ideally, depending on the work product, if you can manage it, certainly more time than half an hour. It's all a function of how much time you have in advance of the deadline.

Say it's Wednesday in Craft. You're due back at 3; your story is due at 5. What time should that draft be done?

You should be writing the draft at minimum in your head, and ideally, not just in your head but on paper on your way back so that when you're on your way back at 3 o'clock you've written it and then you're able to sit and write, assuming you haven't been already. . . . And then you do a second version, and then get up and take a little stretch and then maybe look at it again at 4. But in the meantime, if you can find somebody to look at your piece between 3:30 and 4, you could do that.

There's an old saying: "I didn't have time to write a short letter, so I wrote a long one." Do you find that's true in Craft?

Sure—often. Not always, but often enough that it's noticeable. People always think they'll do better if they have more space, more words, and that's just not true.

Some students—rookie students, newbies—will always say, "It's not as good as it should be because you don't give me enough space, you don't give me enough words." And that's something they need to unlearn. They need to learn that that's not true.

Any other tips for writing on deadline?

Just let the clock be your friend. Students freak out all the time about a deadline, and they need a deadline metabolism. Maybe the way to think of it, the clock is either your friend or foe, and it's just a clock. Students get anxious; they get worried. And the closer the clock comes to being deadline moment, the more anxious they become, and the more worried they become. And they just need to not feel like that.

They need to learn to go sit down and stay calm, not be frightened. It's easy to be frightened, but it's very harmful. Better to just stay calm.

How can writers learn from the editing process?

You learn from comparing what you've done to what's the finished product, after others have edited you. And then try to not have an ego about it, and not to be vain, and not to become angry, and not to be defensive. And just think, "Well, you know, maybe the person who's doing this is a fool, but probably not. There's probably something to be said for the changes that are being made, and it's in my interest to get better, and one way to get better is to see what other people do."

If you like an editor, or you don't like an editor, none of it matters. It only matters what happens on the page. It only matters what happens in the story. So really, just put your ego aside. Don't take things personally—even though in America we joke and say, "Well, how can I not take it personally? I'm a person, and it was directed at *me*." But that's not the point. The point is, don't think that it's about *you* in some specific, harmful way. It's just about the work. It's only about the work—almost always, it's only about the work.

CHAPTER 6

WRITING VERSUS SPEAKING

Whatever the language, native speakers often talk one way—or in a variety of ways—and write in another. This chapter is not about pronunciation, the focus of Chapter 7. Rather, it is about the differences between speaking English and writing it, for publication and other professional purposes. Speech is ephemeral: once out of the mouth, it is gone unless recorded on audio or video, or in a reporter's notebook. Writing lasts longer: a day in a print newspaper before it goes under the cat's litter box; an indefinite period online until the page is deleted or disappears from an archive; years, decades, even centuries for a book. (I own one printed in 1635.) Because writing is more permanent, we want to get it right.

Getting it right applies to the reporting as well as the English. Not so long ago, if a journalist made an error, only the people who read that day's newspaper were misinformed (and even fewer saw any eventual correction). Online, a story may be called up for years, and if an error goes uncorrected, it lives on. "Correction appended" at the top of a story acknowledges that an error was made and has been corrected.

In speaking or writing, what is "right" or appropriate depends on any number of factors—for example, the occasion. Chances are you talk differently when interviewing a news source, being interviewed for a job, making a request for official records and attending a news meeting. You write differently on your personal Facebook page and for your publication, or *its* Facebook page. You speak differently to your colleagues on a camera crew from the way you speak on camera. You might say *yeah* to your friends but *yes* to your boss.

It is the rare speaker of any language who speaks it perfectly 100 percent of the time in terms of grammar, sentence structure and usage. As I often tell students, school English is not street English. In real life, we get excited about what we're saying and talk in *run-ons* (see page 225), barely pausing to take a breath. Our thoughts trail off or we make a mental list, and we talk in *sentence fragments* (see page 206). Dean Sarah Bartlett unquestionably knows how to frame a complete sentence. But in the interview on page 43, she spoke *off the cuff* (that's an idiom meaning spontaneously, without preparation, as if finding the words on the cuff of your shirtsleeve), and her thoughts flowed out as gerund phrases (see page 210). Deconstructed, her answer to the first question might look something like this:

What makes good writing?

Making a story compelling by weaving in those old tools—anecdotes and scene-setting and telling even small stories within a larger story.

Building in little storytelling arcs, mini-arcs, if you will, within a larger piece.

Having a thread that runs through an entire story.

Technically, these are all sentence fragments; that is, they do not have a subject and predicate that add up to a complete thought. If Dean Bartlett were writing an essay on the subject, she would probably make sure each of her sentences did. Yet in conversation her fragments are entirely clear and do not interfere with communicating her ideas. That's how people talk in real life.

Or consider this old English-teachers' joke: "A preposition is nothing to end a sentence with." As Winston Churchill may or may not have said on the subject, "This is nonsense up with which I will not put." That sentence illustrates how awkward and stilted it can sometimes sound to be absolutely, grammatically correct. In the conversation quoted on page 90, Professor Greg David said, "That's not the order I said those sentences in." To be technically correct by not breaking up a prepositional phrase, he should have said, "That's not the order in which I said those sentences." In conversation (or most journalism) that would have sounded too formal; in more formal writing, such as academic writing, it would have been preferred. These are some of the reasons David allows students to clean up quotations, although I doubt he would bother to clean up his; again, it's the way people really talk. When editing text, I opt for the "in which" construction if it can be done simply and gracefully, without sounding as stiff as Churchill's joke.

People also slur their sounds. Americans who know just a little French often complain that the French don't pronounce half the letters in their words. (And they don't, or at least they gloss over some; it's called *elision,* and it's part of their language.) But Americans are no better, nor, I suspect, are speakers of most languages when talking to their countrymen. In short, English-speakers do not necessarily pronounce their words as spelled. (Once again, see Chapter 7.)

In urging students to enunciate clearly, my high school English teacher J. Frederic Knecht (whose word I have never had reason to doubt in 40 years as a professional editor), used to cite the following dialogue he claimed to hear often in the halls around lunchtime:

"Jeetchet?"
"No, joo?"

Translation:
"Did you eat yet?" (More properly: "Have you eaten yet?")
"No, did you?" ("No, have you?")

How does *did you eat yet* turn unto *jeetchet* and *did you* into *joo?* In English, the *d + u* combination often comes out sounding like *j* (as in *education* or *gradual*), while *t + y* comes out as *ch*—especially when said fast. (More on this in Chapter 7.) Thus are four- and three-syllable sentences condensed into two each.

And what about *I'm'na*, as in *I'm'na do a story on that*? That may be what you hear, but what the speaker thinks she's saying is *I'm going to*—an idiomatic expression of future intention—by way of *I'm gonna*. If you were puzzled when you first saw it written, so would your readers be if you wrote it that way for publication.

Informal contractions like *gonna* and *wanna* (want to) are among the most common examples of how Americans slur their words. (Ordinary contractions like the ones on page 22 are now acceptable in American journalism in all but the most formal cases.) As an exercise in listening and quoting accurately, a Chinese student in CUNY's class of 2016 was assigned to pull quotes from President Obama's speech at the 2015 White House Correspondents' Dinner. She quoted him as saying, "I *wanna* point out that when a guy has his face published on a 'Hope' poster . . ." I told her to write it as *want to* because quoting less-than-standard English can make the speaker look bad—uneducated, sloppy or just plain stupid—and you normally don't want to do that to your sources. (For this reason, most publications resist dialect except in special circumstances.) So write *going to, want to* and so on.

Exception: in 1994, when Hillary Rodham Clinton was First Lady, she was asked at a news conference whether she and her husband should have handled their scandal-ridden Whitewater investments many years earlier more carefully. "Shoulda, coulda, woulda," she replied. "We didn't." She meant *should have, could have, would have*, of course, but she chose to say it as she did and was rightly quoted that way. *Shoulda, coulda, woulda* has long been an idiom equivalent to *hindsight is 20/20;* Clinton was saying she might have done things differently had she known before what she knew then.

Another exception: CUNY journalism students are often baffled, at least initially, by a couple of New Yorkisms: *lemmegedda* and *fuhgeddaboudit. Lemmegedda*, as in *Lemmegedda coffee* (sometimes pronounced *cwawffee* by New York natives with a certain accent) translates as "Let me get a coffee," the always-in-a-hurry New Yorker's way of ordering a cup of coffee. (More formally and politely: *May I have a cup of coffee?* or *I'd like a cup of coffee*. And yes, *coffee* is technically an uncountable noun; *a coffee* means a cup, just as *a water* means a bottle of it or *a yogurt* means one cup.) And *fuhgeddaboudit?* It's the New York way of saying *forget about it*—don't even consider the possibility. Expressions like these are so emblematic that they may be written as spoken to underline the speaker's New Yorker status, but like all dialect, they should be used sparingly.

Native English-speakers, especially those who share the regional dialect, would have no trouble hearing these expressions. For international journalists, though, they may be serious obstacles to understanding sources and quoting them effectively. Here's where the recording techniques in Chapter 5 come in handy. If you don't quite understand what a source is saying—or if an editor questions your quote—go back to the recording and double-check exactly what the source said. Sloppy as these elisions may sound, it is crucial to master them and use them wisely.

PHRASING

A sentence is a sequence of words that expresses a complete thought. But—especially if the sentence is long and complex—it is also a collection of phrases that need to be spoken clearly and coherently to make sense. Most CUNY journalism students think of me as a writing coach, but I also work with broadcast students on their scripts and entrepreneurial journalism students on their project presentations. Yes, writing is the basis of all their work, but the delivery—the way they speak to an audience—is even more so. And phrasing is a key to their success.

If readers don't quite understand something in text, they can always go back over it, figuring out the complicated sentence structures, until they get it. Listeners, though, may not have a second chance, unless they are watching TV with recording capabilities or listening to online audio that allows them to back up and replay. Video and audio journalists, then, need to speak in such a way that their words, and their meaning, will be entirely clear to someone with just one chance to hear the report.

In writing, punctuation (see page 223) gives the reader direction, as well as a chance to pause every now and then to digest the information just presented before moving on to the next point. Speech has no such punctuation, except for the signals the speaker gives by pausing or coming to a full stop at the end of a sentence. A long sentence with no pauses or phrasing will be difficult, if not impossible, to understand. "That's a mouthful," I often say of long, complex sentences in writing, and they are even more of a mouthful when spoken.

Now, think about how to make your mouthful more digestible to a listener who has no text to look at. What words group together in phrases? (Two examples: prepositional phrases and dependent clauses.) What phrases work together to create coherent thoughts? Where can you, the speaker, pause to take a little breath and give both yourself and your listener a mini-rest? Mark the breaks on the written sentence. Now say the sentence out loud, observing the pauses and words groupings you have marked. Is it easier to say? More important, is it easier to understand? If so, you have broken it down correctly.

Here's a case study from a script by a CUNY journalism student for a video on abuse of restaurant workers:

When you have dinner at a restaurant, it is customary to leave tips, and if the food or the service is particularly good you might want to leave even more. But it doesn't always go to the person you think you are tipping.

That passage contains only two commas and two periods. Read it aloud, and you'll see how hard it is to take in all at once. To make it easier for your listeners, think first about what words go together in coherent phrases, and then break down the sentence into manageable chunks:

When you have dinner at a restaurant, / it is customary to leave tips, / and if the food or the service is particularly good / you might want to leave even more. / But it doesn't always go / to the person / you think you are tipping.

Similarly, from the same script:

With average restaurant workers earning around seven dollars per hour, tips are a crucial way employees can make enough money to survive.

Again, break it down:

With average restaurant workers / earning around seven dollars per hour, / tips are a crucial way / (that) employees can make / enough money to survive.

And, in the kind of sentence crucial to reporting because it demonstrates that you have tried your best to obtain comment from the other side:

The owners of the restaurant, Xiaotu Zhang and Wenyan Gao, didn't respond to our repeated requests for comment either by email, calls or in person.

Say it more like this:

The owners of the restaurant, / Xiaotu Zhang and Wenyan Gao, / didn't respond / to our repeated requests for comment / either by email, calls or in person.

Grouping the right words is especially important when saying sentences that include phrasal verbs (see page 219). From a *New Yorker* article on Islamist poets:

Hamza goes on to recall the odyssey of bin Laden and his family.

A Polish student reading it aloud broke it down this way:

Hamza goes / on to recall the odyssey / of bin Laden and his family.

But *go on* is a phrasal verb meaning *continue*, so she should have said it this way:

Hamza goes on / to recall the odyssey / of bin Laden and his family.

Another student read a sentence as *We are thinking about moving / in together.* But those last three words are an idiom meaning starting to share living quarters, and the phrasal *moving in* needs to stay together: *We are thinking about moving in / together.*

Too often, American newscasters reporting breaking stories sound breathless, as if they are racing to tell you the story and cannot stop. That gives a sense of immediacy, but their storytelling would be far more effective if they slowed down and broke their sentences into chunks. Anchors also have a bad habit of moving from one story to another without coming to a full stop—putting a mental period at the end of one sentence or topic—and taking a breath before moving on to the next story. This technique can also help you detect run-ons (see page 225). If you go through two or three thoughts without pause and find yourself out of breath, your "sentence" is probably a run-on that needs to be broken up.

REGISTER

When Obama said *I wanna point out,* he was speaking at a relatively informal setting, for Washington. The president's speech at the annual correspondents' dinner is essentially a chance to do stand-up comedy, making fun of himself, the media, the entire Washington political scene. Obama, with his deadpan face and dry delivery, is a natural at it. (Witness his cool performance at the 2011 dinner, when the operation that would kill Osama bin Laden the next night was already in progress.)

This graduate of Columbia University and Harvard Law School is certainly capable (unlike some other recent presidents) of enunciating *I want to,* but here the less formal *wanna* suited the occasion. Similarly, it has been widely noted that Obama spoke in a less formal, more folksy manner on the campaign trail—presumably because he wanted to come across as less intellectual and more connected with ordinary citizens. In the July 2015 *Vanity Fair,* Graydon Carter noted in his "Editor's Letter" that when candidates are running for president, "you start hearing a lot more 'gotta's and 'lemme's from the lips of people who went to Wellesley or Yale" (two elite colleges).

In such cases, politicians are proving their ear for *register*—the degree of formality suitable to a particular occasion. In English, as in most other languages, successful communication depends heavily on knowing which words and usages are formal and which are informal, and when each is appropriate. Americans tend to be less formal than people from many other cultures. Their speech is less formal than their writing, and their journalism less formal than academic writing. Even within that framework there are varying degrees of formality.

Sometimes slang is acceptable, sometimes not. Sometimes even profanity is acceptable in certain circumstances, at editorial discretion. Even a magazine as traditionally high-toned as *The New Yorker* now regularly prints swear words and what were once considered unprintable obscenities—but probably only with the explicit approval of a high-ranking editor, as is the case at *The New York Times.* Or consider this passage from an episode of Sarah Koenig's "Serial" podcast from National Public Radio:

> *About a month later, on Feb. 9, Hae's body was found in a big park in Baltimore, really a rambling forest. A maintenance guy, who said he stopped to* **take a leak** *on his way to work, discovered her there.*

Take a leak is slang, generally considered vulgar, for *urinate.* (More politely, *going to the bathroom* in American English, *to the washroom* in Canadian or *to the loo* in British.) It is also more commonly used by men than women, suggesting that it was the maintenance worker's phrasing rather than Koenig's. In the old days, the phrase—or even the universal biological function behind it—would have been too vulgar even to mention in many publications such as *The New Yorker* or *The New York Times*, let alone to use the slang. But it was acceptable in an NPR storytelling podcast in late 2014, possibly because podcast audiences tend to be younger and less likely to be offended. (Even so, on the day I was writing this paragraph, *The Times* posted a story on public urination in New York City that used two other common synonyms it would have considered unfit to print 30 years before.)

As that case suggests, the degree of formality in storytelling may vary by medium as well as occasion. In May 2015, *The Times* published a front-page investigative series on the city's nail salon industry. The story by Sarah Maslin Nir started with a five-paragraph anecdotal lede before coming to its nut grafs:

> *Once an indulgence reserved for special occasions, manicures have become a grooming staple for women across the economic spectrum. There are now more than 17,000 nail salons in the United States, according to census data. The number of salons in New York City alone has more than tripled over a decade and a half to nearly 2,000 in 2012.*
>
> *But largely overlooked is the rampant exploitation of those who toil in the industry. The New York Times interviewed more than 150 nail salon workers and owners, in four languages, and found that a vast majority of workers are paid below minimum wage; sometimes they are not even paid. Workers endure all manner of humiliation, including having their tips docked as punishment for minor transgressions, constant video monitoring by owners, even physical abuse. Employers are rarely punished for labor and other violations.*

Note the formal language (words like *indulgence, spectrum, toil* and *rampant;* expressions like *all manner of*), the reverse construction *(largely overlooked is . . .)* and the long sentences. Now consider the equivalent of the nut graf in a follow-up story on NBC (http://www.nbcnews.com/news/us-news/ny-governor-cracks-down-nail-salon-after-abuse-exposed-n357041):

> *Pick a color—that's the toughest choice a customer faces at the nail salon. But according to a stunning report, the workers putting on the polish may feel like they have no choice but to sit on a stool for hours on end . . . [Workers] said they initially paid salon owners for the right to work and then, after months of free labor, made as little as $3 an hour.*

Here both language and concepts are much simpler and conversational. Part of the reason may be that *The Times* report ran thousands of word in print—more than 6,000 for just the first part of the series—while the entire TV report, including lead-in, lasted just 3 minutes and 6 seconds, and thus needed to get its message across faster and more directly. Again, in audio and video, the audience is hearing the information, not reading it, and is less likely to be able to go back and listen again to what it missed the first time. Since TV reporters, like Koenig on the "Serial" podcast, are essentially telling a story rather than writing it, they not only can but should be more conversational.

Legal and governmental language tends to be highly formal, making it precise for legal scholars and public officials, perhaps, but often all but incomprehensible to the average reader. An early paragraph in the U.S. Supreme Court's landmark 2015 majority opinion on gay marriage read in part:

> *The history of marriage as a union between two persons of the opposite sex marks the beginning of these cases. To the respondents, it would demean a timeless institution if marriage were extended to same-sex couples. But the petitioners, far from*

seeking to devalue marriage, seek it for themselves because of their respect—and need—for its privileges and responsibilities, as illustrated by the petitioners' own experiences. (68 words)

Journalists, especially broadcast journalists, would paraphrase the passage for readers interested mainly in what it meant to their own lives:

These cases stem from the traditional definition of marriage as a union of a man and a woman. Opponents say same-sex marriage devalues this timeless institution. But the people who brought the cases value marriage enough to want to share in its benefits and responsibilities. (45 words)

The decision was based on the Equal Protection Clause in the Fourteenth Amendment to the Constitution, which says: "No state shall make or enforce any law which shall abridge the privileges or immunities of citizens of the United States; nor shall any state deprive any person of life, liberty, or property, without due process of law; *nor deny to any person within its jurisdiction the equal protection of the laws.*" Less formally, that says *the government must treat all citizens equally.* You may want to quote the original text to make a point, but in most cases, the simpler paraphrase will serve your audience better.

Curiously, some of the most elevated language American journalists encounter comes from the lowly police *blotter,* or log of crimes, arrests, accidents and other, often petty, police calls. Officers tend to write their reports in very formal language to conform with language in the penal codes, so they use phrases like *the alleged perpetrator was apprehended* to say *the suspect was arrested.* From a story on an Indiana news website about a mother charged with child abuse:

A medical examiner at Kosair Children's Hospital reported the toddler had extensive bruising, abrasions, contusions and scratches over much of his body.

Abrasions are more commonly called *scrapes*. *Contusions* are bruises, and the use of both words suggests that neither the reporter nor the editors knew that. Such language indicates the information was taken straight from the blotter, which may also have used words like *lacerations* (cuts) or *fractures* (breaks). In an article about a car crash that seriously injured the governor of New Jersey, *The New York Times* reported:

> *Gov. Jon S. Corzine underwent surgery on Thursday night after a car accident in which he broke his left leg, sternum, collarbone, six ribs on each side and a lower vertebra, state police and other government officials said.*

I would bet money that the original police or emergency medical report, and possibly the surgeon who spoke at a news conference, said Corzine had *fractured* these bones, and that he had fractured his *clavicle* rather than his collarbone. And I would have further edited the *sternum* to *breastbone*. Whenever possible without violating register or accuracy, simplify to make things easier for the reader.

As a journalist, you may find yourself not only changing register in different situations or with different people, but also becoming progressively less formal with your sources as you establish relationships. Here's an abridged e-mail chain from my own recent request to a press agent for an interview with a Broadway actor to discuss a show in which he had starred a decade earlier:

> *Dear Ms. ---------:*
>
> *I am writing to ask the best way to set up an interview with Michael Cerveris about his memories of "Assassins."*
>
> *The Sondheim Review is doing a special issue on "Assassins" and has assigned me the interview, with a July 10 deadline. By way of introduction, I am a freelance writer in New York specializing in the arts. I spent 20 years as an editor at The New York Times, primarily on the culture news*

desk. My most recent article for The Sondheim Review was an interview with David Loud in advance of the Lyrics & Lyricists program at the 92nd Street Y on the Sondheim-Prince partnership.

Thank you for any guidance, and I look forward to hearing from you.

Sincerely . . .

In this initial contact, I chose relatively formal language and structure to introduce myself, clearly state the purpose of the interview and present my credentials. Once I had established a professional basis (and probably after checking me out independently to make sure I wasn't a stalker), the press agent felt comfortable enough to respond less formally:

Hi Diane,

Hope you're well! I'm happy to arrange. He's asked if we can do it next Thursday, June 25 from 5:15–5:45 PM, at Citizen M on 50ᵗʰ ST.

Let me know if that works, and we can confirm. And just to clarify—it's for print only... no photos or video, right?

Thanks.

My response:

That's all perfect. Yes, text only. The Sondheim Review *will want to use a photo of him in "Assassins," of which the editor is sure to have many in hand. Looking forward, and I'll reconfirm next week.*

And finally:

Great, then it's confirmed for 5:45–6:15 PM. If that ends up not working for you, let me know ASAP and we can hopefully adjust a little.

A telephone request could proceed in much the same way, but it might even start out a bit less formal because it's speech.

That interview negotiation, for a magazine feature with a three-month *lead time* (in this case, the time to the reporter's deadline, as opposed to the time until publication), took place over nearly two months. Breaking news is more urgent, and you may not have time for all the formalities on every occasion. Imagine that you have been granted an exclusive sit-down interview with the president of the United States; as you sit facing him in the Oval Office, you will probably take a respectful, even courtly tone befitting the setting and the courtesy he has granted you. (Sir David Attenborough's for the BBC, https://www.youtube.com/watch?v=NZtJ2ZGyvBI, may be an extreme example; more usual is David Muir's for ABC, http://abcnews.go.com/Politics/obama-rule-presidential-visit-cuba-lets/story?id=27675478, or Thomas L. Friedman's for *The New York Times*, http://www.nytimes.com/video/opinion/100000003048414/obama-on-the-world.html.) At a press conference—where the pace is faster and you are competing with other reporters to have your questions heard and answered—your tone may be less formal, especially at a time of crisis. Trying to get the president's attention as he steps off a helicopter on the White House lawn, you may only be able to shout out a brief question. The circumstances will help determine your register.

Sometimes reporters do need to be aggressive, though perhaps not so aggressive as in the video showing the high-finance swindler Bernard Madoff being pushed by a news photographer as reporters shouted questions (https://www.youtube.com/watch?v=ZnMAMjhqpyM). But there is a very thin line between being effective and offensive. At a news conference on the 2015 Iran nuclear arms deal, CBS reporter Major Garrett seemed to be using the occasion to challenge Obama (https://www.youtube.com/watch?v=oMI7HPq3tXI):

Thank you, Mr. President. As you well know, there are four Americans in Iran—three held on trumped-up charges

*and according to your administration and one whereabouts
unknown. Can you tell the country, sir, why you are content
with all the fanfare around this deal to leave the conscience
of this nation, the strength of this nation, unaccounted for in
relation to these four Americans? And last week the chairman
of the Joint Chiefs of Staff said under no circumstances should
there be any relief for Iran in terms of ballistic missiles or con-
ventional weapons. It is perceived that that was a last-minute
capitulation in these negotiations. Many in the Pentagon feel
you've left the Joint Chiefs of Staff hung out to dry. Would you
comment?*

Whether or not the question itself was appropriate, Garrett's tone,
both on video and in the transcript, was mostly measured and digni-
fied, appropriate to the occasion. (That said, *trumped-up* and *hung out
to dry* are fairly informal idioms, meaning *made up or invented* and
left to suffer the consequences.) Garrett did not come across as angry or
inflammatory, like a reporter from, say, the conservative Fox News. He
did explain the next day: "I provoked the president to reconcile what I
believe are two issues that any president under the circumstance should
have to address. . . . All I was trying to do was elicit from the command-
er-in-chief where these four Americans in Iran fell in his prioritization of
obtaining a nuclear deal and whether he fought for their release." Even
so, media websites were ablaze for a day or two over whether Garrett had
overstepped his role and been disrespectful.

Whatever your deadline, choose a register appropriate to the occasion. Don't follow the example of the old-time reporter for *The Boston
Herald* (not a native English-speaker) who was notorious for opening
phone interviews with questions like, "Hello, you the mother of the dead
kid?" More appropriate (and effective):

Hello, this is ----- from The Boston Herald. *Am I speaking to
Mrs. -----? And you're the mother of ------? Ma'am, I'm very
sorry to hear about your loss. I'm working on an article about*

the shooting, and I was wondering if you feel up to telling me
a little about your son.

And then proceed as gently as possible; the questions are sure to be painful to your source. Always apply sensitivity and good judgment. Remember that you represent your publication. Any missteps you make will reflect on it and reduce your effectiveness.

LONNIE ISABEL

PAINTING VISUAL PICTURES

Before joining the Columbia School of Journalism in 2015, Lonnie Isabel was a professor and distinguished lecturer at CUNY. There he trained about 100 future foreign correspondents, drawing from his own experiences reporting from Cuba, India and the Middle East. In his 30-year newspaper career, he was a reporter and editor at *The Oakland Tribune*, *The Boston Globe* and *Newsday*, leaving in 2005 as deputy managing editor in charge of foreign and national coverage. At *Newsday*, he supervised coverage of the O.J. Simpson case, the impeachment of President Bill Clinton, the 2000 presidential election and the Iraq War. He is co-writing a textbook on new ethical challenges in video reporting and documentaries.

What makes good writing? Or, in this day and age, good communication?

I think "in this day and age" is a key part of it. Good writing has always been the same: it's been a human connection. It's a human voice; it's warmth; it's personality. The ability to show that, in your writing, is something you can acquire, and it's something that, for some people, comes fairly naturally. But I think that in this day and age, it means that it must be quick, that it must be attractive on the Internet, that it almost has to have extra visual quality. So writing has changed because you have to almost always have pictures or film. And so some of that need to be so descriptive has disappeared. But I would have to say . . . anyone who thinks that this new age and the Internet have changed writing irretrievably, I think, is very wrong because we're in sort of a golden age of writers.

Are there differences between writing for print, for broadcast, for online?

Yes, there are, and they're subtle and very strong. All of it is painting visual pictures. With audio, with radio, painting visual pictures is extremely difficult because you're not getting a chance to actually *have* pictures. With visuals, your language is basically augmenting what you see, and so I think there is a great fascination with all the new technology and the things that make us want to put things evocatively online. But really, *really* compelling writing online can work.

I was rereading Ta-Nehisi Coates's very long, voluminous essay calling for reparations. ("The Case for Reparations," the *Atlantic*, June 2014; http://www.theatlantic.com/features/archive/2014/05/the-case-for-reparations/361631/) And it was brilliant writing. It was all online; it had all of the whiz-bangs and graphics and pictures and clicks and the things that may be distracting—would have been distracting reading Shakespeare. But it was also really brilliantly written.

So I don't think writing has suffered; it's just changed. Those different media all have had an impact.

What do we, as writers, have to do to change with it?

The thing about writing, and the thing that makes it so great, is that it's always about reinvention. It's always about trying to find a way not to find yourself, but to reach the people where they need to be reached, and to find an audience that is willing to partake of your work. I think that finding that audience, in a way, has become easier and not so easy. It's become easier because we can distribute it, but not so easy because we can't specify and find the very people who might have gone to a bookstore and looked around and figured out what they could get. So I think we have to realize that the reader has changed: that the reader is hungry for more visual imagery. The reader wants to be involved with characters. Most readers love people more than ideas. But we *must* have ideas that match people, and vice versa. So it makes it much more of a challenge.

We have to change, somewhat, our pace because we're at a rapid, rapid pace now. I've been rereading some novels that I read and loved when I was younger, and they're so slow! Even Ralph Ellison's *The Invisible Man,* which is such a dynamic novel—if you read it and read Annie Proulx or somebody, it's so slow. It's brilliant, but I think we have to adapt to the fact that people want to move.

You've worked a lot with international reporters and international students here. In terms of the English language, what advice would you have for a foreign journalist working with American media?

One of my favorite writers of all time is, of course, Joseph Conrad, who never spoke a word of English until he was an adult. In the things I've read about him, he just read every damn thing he could get his hands on. He read, you know, the back of a Cracker Jack box. And I think that listening is really important—listening not just to what the words may mean, but to the inflection and the rhythm and the pace of a language. As writers, we have to have that.

The thing a non-English-speaker kind of gets trapped on is clichés. Well, all of us do. But I think you have to rigorously kill them because that's how you learn the shorthands of language, when, really, they don't really say much and they're sort of like empty boxes. That's particularly a challenge for people with other languages because they experience our own conversational clichés. And writing is how we wish we could speak—all of us, *all* of us. If you wish you could speak English as much as Joseph Conrad wished that he could write it, you'll be OK.

CHAPTER 7

PRONUNCIATION PITFALLS

First, the noun (or adjective, as used above) is *pronunciation*. But the verb is *pronounce*—not *pronunciate*, as any number of students have tried to pronounce it.

It's an understandable mistake. The noun *enunciation* comes from *enunciate*, so why not *pronunciate*? But then, from the same Latin root (*nunc-* for *speak* or *declare*, not to be confused with the adverb *nunc*, meaning *now*) also come *announce*, *denounce* and *renounce*. Anyone learning a foreign language prefers to think there are hard-and-fast rules. But as you may have noticed, English has lots of rules and at least as many exceptions; regular verbs (those that form past tense by adding *-ed* or *-d*), but also hundreds of irregular ones that follow no consistent pattern, like *see/saw, run/ran, keep/kept, sing/sang, think/thought, teach/taught, lead/led, read/read* (past tense pronounced *red*). And no aspect of the language is more irregular than pronunciation.

The noun *nation* is pronounced with a long, or tense, *a* sound, but when the part of speech shifts to the adjective *national* or another noun derived from that, *nationality*, the *a* sound becomes short, or lax. Same with the *y* in *cycle*, which becomes short *i* sound in the adjective, *cyclical*. In *society* the *ci* is pronounced like *sigh*, but in the adjective *social* and other words derived from it (*socialize, socialism*) the *s* sound turns into *sh*. The *-ate* ending is pronounced like the past tense of *eat* in verbs but more like *uht* in nouns and adjectives. (See page 142.) Non-native speakers often say that they are *ti-red*, or that something is made of *i-ron*, when the words they want—*tired* and *iron*—are correctly pronounced more like *TIE-erd* and *I-ern*.

Journalists no longer report the news only, or even primarily, in writing. Today even print reporters may also be expected to become video or podcast personalities. Mistakes annoy the target audience and undermine credibility, so media figures need to pay close attention to their pronunciation—among them the veteran New York television reporter who talked about the mayor's *clap-board* house—one covered with *clapboard*, overlapping strips of wood. (It's pronounced *KLAB-erd*.) And she's a native speaker, but she apparently wasn't familiar with the word.

Everyone makes errors in English related to his or her own language. In our native languages, we never have to think about how to make sounds; we've been making them since early childhood. But when studying foreign languages, we do.

One Japanese student at CUNY worked for a year on the difference between *walked* and *worked*, and *collaborate* and *corroborate*. Japanese has no *l* sound, and since *l* is a liquid sound (made largely by air flowing around the tongue) closely related to *r*, she had trouble first hearing those sounds and then saying them correctly. And the *mayoral elections* she had once covered? Let's not go there. (Americans have been known to make fun of Japanese-speakers with the phrase *flied lice*—fried rice—apparently unaware that fried rice is Chinese.) Spanish-speakers find it difficult to start words with an *s* sound, since their language does not; "*I espeak eSpanish*," they say, or at least that's how Americans hear them. The Chinese tend to speak English in a choppy way, as if lowering a meat cleaver between words and often syllables. Poles have trouble getting the accents within words right because in Polish the accent is almost always on the second-last syllable, and they carry the habit over into English. French-speakers tend to accent the last syllable, as they do in French.

Scott Thornbury, an internationally recognized expert in English teacher training, suggests using movies or TV in English—popular the world over—as a learning tool. As you imitate the accent you hear onscreen, he says, think about how you form its sounds differently from the closest equivalents in your native language. Practice, and then transfer them to your spoken English. (For more ways to learn from movies and TV, see Chapter 14.)

Some pronunciation problems cross borders: misplaced accents, rhythms, choppiness, past tenses, difficult or easily confused sounds that may not exist in other languages. This chapter is not intended to be a comprehensive pronunciation guide addressing every problem stemming from every language. (For an excellent language-by-language summary that I consult regularly, see *Teaching American English Pronunciation*, by Peter Avery and Susan Ehrlich, Oxford, 1992.) Nor should you expect it to perfect your pronunciation; for that you need practice with a teacher or native speaker who can give you feedback. Rather, it is a guide to attacking some general problems with English pronunciation common to speakers of various languages, based on those I hear repeatedly among the international students at the CUNY journalism school. Not every student suffers from every problem listed, but there is probably something here for everyone. Sounds are rendered not in the phonetic alphabet you may have studied in language classes, but as they would more likely be rendered in "pronouncers" in text journalism.

One general observation: over the centuries, English has evolved in such a way that the "correct" pronunciation is often the one that is easiest for the mouth to form. *Woman,* for example, came from *wiffmann,* or "female human" in Old English (not *womb-man,* meaning a human with a womb, or uterus, as some feminists say); *Mrs.* (MISS-iz) is a contraction of *Mistress,* the feminine form of *master,* both used as courtesy titles hundreds of years ago. If your mouth is having trouble moving from one sound to the next to the next in a word, chances are you're trying too hard and saying it wrong. Check the pronunciation in a dictionary, especially an online one with audio, and practice. As Polly Merdinger of Columbia University's American Language Program said on the first day of Sound Systems of English, her teacher-training course at the New School in New York: "It's OK to make funny noises in this class."

REVIEW: THE ALPHABET

American children learn their ABC's to the tune known to French speakers as "Ah, vous dirai-je, maman" and to English speakers as "Twinkle, Twinkle, Little Star." For that reason, some kids think *elemeno* is one letter, like *double-u* (*w*). Actually, it's four—*l, m, n, o*; it's just that the tempo speeds up at that point in the song. To hear the alphabet spoken in both British and American English, look no further than YouTube: https://www.youtube.com/watch?v=hommWz1qKGk.

In spellings of words and especially names, it is important for journalists to hear and say the letters as we do in English, or their work may contain errors. French-speakers often confuse *g* (pronounced *jee*) and *j* (pronounced *jay*) because their French pronunciations are the opposite (*zhay* and *zhee*). Europeans pronounce the last letter of the alphabet *zed*—which is fine if they're dealing with the British, but Americans pronounce it *zee*, and those who don't know foreign languages may have no idea what *zed* means. A Polish student, reading aloud a story about new apps, pronounced the X in the phrase "Ubers for X" as *eex*, not the English *ex*.

Vowels—*a, e, i, o, u* and sometimes *y*—are the letters whose sounds are produced by air flowing freely, without obstruction, from the lungs up through the throat and out the mouth. All the others are *consonants*, whose sounds are produced when the air is blocked in some way by the tongue, teeth or lips. Vowels may be either *long* (your English teachers may have said *tense*) or *short* (*lax*). Long vowels sound like the letters: *a, e, i, o, u: same, be, I, owe, cue*. Long *u*'s are sometimes pronounced *oo* as in *mood*, and sometimes *yu*, as in *popular* and *regular*. Short vowels are said more quickly and with a more open mouth, as in *bag, beg, big, bog, bug*.

Variations in vowel sounds largely account for different accents in English. In the word *plate,* I say the long *a* the way I learned growing up in Pennsylvania; a friend from Melbourne, Australia, says it in a way that is standard to her but sounds like *plight* to me. While I say *right,* she says what I hear as *roight*. A Polish student confused me when I heard her say *blood concert,* which I interpreted as a benefit concert for victims of some blood disease. Well, close: she meant *blood cancer,* or leukemia.

My confusion was due to her pronunciation of that *a* in the European way—*ah*—instead of the flatter short-*a* sound.

It is important to get vowel sounds right, or you may be misunderstood. In *wander* and *wonder,* the first-syllable vowels are very close in sound and need to be very clear—*WAHN-der* for the first, *ONE-der* for the second. And be especially careful with the distinction between long-*e* and short-*i* sounds. If you say *ship* for *sheep,* you may cause only momentary confusion, but the same vowel error in words like *beach* and *sheet* will produce words that may offend your listener. (Try it and see what you hear.)

VOICED AND UNVOICED SOUNDS

Now, think about that column of air that comes up from your lungs. It flows through the larynx, or voice box, which contains your vocal cords. (Note that spelling: *cords,* not *chords,* which refers to musicals sounds.) The cords' vibrations affect the air flow and help produce the sound, but not every sound requires them to vibrate. *Voiced* sounds involve vibration; *unvoiced* sounds do not. All vowels sounds are voiced, but consonants may be either voiced or unvoiced. To determine which are which, put two fingers on that soft indent at the base of your throat and go through the alphabet, saying the sounds—not the letters themselves, most of which end in vowel sounds. If you say the letter *p,* for example, it will come out as a voiced sound; if you say just the sound, you will find it is an unvoiced puff of air through the lips.

Knowing the difference between voiced and unvoiced sounds is important because it affects pronunciation of particular words and gives you a perhaps unwanted accent. The letter s may be pronounced as an *s* or a *z,* depending on the word—for example *decisive* (*s*) but *revise* (*z*). Both sounds are made by touching the top of your tongue to the ridge behind your top teeth, but the *s* sound is unvoiced, while *z* is voiced. If you are a TV reporter covering a story on New York City rent guidelines, you don't want to say that legal rents *increazed*; that would mark you as a non-native speaker. It's *increased.*

THE WEAK VOWEL SOUND: UH

In America my name is Diane, but among my German friends I also answer to *Diana*. It's not that the spelling changes when I land in Berlin, but rather the way that final *e* is treated in their language: as an *uh* sound. (In English, a final *e* tends to be silent. It also tends to lengthen the vowel preceding it—though not in *Diane,* where the *a* is short. English has exceptions to every rule.) In a dictionary or the phonetic alphabet, that would be written as a schwa, or upside-down *e*, and pronounced like a short *u* sound: *uh,* as in *bug.* "Think of how you feel," I often tell students in New York, "when you come home exhausted from a long day of shopping. You drop your bags, you fall into a chair and you say 'Uh!' That's the sound"—as if everything simply drops, including your jaw.

It's a weak sound, but it is one of the most important in English for a simple reason: the vowel(s) in the unaccented syllable(s) of thousands of words are pronounced simply *uh.* Any vowel may be pronounced *uh* depending on the word. If you pronounce every vowel in a word exactly as it's spelled, you will tend to draw out each syllable, throwing off the accent and ultimately the rhythm of both word and sentence—crucial to good English. (See below.)

Not every unaccented vowel is a weak vowel—for example, *campaign, vacation, icon, compensation.* When in doubt, consult a dictionary or the nearest native speaker.

ACCENT AND RHYTHM

To American ears, Indians and Scandinavians speak English with a singsong lilt, their voices going up and down in pitch in no apparent relation to the rhythm of a sentence. Spanish overheard on the New York subways sounds *rat-a-tat-tat*, as if syllables are being fired from a machine gun. The Chinese sound choppy, each word or even syllable disconnected from the last. The Japanese seem to have no rhythm at all, speaking in an even monotone with no apparent change in pitch and volume.

Every language, even Japanese, has its own rhythm that may sound, well, foreign to speakers of other languages. In English, a rhythm that is slightly off may not interfere with comprehension, but it will give the speaker an accent, which may affect the impression he makes. Sadly, Americans do judge foreigners on the way they speak English. One CUNY student from Asia, starting her beat reporting for Craft, said she felt the sources she approached didn't take her seriously; whether because she was a student or because she spoke with an accent, she wasn't sure. While we may never completely master the rhythms of a second, third or fourth language, improving your rhythm is a big step in improving your English overall—and thus your credibility as a reporter.

In teacher talk, languages are either *syllable-timed,* with each syllable taking about the same amount of time, or *stress-timed,* in which some are shorter and some longer. Japanese, with its evenness, and Spanish, with its rapid fire, are syllable-timed; English is strongly stress-timed. To communicate effectively, you may have to adapt your speaking rhythms to those of English. Otherwise, native speakers may perceive you as uninterested, as the Japanese monotone suggests to Americans, or even comical, as they find the Indian singsong.

Even if your language is stress-timed, the stress may not be the same as in English. In French the last syllable of the word almost always gets the accent; in Polish it is the second-last. The four tones of Chinese in some ways take the place of English rhythm.

In English, we accent a syllable three ways: by raising the pitch—that is, saying it on a higher musical note; by saying it a little louder; and by sometimes drawing it out. (The Japanese come closest in words that hold a vowel sound for two beats instead of one, as in *sayonara,* which is properly pronounced not *sa-yo-NA-ra,* as stress-timed English-speakers think, but *sa-yo-o-nara.*)

Here's where that weak vowel sound in English becomes so important. Remember that often, though far from always, the vowel in an unaccented syllable gets the weak *uh* sound. It's a short sound, and if you draw it out to pronounce the letter as written, it will compete with the accented syllable, and thus the rhythm of the word. I often have to correct students' pronunciation of words like *consumer* and *computer.* They come out as *CON-sumer* and *COM-puter* because the students are trying to make that *o* sound like an *o;* in doing so, they hold the sound a fraction of a second too long and give the syllable too much weight. The weak vowel will give the words their correct pronunciations: *cuhn-SU-mer, cuhm-PU-ter.*

A long word may require accenting more than one syllable. The *primary accent* takes the strongest stress; the *secondary accent* gets somewhat less but still a recognizable accent. Once when I was teaching in Poland, the word *extemporaneously* came up in a reading, and students were baffled by both the meaning and the pronunciation of this seven-syllable word. First, for meaning, I broke it down into its Latin roots and English suffixes: *ex + tempor + aneous + ly. Temp-* comes from the Latin word for time; *ex-* means from or out of; *-aneous* makes it an adjective, and *-ly* into an adverb. So if you are speaking *extemporaneously*, you are speaking *from the time* or *the moment*—that is, without preparation. Now, how to say it? You might be tempted to accent the syllable with the most important root—*temp-*, as in *temporary*—but you'd be wrong; try it and see how the rest of the word comes out. Instead, the word sounds more like *ex-**tem**-po-**RAY**-ne-ously*, with the **RAY** getting the strongest accent and the **tem** a lighter one. The remaining five syllables get just about equal, unaccented weight, giving the word its distinctive rhythm. Many, many words have similar primary and secondary accents, among them *Mediterranean, globalization* and *serendipity.*

Phrases and sentences also have rhythm. Once again, think about how a word is spoken: one or two syllables are accented, while the rest are not. Now extend that idea to sentences: we tend to accent the important words and drop the pitch and volume for the others. The important, accented words are generally the nouns and verbs; the less important are articles, prepositions and *parenthetical* expressions (those that could be placed in parentheses or lifted out of the sentence completely—*for example, however, nonetheless, you see*, etc.).

Speaking English like a native requires mastery of these rhythms. Even if you pronounce individual sounds or even words flawlessly, poor rhythms will mark you as a non-native speaker, and therefore suspect in some Americans' eyes. Listen to native speakers' rhythm patterns, and make them your own.

LINKING SOUNDS

When Qingqing Chen from China arrived at CUNY in 2013, she had already lived in Paris for several years and was fluent in French but a little rusty in English. As we worked on her pronunciation, I occasionally made a point about English by relating it to French, which after all is one of its roots. Chief among these was the concept of *liaison,* or linking of sounds. The French rarely pronounce words exactly as written, given the large number of silent letters that drive American learners mad. But they move smoothly from one word to another by linking a consonant in one to a vowel in the next, and vice versa. Smoothness is valued in English, too, and we do much the same. Liaison is a skill that speakers of languages like Chinese, especially need to master.

One of the simplest illustrations is the article *a/an* (see page 198). It's easy to say you work for *a newspaper,* but much harder to say your website is *a aggregator.* Since that noun starts with a vowel, *a* becomes *an,* which links to the vowel as if the two words were one: *anaggregator.* Exception: the long-*u* sound really starts with a *y* sound and is generally treated like a consonant. So it's *a university,* not *an.*

There's no equivalent change in spelling for *the,* generally pronounced *thuh* when followed by a consonant. When followed by a vowel, however, you don't want an awkward pause between vowels, so it becomes *thee,* with a little *y* sound added to move smoothly from one *e* to the other. So the aggregator becomes *thee(y)aggregator; the envelope* becomes *thee(y)envelope; the international* becomes *thee(y)international;* and the satirical website The Onion becomes *Thee(y)Onion.* But *thuh* works just as well as *thee* for *the university* or *the United States.*

The phrase *a string of attacks* contains three opportunities for linking: *a* to *string, string* to *of* and *of* to *attacks.* So an American newscaster would say *astringtofattacks,* as if it were one long, smooth word, rather than saying each word distinctly—though for emphasis she might say *a **string** / of **attacks***.

INTONATION

In writing, the punctuation at the end of a sentence indicates what kind of sentence it is. A declarative sentence—one that makes a declaration, or statement—ends in a period; a question with a question mark; an exclamation with an exclamation point. In speaking, there are no such obvious markers. Some languages use particles, or marker words, for this purpose. In English, we use our voices.

Think back a few pages to what I said about using pitch and volume to accent syllables and important words. English-speakers do something similar with parts of sentences. A declarative sentence tends to have an even tone and end on a lower pitch. From a story in *The Guardian* about the transformation of a Pittsburgh neighborhood:

> *In 2003, ELDI decided that the only way to stop that problem was to remove the slumlords.*

Here's how a TV reporter might say it on camera:

> *In **2003**, **ELDI** decided that the **only way** to **stop** that problem was to **remove** the **slumlords**.*

In bold are the "important words" (see page 138) that he would stress by saying them louder and at a higher pitch than the others. But even though *slumlords* is an important word and would be said slightly louder, the reporter would probably drop it to a lower pitch because it ends a statement.

In contrast, a question tends to end with an upswing in pitch:

> *Mr. Mayor, do you think getting rid of the slumlords is the best way to solve the problem?*

Instead of ending on a lower pitch as in a statement, the reporter's voice would rise on *problem*.

Be careful with these upswings, and do limit them to questions. Ever since the stereotype of the Valley Girls—young Southern Californians whose voices rose at the end of every sentence? As if they were asking questions?—emerged in the early 1980s, more and more Americans of various ages have taken to ending seemingly every sentence on an upswing, as if implicitly asking, "You know?" or "Right?" or "Don't you agree?" Make statements sound like statements—firm, confident, not asking for agreement. Reserve the higher-pitched ending for questions—or exclamations.

An exclamation expresses surprise, excitement or shock. It also tends to end on a higher pitch, and with greater force or volume. A CUNY student covering a protest of a dispute between Dominicans and supporters of undocumented Haitian immigrants to their country quoted the signs the Dominicans carried:

It's not about race! Stop spreading lies!

Now think about how the protesters must have sounded when they were shouting those slogans. They would have emphasized *race!* and *lies!* with a higher pitch and and a louder tone. That's the spoken equivalent of the exclamation point.

Intonation can also be used for other purposes, like expressing sarcasm. *He had to go the dentist today* is a straightforward declarative statement, but if I stress certain words in a particular way—*he **HAD** to go to the dentist **today** (**RIGHT** when I **NEEDED** him)*—I'm expressing sarcasm. Again, if your intonation is off, you may be misunderstood and unintentionally cause offense.

-ED IN PAST TENSE

In English, regular verbs form the simple past and past participle by adding *-ed*, or just *-d* if the base verb ends in *e*. (Irregular verbs have widely different forms, and the only way to learn them is to memorize. One good list: https://www.englishclub.com/vocabulary/regular-verbs-list.htm.) International students assume that adding that suffix automatically adds a syllable in pronunciation, and thereby identify themselves as non-native speakers when they say they *talk-ed* to a source or *work-ed* on their stories.

The rule for pronouncing past tenses with -*ed* is really quite simple, with only three categories and very few exceptions:

If the base verb ends in a *t* or *d* sound, say the extra syllable: *reported, edited.*

If it ends in a voiced sound, the past tense ends in a *d* (voiced) sound: *interviewed.*

And it if ends in an unvoiced sound, it ends in a *t* (unvoiced) sound: *talked, worked, clicked.*

That's all there is to it. Note that I emphasize the sound—not the letter—that ends the base verb. Those that end in a silent *e* match the sound of the consonant before (*approved, forced,* etc.). How can you tell if the end sound is voiced or unvoiced? Just put your fingers on your throat and see if you can feel your vocal cords vibrating, as discussed on page 135.

And those few exceptions? One is *beloved,* pronounced *bee-LUV-ed* when used as a noun or adjective. Another is *revealed* in old-fashioned usages as in the King James Bible, poetry or Handel's "Messiah": "*And the glory of the Lord shall be re-VEAL-ed.*"

-ATE

Once you *graduate* from a university, you are a *graduate,* and you may want to go on to a *graduate* school like CUNY Journalism. At first, you may not be able to *articulate* easily what you want to say, but with practice and editing you will surely become more *articulate.* In the process, you will learn the skills to *elaborate* on more complex issues, and your reports may become more *elaborate.*

Those italicized words look exactly alike in text, but they have different pronunciations. For words ending in -*ate,* there's a general rule: if it's a verb, -*ate* is pronounced *ate* (long a). If it's a noun or an adjective, it's more like *uht*—in other words, that weak vowel sound. Here's a sampling of -*ate* words and their pronunciations. Note that not all -*ate* words have all three forms, or even two; *certificate,* for example, is the noun of *certify,* and the adjective of *incorporate* is *incorporated* or *corporate,* depending on the meaning.

Verb (*ate*)	Noun (*uht*)	Adjective (*uht*)
advocate	advocate	
aggregate	aggregate	aggregate
alternate	alternate	alternate
appreciate		
articulate		articulate
	certificate	
decorate		
dedicate		
deliberate		deliberate
designate		designate
elaborate		elaborate
estimate	estimate	
graduate	graduate	graduate
incorporate		corporate
intimate	intimate	intimate
moderate	moderate	moderate
separate		separate
situate		
sophisticate	sophisticate	
suffocate		

SIBILANTS

Think of the sound a snake makes in English—*hiss!*—and you have the basis of the sibilants. These four sounds—*s, z, sh* and zh—are made by touching part of your tongue to the top of your mouth. For the *s* and *z* sounds, curl the tip of your tongue slightly downward and touch the top of the curve to the ridge behind your top teeth; *s* is the unvoiced sound, *z* the voiced. For *sh* and *zh*, touch the top of the curve to the palate right behind that ridge; *sh* is unvoiced (*ship, sheep, ssh!*), *zh* (the sound in *measure, pleasure* and *treasure*) is voiced. These sounds may take some practiced if they, or the distinctions between them, do not exist in your language.

With sibilants, the tricky part is knowing the correct sound in a particular word, especially since sibilants may be spelled in any number of ways: not just *s, z, sh* and *zh* (the last is rare in English), but also *se* (as in *these* and *those*); *si* (*decision, revision*); *ss* or *ssi* (*session*); *ti* (*nation*); *ce* (*once*); even *ge* (*beige, loge*). Nor are the pronunciations of a given spelling consistent: the sibilant in *nation* is *sh*, but *equation* is *e-QUAY-zhun*. Getting a sibilant wrong will mark you as a non-native speaker, so when in doubt, check with a dictionary or a native speaker. One private student of mine, a high-level executive with J.P. Morgan Chase whose native language was Portuguese, discovered in our lessons that he had been pronouncing the name of his company wrong all along—*Chaze* instead of *Chase*. He was mortified by the thought of how many times he had made that mistake in business situations. As a journalist who mispronounced it on the air, you would be, too.

OTHER PROBLEM SOUNDS

Early in this chapter, I mentioned the problems speakers of various languages have pronouncing words like *tired* and *iron*. Remember what I said about the right pronunciation often being the easiest for your mouth to form? That's the case with these *long i* + *ir* combinations. It's simply too awkward for the mouth to follow long *i* sound immediately with an *r* sound, so it breaks the syllable into two: *i-er*. The same happens in many, though far from all, words with a long *a* sounds followed by an *r*, like *care, share* and *parents*. It's tempting to say the combination as in the word *are*, but it's really more like *air*—so *parents* becomes *pair-ents*.

English being English, it includes a number of sounds that aren't pronounced exactly as their spellings would suggest—or anywhere near. Here are some of the sounds with which CUNY journalism students have the most problems.

-CALLY ADVERBS

A common suffix to turn a noun into an adjective is *-al (type, typical)*; the suffix *-ly* almost always means a word is an adverb. (Exceptions: *friendly, likely* and *lively* are adjectives.) Put them together in an adverb ending in *-ally*, and pronunciation problems ensue. Why? Because non-native speakers tend to give that *-al* syllable full weight, whereas native speakers do not. It should have that weak vowel sound, except that in this case it is so weak that it's not even pronounced. So even though words like *politically, psychologically, typically, technologically, grammatically, dramatically, magically, theoretically, authentically* and many others are spelled *-cally*, they are spoken more like *politicly, psychologicly, typicly, technologicly, grammaticly, dramaticly, magicly, theoreticly,* and *authenticly*.

Note that this is true mainly of words ending in *-cally*; we do not say, for example, *marginly* for *marginally*. And *publicly* is both spelled and pronounced as *publicly*, not *publically* (as many native speakers assume) because the adjective is *public*, not *publical*. But someone who is *athletic* is *athletically* inclined.

CONSONANT CLUSTERS

If you speak a language like Japanese that almost entirely alternates consonant sounds with vowels (at least by English definition), as in *domo arigato*, you may have trouble saying multiple consonants in a row. The most obvious examples are verb contractions: *it's, can't, won't, didn't, wasn't,* etc. The easy solution is to avoid the contractions and say *it is, cannot* (the only one written as one word), *will not, did not* and *was not.* They're not incorrect, but they do sound overly formal and sometimes stilted in conversation. In America, land of informality, contractions are our normal way of speaking in most situations, so do your best to master them.

When confronted with any word containing clusters of consonants—like *confront,* with three in a row—resist the temptation to insert a vowel sound between the consonants. Instead, break the word into syllables—*con-front*—and say each one distinctly in sequence. Once you feel comfortable with each one individually, say them together quickly and they form a single, smooth word. Those whose native structures make them sound choppy in English can also benefit from practicing this technique.

ER SOUNDS

In many languages, especially European ones, the *er* combination is pronounced like *air,* but in English, it's, well, *er.* Think of a word that is now almost as universal as *OK: burger.* Does anyone in the world say *boorgair?* I very much doubt it. That *er* sound in both syllables of *burger* is the one you want in most words containing *er,* so do practice and master it.

To confuse you further, it's not only the *er* combination that's pronounced that way, but often *ar, ir, or, ur* and occasionally even *yr.* That's right: any vowel followed by an *r* may be pronounced *er.* Once again, consider *burger,* in which the *ur* in the first syllable is pronounced exactly like the *er* in the second. The same is true of the fourth word of this paragraph: *further.* A very few of the many examples:

  ar   *familiar, peculiar, particular*
  er   *better, butter*
  ir   *Birds chirp. (Chirp* is one English word for the sound birds make.)
  or   *word, work, world*

ur   *burn, turn, urge, urban, hurricane*

yr   *martyr*

Pronounced as spelled without that *er* sound, *firm* may be misheard as *film,* or *Thursday* as *Tuesday,* especially if the *th* sound is not part of your native language and comes out sounding like *t.*

Note that I said above that with these vowel/*r* combinations *r may* be pronounced *er.* This is by no means true 100 percent of the time. *Martyr* is pronounced *MAWR-ter;* giving that *ar* an *er* sound would make it sound like *murder*—yet another word containing two *er* sounds. When in doubt, consult a dictionary (especially an online one with audio) or a native speaker.

H SOUNDS

The French tend to drop their *h*'s in English because they're silent in French; the Italians because few if any words of Italian origin start with *h.* Slavic-speakers tend to overpronounce *h*'s with a strong vibration that sounds as if they're clearing their throats, as in the *chleb,* the Polish word for bread. Wherever your language falls on that spectrum, you need to master the English *h*—unless, of course, you want to sound like the London Cockneys, whose dropped *h*'s are a hallmark of their dialect.

The English *h* is an odd consonant because we're really just blowing air up from our lungs through our throats and mouths without an obstruction—which is the definition of a vowel. (See page 134.) Even so, in most cases *h* is treated like a consonant; for example, it takes *a* rather than *an* as its article (*a house, a home*) and the *the* before it is pronounced *thuh,* not *thee,* with no linking. (See page 139.) Exceptions: in *honor* the *h* is completely silent; the noun *history* is pronounced with a definite *h,* but its adjectives, *historic* and *historical,* may not be (and may take either *a* or *an*); and phrases like *would have, could have* and *should have* are usually said like their contractions, *would've, should've* and *could've*—which are *not* spelled *would of, could of* and *should of,* as many poorly taught Americans think.

-IETH IN ORDINAL NUMBERS

Cardinal numbers are the ones you use to count: *one, two, three*, etc; *ordinal numbers* indicate order: *first, second, third*, etc. The cardinals 4 to 19 form their ordinals by adding *-th*; 20, 30, 40, 50, 60, 70, 80 and 90 do it with *-ieth*. Many English language-learners, even advanced ones, see that *ie* combination and, knowing it is often pronounced *ee*, as in *believe*, do so in ordinals. In fact, *-ieth* is two syllables—*i-eth*—and needs to be pronounced that way, or it will confuse the listener. *Seventieth*, if pronounced *seven-teeth*, is much too close to *seventeenth* for comfort.

The syllable accent is also very important in distinguishing the teens from the higher numbers. In *20, 30,* etc., the accent is on the first syllable. (And the middle *t* sounds closer to *d* than *t*; see below.) In the teens, the accent is also on the first syllable, but in the ordinals, the *teenth* is drawn out and may, depending on the speaker, receive a slightly stronger accent. When saying these numbers, accuracy and clarity are paramount to both speaking and listening comprehension. If you're a reporter in New York sent to cover a fire at 219 West 40th Street but hear "14th Street," you're going to get lost—and may miss the story.

-ISM

This one-syllable suffix in *catechism, chauvinism, Darwinism, extremism, heroism* and many others we use in *journalism* is really pronounced as two: *-isum*. Remember, in English the correct pronunciation is usually the one that's easiest for the mouth to form. English language-learners tie their tongues in knots trying to say *-ism* as one syllable, moving smoothly from one consonant to the next without a break, but an American would never even try. Instead, we insert a little *uh* sound—that weak vowel again—between the *s* and the *m*, essentially breaking the syllable in two. (The same holds true for words ending in *-asm*, like *enthusiasm*.) So journalism becomes *JOUR-nuh-liz-um*, and hundreds of other *-ism* nouns follow the same pattern. But when syllables are added to create the adjective form in words like *prismatic* and *spasmodic*, that *uh* sound is dropped and the syllable break falls between the *s* and the *m*: *priz-MA-tic* and *spaz-MAH-dic*.

NG SOUNDS

As previously noted, multiple consonants can be a challenge, and one of the most difficult—especially for Slavs and other Eastern Europeans— is the *-ng* sound. Like some New Yorkers who say they're going to Long Guyland for the weekend instead of Long Island, they have trouble making a smooth *ng* sound without adding a hard *g* sound, or even a *k*, as in *think*. So *singer* comes out as *sing-guer*, or even *sinker*.

Ng is one of the three nasal sounds in English, along with *n* and *m*, all made by closing off the air flow so that the sound has to come out of the nose. *N* and *m* are made by closing off the front of the mouth, *ng* the back at the top of the throat. The sound needs to come from that high point in the throat—not the base, where the *g* and *k* sounds come. Especially when linking to a vowel sound, as in *thinking about*, be sure not to pause after the *ng*. Making this sound correctly takes a great deal of practice and feedback, but it is a giant step forward in sounding more like a native speaker and reducing your accent.

There are, of course, exceptions. The adjectives *long* and *strong* need to end with a smooth *ng*, but their noun forms, *length* and *strength*, need a *g* sound or even a *k*: *lenkth* and *strenkth*. (Some Americans do eliminate the *g* altogether, saying *lenth* and *strenth*, but that doesn't sound right to us either.) And what better exception than the very subject of this book? The *English language* is pronounced not *Ing-lish language*, but *Ing-glish lang-gwage*.

T, D AND COMBINATIONS

Both *t* and *d* sounds are made by placing the tip of the tongue on the ridge behind the upper front teeth; *t* is the unvoiced sound (see page 135), *d* the voiced. *T* tends to sound very precise—too precise, to a lot of

Americans, though perhaps not to upper-class Britons. If that phrase *a lot of* is spoken with a full *t* sound, it sounds unnatural to us, so instead we say the phrase more like *a loddov*, or even more casually as *a lodda*. In the numbers cited above—the teen numbers *13* through *19*—that middle *t* sound needs to come through very precisely as a *t*. But in 20, 30 and so on, the *t* is closer to a *d*, or it sounds prissy.

In keeping with the idea that the easier pronunciation is likely to be the right one, the language has evolved among native speakers—especially Americans—so that these sounds are often slurred when followed by certain vowels. A *tu* combination may produce a *ch* sound, as in *nature, culture, virtual* and *situation*, while *du* may produce a *j* sound, as in *education* and *individual*. Say *sit-you-A-tion* or *in-di-VID-you-all* to an American, and he is likely to think you are overeducated, pretentious or British. Similarly, *ti* often takes on a *sh* sound, as in *nation, motion or rational*. Again, when in doubt, check a dictionary.

USED TO

This deceptively simple phrase actually has two different pronunciations, with three different meanings. If you talk about *the sources I used to research the story*, it's pronounced *yoozed too*, meaning employed, with a slight break after *used*. If you want to say you did something over a period of time in the past but don't anymore, it's pronounced *YOOSS-too*, or even *YOOSS-tuh*. And if you mean you're accustomed to writing on tight deadlines, you say *I'm used to (YOOSS-too) it*.

Finally, avoid saying *nuclear* the way a former president of the United States not known for his diction did: *nucular*. "But we say *spectacular*," some of his defenders said. Yes, because it's spelled that way. *Nu-cle-ar* is not.

As I said above, this is not a comprehensive guide to pronunciation—just points to be aware of and work on in your own speech. In the media, checking the correct pronunciation is part of the reporting, and pronunciation errors, like any other fact errors, cost you credibility. In a

2015 CBS News report on sea turtles stranded ashore in Massachusetts, it was obvious to me (a former resident) that the on-air reporter hadn't done enough homework when the name of the Boston suburb Quincy came out as *QUINT-see*. While that's the usual pronunciation in most of the English-speaking world, in Massachusetts, it's *QUIN-zee*. Another TV reporter, this one for a New York local station, once spoke at a gala tribute to Judith Jamison, who was retiring as director of Alvin Ailey American Dance Theater. This reporter, too, used the most common pronunciation of the name—*JAME-ison*—but Judith happens to pronounce her name *JAM-ison*. The reporter didn't bother to learn the name of the person she was honoring, and I have never trusted her on camera since. If you have the slightest doubt, ask a variation of the follow-up question on page 78 about spellings:

> **Reporter:** *"Could please I get your name?"*
> **Source:** *"Sure, John Quincy Adams."*
> **Reporter:** *"That's Q-u-i-n-c-y? And you pronounce it . . . ?"*
> **Source:** *"QUIN-zee."*
> **Reporter:** *"Thanks."*

CHAPTER 8

THE RIGHT WORD

CUNY writing coach Deborah Stead (see page 243) was chatting in the hallway with a student from India a few weeks into his summer internship as a copy editor at *The New York Times*, "where he is succeeding terrifically," she said. "Every once in a while, though, he reaches for a word, and it's not the right one. So he was telling me about a story he did about the 200th anniversary of the Battle of Waterloo, and he said, 'I wrote about the re-enactments, and this year that story is especially poignant because it's been 200 years; it's an anniversary.' I said, 'Do you mean *pertinent*? *Poignant* means moving, and you don't want to use that.' And of course he said, 'So you're always an editor?' " As a matter of fact, she is. (By the way, the word is pronounced *POYN-yant*, not *POIG-nant*, as a New York TV reporter butchered it while covering the first anniversary of 9/11. English has kept the *nyuh* sound for the *-gn-* from the French original, meaning pointed or sharp, according to the Online Etymology Dictionary.)

Being an editor is hard to turn off. When I send back students' e-mails with corrections, I often excuse myself by adding, "English teachers never sleep!" Nor do editors. Try going to a restaurant with one; any errors (*Ceasar salad, potato and leak soup*) leap off the menu. When wearing either hat (*wearing two hats* is an idiom meaning doing two jobs or filling two roles at the same time), they can't help noticing mistakes in speaking and writing, and feel compelled to correct them—especially with students as good as this one. Stead was teaching him the distinction between two words that must sound very much alike to a non-native English-speaker. But the difference in meaning is crucial.

In the media, words are your *stock in trade*—what you have to offer in exchange for making a living. The average English-speaker has a vocabulary of as many as 30,000 words, according to numerous sources. We don't use all of them in our everyday lives, and we all have our personal vocabularies: the words we use all the time, and the ones we recognize and understand but tend not to use ourselves. Journalists need at least that many—not only to report the facts of a story, but also to convey the nuances, the shades of meaning that separate a good-enough writer from a great one. As the American writer Mark Twain put it: "The difference between the almost right word and the right word is . . . the difference between the lightning-bug and the lightning." Remember that as a mongrel among languages, English has multiple ways of saying just about anything. For any writer, native speaker or not, the key to making the right choice is vocabulary-building.

Just as you must be accurate in the facts you report, you must be accurate in your language—as an incoming CUNY student from Italy learned when he wrote:

Just hours before, he had broadcast a recorded interview with a man claiming to be one of the perpetrators of the slathering of the three Italian missionary nuns killed in September 2014.

In my comments, I wrote: "You mean *slaughtering*, or better yet, *slaughter*. *Slather* means to put a lot of something on something else—for example, slathering cream cheese on a bagel (you'll learn about this in New York), or slathering yourself with sunscreen."

That particular error is not common, but that kind of confusion is. Two words start and end with the same combination of letters, with just a few different in the middle. Yet they are a world apart in meaning. More commonly, getting a word wrong is a matter of being just slightly off target, as in this sentence from another story by the same student:

As the arrival point of thousands of migrants escaping war, dictatorship and famine, the Mediterranean island of Lampedusa became the symbol of a certain idea of Africa: an idea of sufferance and despair.

I changed *escaping* to *fleeing* and wrote in my comments: "A very fine distinction, but worth making, I think. *Fleeing* means running away, which they've done. *Escaping* means they've succeeded—have they?" I also changed *sufferance* to *suffering*, the noun for what these refugees have suffered. *Sufferance* means tolerance or acceptance; it comes from a second definition of the verb *suffer*, to tolerate or allow. In the early 17th-century King James Version of the New Testament, Jesus is quoted as saying, "Suffer the little children to come unto me." Modernized versions word it, "Let the little children come to me."

Similarly, in a story on the treatment of youthful offenders in Brazil, another incoming student wrote:

The interns should have been at school at the time they were torturing Felipe.

Interns are apprentices learning a job or profession by doing it, like the Indian student mentioned at the beginning of this chapter. The writer meant *inmates*, those held legally, but presumably against their will, in a prison or sometimes a mental asylum.

Some errors result from simple confusion about spelling, or the way the writer has heard the word and then envisioned its spelling. A native French-speaker—who is far from the only writer ever to have made this mistake—wrote:

Ever since the Dominican Supreme Court issued the decision of striping citizenship to more than 200,000 immigrants of Haitian descent in 2013 . . .

"You mean painting them with stripes?" I wrote in my comments. "Or do you mean *stripping*?"—taking away. She did. When the vowel sound in a verb is short, as in *strip*, the consonant is doubled in the *-ed* and *-ing* forms; if the words ends in an *e* that lengthens the vowel preceding it, it is not, and the *e* is dropped. (Exception: the present participle of *dye*—to change color—is *dyeing*. *Dying* is the participle of *die*.) Better and tighter:

> *Ever since the DSC stripped more than 200,000 immigrants of Haitian descent of their citizenship in 2013 . . .*

A Danish student made two similar mistakes:

> *The tears ran down her chicks as the sparkles from the fire-works fell to the ground.*

Instead, of *chicks* (baby chickens, or male slang for young women, as in "Let's go cruise some chicks"), she meant *cheeks*. Like speakers of many languages, this writer may have confused the long-*e* sound with the short-*i* sound. (See page 134.) By confusing the sounds, she also confused the spellings and ultimately the words.

From the same piece:

> *They were colleges in a day care center and pregnant at the same time.*

Rather than *colleges*—institutions of higher education—she meant *colleagues*, or co-workers. If speaking, she probably would have pronounced the word correctly, but being unsure of the correct spelling, she reached for the simplest, in her mind most likely spelling—and was wrong. (A variation from China: a student wrote of "working for my *collage* newspaper" when she meant *college*. A collage is an artwork made of bits and pieces of unrelated materials glued together. If I were writing a Chinese character and put in a tiny extra line, or left one out, that changed the character's meaning, it would be the equivalent of her misspelling.)

Errors like these are prime examples of what spellcheck won't catch. *Colleague, college* and *collage* are all real words in English, found in dictionaries, as are *cheek* and *chick*, and spellcheck cannot distinguish between them.

In e-mail, I often catch a certain friend of mine (not a journalist or professional writer) writing *loose* (the opposite of *tight*) when he means *lose* (the opposite of *find* or *win*), as in: *Obama is certain to loose the election*. (That's not a real example, though my friend is a diehard Republican.) He once wrote about *when I traveled in the East Block;* he meant the *Eastern Bloc*. He excuses such errors by saying he relies on spellcheck.

In cases like these, spellcheck is not enough. It won't flag you on *block* and *bloc* because, like the examples cited above, both are actual words in its dictionary. (Not sure of the difference? Look them up.) A really thorough grammar-checker might; the one on my version of Microsoft Word doesn't.

Often the culprits are homonyms (words with the same spelling but different meanings) and homophones (words that sound alike but have different spellings and meanings). *You're* and *your* are homophones— the contraction for *you are* and the possessive form of *you*, respec- tively—and *you're* going to get in trouble with *your* editors if you keep getting them wrong. A parallel case is *it's* (contraction for *it is*) and *its* (possessive pronoun). And then we have *their* (possessive pronoun), *there* (adverb) and *they're* (contraction of *they are*), as in: *They're* doing *their* interviews over *there*.

Desert (to abandon) and *desert* (a dry sandy place, like the Sahara) are homonyms, while *dessert* (sweets at the end of a meal) is the first one's homophone. *Feet* and *feat* (an act of skill, an achievement, an accomplishment, as in *That's quite a feat!*) are homophones. So are *council* (a decision-making or advisory panel) and *counsel* (*advice* as a noun, *advise* as a verb). Neither should be confused with *consul,* slightly different in both spelling and pronunciation. One international student confused me for a moment when she said she had to go to her *council* when she meant the *consul,* her country's representative in New York.

As that example illustrates, non-native speakers sometimes confuse words that sound close. A Russian student wrote, *Traditionally, Russians don't thrive for self-governance;* she meant *strive.* A Chinese student wrote, *Thousands of Americans were presented at the speech;* she meant *present* (in attendance) instead of *presented* (introduced to the audience). And phrases that sound exactly alike may be written differently. New Yorkers wait *on line* for buses, theater tickets and just about everything else, but you post your blog *online.* (Outside New York, Americans wait *in line;* the British *queue.*)

It is part of your job as a communications professional to know such differences, make the correct choice and be able to spot errors when proofreading your work.

WORD CHOICE

A student doing a news writing exercise about the 2010 plane crash that killed many of Poland's leaders wrote:

> *Polish President Lech Kaczynski's plane crashed about a half-mile from the the airport in Smolensk, killing all 97 passengers aboard.*

I changed *passengers* to *people.* Normally, I would tell writers to find a more precise, descriptive word than *people,* but not in this case. Why? Because in the transportation industry *passengers* are those holding tickets—not the pilots and crew, who were also killed. *People* covers them all.

This case is not so much a matter of being wrong—*council* for *consul, intern* for *inmate*—as being not quite as right as you can be. Precision in language is often a judgment call, and unfortunately for language-learners, who yearn for hard-and-fast rules, precision is often a judgment call—what sounds right or best to a native speaker's ear.

A Chinese student doing that same exercise wrote that *Russia's leaders were soon aware of the potential political fallout of the crash and showed their condolences.* In English we don't *show* condolences; we *send, give* or *express* them.

A student from Latin America wrote in a story on tinnitus:

> *According to the U.S. Centers for Disease Control, about 45 million—nearly 15% of the population—suffer from this illness, commonly referred to as "ringing in the ears."*

In this sentence I questioned two word choices. I would call tinnitus a *problem,* a *syndrome* or a *condition* rather than an *illness,* which implies sickness, like the kinds caused by germs or organ failure. Tinnitus patients aren't sick; they just hear sounds that don't exist outside their heads. And rather than *referred to,* I would say *described as. Refer to* (a noun) *as* implies that you are mentioning or naming it: *Doctors refer to the condition as tinnitus,* or, two words tighter, *Doctors call the condition tinnitus. Describe* implies the opposite, that you are giving more information about what you have already named: *Tinnitus is described as ringing in the ears that no one else can hear.*

Another Spanish-speaker, this one from Spain, wrote in an exercise on Barack Obama's election as president:

> *On a bitter note, his grandmother Madelyn Dunham, a white woman who helped raise him during his teenage years, died last Saturday.*

Bitter struck me as the wrong word; it means having hard feelings or resentment, often in reaction to perceived unfairness or mistreatment. Perhaps this writer was reaching for *bittersweet,* a word she did not quite know; it means a mixture of sadness and happiness, and would certainly have been appropriate to this occasion. I suggested she simply say *sad.*

Register (see page 116) may also help determine word choice. Another Danish student, translating her own article on a serious political issue, used the word *busted*—slang for *arrested*. Both words mean the same thing, but the context made her choice inappropriate.

BUILDING VOCABULARY

"How can I increase my vocabulary?" international students often ask, especially those arriving for their first semester. Short of having your own personal editor to perfect your copy before you file it, building vocabulary is the one sure way to avoid the mistakes above and thousands of others like them. It is crucial to finding the right words for the facts you need to report, the ideas you want to express and, ultimately, the voice you want to project as your own.

Language-learners do it in all manner of ways. In school, teachers drill and test them endlessly. Many teachers also encourage students to figure out an unfamiliar word from its context: seeing how it fits into the words, sentence or paragraph surrounding it; guessing the meaning, and then checking a dictionary. Later, often on their own as adults, they may learn by reading in the new language, noting words they don't understand and looking them up. Hearing new words in conversation, the shy ones pretend to understand and, maybe, look them up later; the brave ones come right out and say: "I don't know that word. What does it mean?" Media professionals have almost unlimited materials available: all they need do is look at a news website or a TV newscast in English.

These are all good techniques for increasing vocabulary. I would like to suggest three others that may appeal more to language nerds than to busy professionals who simply want to memorize what's the right word to use when. These techniques are based on the building blocks of English: recognizing the roots of words in other languages; breaking down unfamiliar words, especially multi-syllable ones, into their component parts and seeing how those parts work together; and finally recognizing how words change form—verbs morphing into nouns, nouns into adjectives, adjectives into adverbs—to create word families. You know one English word; then, suddenly, you know four, or even more. *That's* vocabulary-building.

ROOTS

Teaching at Jinan University in Guangzhou, China, in fall 2015, I was escorted to my mandatory medical exam—a circuit of seven or so stations, each of which checked one aspect of my health, from blood pressure to a blood test to a sonogram of my internal organs—by an undergraduate whose English was admittedly limited. After two hours, he reassured me: "Now we are coming to the terminal exam." I smiled and said an American wouldn't use *terminal* in a medical context, where *terminal* means *fatal*, or leading to death. "Doesn't it mean *last*?" he asked. "Yes," I said, "but we wouldn't say it in this case, and here's why." I whipped out my reporter's notebook and wrote *terminus,* the Latin word for *end* and the root (here I sketched a tree with roots) of English words including *terminal* (adjective and noun, as in Grand Central Terminal), *terminate* (the verb meaning *end*) and *termination* (the noun meaning being let go from a job), I did not mention the word the young man probably knew best of all: *Terminator,* the Arnold Schwarzenegger movie character.

Terminus is just one of thousands of words in Anglo-Saxon, Latin, German, Scandinavian and French that became the roots, or ancestors, of modern English words and their families. I was able to sketch out the family descended from *terminus* because, at age 11, I had made one of the pivotal decisions of my life: I opted to study Latin in junior high the next year, and thus had the great fortune to be assigned to Frances Chase. Mrs. Chase was an English and Latin teacher of the old school, which means she made the lives of 30 seventh graders hell for a year until either she mellowed or we shaped up. But in the process, we learned the discipline of a highly structured language and the importance of roots. For that reason, as many of my students will confirm, an English lesson with me often feels like a Latin class.

A root from any language is a possible clue to the meaning of an unfamiliar English word. In Chapter 7, I mentioned some of the words derived from the Latin root *nunc-*, for *speak* or *declare: announce, denounce, pronounce, renounce, enunciate.* So if a word contains

-nounce or *nunc-* it may well have something to do with speaking, or communicating. Or consider *vert-*, from the Latin for *turn*. As all journalists know, an *inverted pyramid* is a news story written in the form of a pyramid turned upside down. A ballet critic knows that a *divertissement* (a French word, also rooted in Latin) is a light dance interlude intended to do nothing more than entertain, or *divert*—turn away—the viewer's attention from the drama of the ballet, or the worries of everyday life. If a travel writer's plane is *diverted* because of bad weather, it is turned away from its destination—sent to another airport where conditions are safer. If a legal correspondent suspects justice is being *perverted*, he thinks it is being turned away from its intention.

English words containing roots like *fract-*, from the Latin word for *break,* often have something do with being broken: *fracture* (a break, as in a bone), *fraction* (a part of a whole), *fragile* (easily broken). Words containing *sens-* are related to feeling: the five *senses* (which help us "feel" the world around us), *sensitive* (feeling easily), *sensible* (perceptible through the senses), *sensation* (feeling). *Consensus*—a general agreement—is achieved by people feeling together as similarly indicated by the prefix *con-*, from the Latin *cum* for *with.* Words containing *spir-* are rooted in the Latin for breath—not just *respiration* (another word for breathing) but also *aspire* ("breathe to"), *inspire* ("breathe into"), *conspire* (literally "breathe together") and *expire* (die as the breath leaves the body). The Latin word for farmer is *agricola*, which has come down to us in the 21st century in *agriculture.*

Foreign roots of English aren't limited to Latin. From French we have simple words like *juice*, from *jus*, and more sophisticated ones like *reconnaissance* (information-gathering) from *connaitre*—to know, as in be familiar with. German has given us *hamburgers, frankfurters* and *delicatessens*; *noodles* and *poodles; wunderkinds* and *wanderlust; flak, ersatz* and *kitsch.*

Once again, roots are clues, not hard-and-fast rules. *Vertical* comes from *vertex,* or highest point, rather than *vert-* for turn, and while *t*'s often become *d*'s in English, words containing *verd-*, like *verdure* and *verdant,* actually have to do with green, from the French *vert* (from the Latin *viridian*). When a student at Columbia University asked me about *penthouse*—a most desirable piece of New York real estate, a private home perched atop a large apartment building—I guessed that it came from *paene,* the Latin word for *almost* "almost a house." (*Peninsula* comes from *paene insula,* or almost an island: *Brittania est insula. Europa non est insula, Italia est paeno insula; Itulia paeninsula est.*) When I looked up *penthouse,* I found I was *in the right church but the wrong pew.* (That's an idiom meaning close but not quite right—or, in another related idiom, *close but no cigar.*) It actually comes from *appendere,* Latin for *hang,* also the root of *append* and *appendix.* (An *appendectomy* is the surgical removal of an inflamed appendix—*appendicitis*—while a *tonsillectomy* is the removal of tonsils.) A *penthouse* hangs on another building, just as a *pendant* is a piece of jewelry hanging from the wearer's neck, or a *pendulum* swings from the point above where it hangs.

"Oh, no!" you're probably thinking. "Now I have to learn Latin to understand English?" Not at all—or at least, only a little. When you look up a new word in a dictionary, pay attention not only to its modern-day definition, but also to its *derivation*—its history as it has evolved through the centuries and cultures. That's the part that looks like this: for the word *derivation,* from Dictionary.com:

1375-1425; late Middle English *derivacioun* < Latin *dērīvātiōn-* (stem of *dērīvātiō*) a turning away, equivalent to *dērīvāt* (*us*) (past participle of *dērīvāre;*see derive, -ate[1]) + *-iōn-* -ion

And that's where you'll find roots like *term-* and *nunc-* and *pend-.* You can then confirm the new word's relationship to words you already know—or not, as with me and *penthouse.*

BREAKING WORDS DOWN

Right around now, the process of learning English may seem *interminable.* What on earth does that five-syllable word mean? Look for the clue you already know from above: the root *termin-*, meaning end. *Interminable* adds a prefix—*in-*, here meaning *not*, or the opposite—and a suffix, *-able*, meaning just what it says. So an interminable process seems unable to end, or never-ending.

By breaking big words down into their components, you can figure out their meanings surprisingly often. For an easy example, some prefixes from Latin or Greek indicate numbers: *uni-*, *bi-* or *di-*, *tri-*, etc. An old European joke:

> *What do you call someone who speaks two languages?*
> *Bilingual.*
> *What do you call someone who speaks three languages?*
> *Trilingual.*
> *What do you call someone who speaks one language?*
> *American.*

Actually, it's *monolingual*, from the Greek *mono-* for one or alone, not *unilingual*, using the Latin. *Lingua,* the Latin word for *tongue*—which in English sometimes means *language* (your *mother tongue*) as well as the body part that enables us to speak it—has come down to English in words including *linguistics,* the study of language.

Specific prefixes help us create nouns, verbs, adjectives and adverbs. (Prefixes, by the way, are so named because they go *before* the root; *suffixes*—from *sub-*, meaning *under*—go after.) Some common examples:

ADJECTIVE PREFIXES

anti-: against, as in *antiwar* (not to be confused with *ante-*, meaning before, as in *antebellum*, before the U.S. Civil War)

con-: with, together (*conspiratorial*)

contra-: against, as in *contradictory* (speaking against or opposite)

dis-: not, opposite (*disparate, disproportionate*)

ex-: former (*ex-husband, ex-mayor*)

ex-, e-: out of, away from (*elusive*)

extra-: outside (*extracurricular*) or more than (*extraordinary*)

hyper-: over in the sense of more than or unusually, as in *hypersensitive.* The opposite is **hypo-,** or under, as in *hypodermic needle,* one that goes under the skin. (*Hyper* is also American slang for overly excited or agitated.)

in-, im-, il-, ir-: opposite or not (*insensitive, impractical, illogical, irregular*)

inter-: between (*international*)

intra-: within (*intramural*)

mal- or mis-: bad or wrong (*malevolent, misunderstand*)

multi-: many (*multiple, multinational, multisyllabic*)

neo-: new (*neoclassical, neoconservative, Neolithic*)

non-: not (*nonconformist, nondenominational*)

omni-: all (*omnipotent, omniscient*)

post-: after (*postwar, postgraduate*)

pre-: before (*predict, predestined, prefix*)

re-: again (*recreate, redraw*) or back (*return*)

sub-: under (*submarine, subterranean*) or after (*subsequent, suffix*)

un-: not (*unbelievable, unreasonable*)

ADJECTIVE SUFFIXES

-able, -ible: (*formidable, reasonable, risible*)

-al: (*rational, typical*)

-ful: (*useful, truthful*)

-ish: a little or around (*purplish, 30-ish*)

-istic: (*characteristic, futuristic*)

-ous, -ious: (*dangerous, injurious*)

NOUN SUFFIXES

-ance, ence: *An independent nation celebrates its independence*

-ant, -ent: *attendant, superintendent*

-ee: someone who receives something (*grantee*) or sometimes someone who performs an action (*attendee, escapee*)

-er, -or: *A dancer dances. A director directs*

-ess: makes a noun feminine (*actress, sculptress*). Now often avoided on grounds of sexism

-ism: *activism, conservatism, journalism.* Someone who practices an *-ism* is often an *-ist*: *activist, journalist*

-ment: *contentment, resentment*

-ness: *togetherness*

-ship: *relationship, partisanship*

-tion, -ation: *detention, retention, congregation, representation.* (in pronouncing *-ation* words, the *-a-* syllable is almost always accented.)

VERB SUFFIXES

-ate: *affiliate, moderate, separate, regulate, etc.* (See page 142 on pronunciation.)

-ify: *dignify, rectify*

-ize: *familiarize, hypothesize, recognize, sanitize.*

As for adverbs, almost any adjective can be turned into an adverb by adding *-ly* or, depending on the spelling, *-ally*. (See page 145 on how to pronounce *-cally* adverbs.) But not if it already ends in *-ly* (*friendly, likely, portly*).

Now, put the theory into practice. *Influx* (*in* + *flux*, meaning *flow*, from the same root as *fluent*) means a flowing or pouring, as in the *influx of refugees* (people seeking refuge) in Europe in 2015. *Contradict* breaks down into *contra-* (against) + *dict-* (say). When the American poet Walt Whitman says, in "Song of Myself," "Do I contradict myself? Very well, then I contradict myself, I am large, I contain multitudes," he means he says two opposite things at the same time. *Emasculate* breaks down into *e-* + *mascul-* + *-ate*—literally, take (*-ate*) away (*e-*) manhood (*mascul-*) or weaken. This technique doesn't apply only to Latin-based words; those Syrian refugees were seeking *resettlement*, the condition of being settled again, or in a new place.

These same building blocks you use to break words down can also be combined to create words. But be careful. Sometimes the parts do not add up to a recognized whole. Or one adjective may have two different negative forms, such as *uninterested* (lacking interest) and *disinterested* (having no stake). When using these parts to build words, check a dictionary to see if your creation is a real word, or the right one—*monolingual*, not *unilingual*.

BUILDING WORD FAMILIES

A private student in Poland had a *sickly* (an adjective tending to get sick easily) 3-year-old and was struggling to talk about the problem: "something to do with her *IM-mun-* . . . *im-mun-OL-o-gic* . . ."

"*Immuno-LOG-ical* system," I corrected her. "But we just say *immune system.*"

Yes, even native speakers struggle with six-syllable words, and simplify them whenever possible. (This student was also struggling to say she had taken her daughter to an otolaryngologist. I told her Americans tend to say *ear, nose and throat doctor,* or even *ENT.*) But if I may be excused just this once for mixing metaphors (see page 258), *immunological* is a perfect illustration of how these building blocks can make one word into a family of four, or even more. The adjective is *immune*—unaffected by disease, or some other form of trouble. If you are *immune to* poison ivy, you don't develop an itchy rash from contact with it; if you are *immune to someone's charms,* you aren't charmed. The verb is *immunize*; if you have been *immunized against* polio or smallpox, you will not catch it.

The noun for the act of being immunized, when a doctor sticks a needle into your arm, is *immunization.* Then you will develop another noun, *immunity* to the disease. If you have been involved in a crime but agreed to testify against another defendant, you may be granted a different kind of *immunity,* from prosecution. And that mouthful *immunological?* An adjective meaning related to the science of the immune system.

Note how the different family members are formed. The main Latin root of *immune* is *mun-,* meaning common, as in *municipal*; the prefix *im-* means not or opposite. So if you are *immune,* you are exempt from the common effect, like a contagious disease. The verb suffix *-ize* means make, so *immunize* means make immune. There are two possible noun suffixes, *-ity* and *-ation,* with two different meanings, both rooted in *immune.*

Many international students come to CUNY for its concentration in business and economic reporting. They need to master the various words that come from the noun *economy,* the exchange of money, goods and services in a society. A scholar in that field is an *economist* (noun) and may specialize in *economic* (adjective) theory or developments. But, like *immunity, economy* has a second meaning: thrift. So it also has a second adjective form: *economical,* meaning thrifty (*When the economy is bad, people tend to be more economical*) or comparatively inexpensive (*One large box of detergent can be more economical than two small ones*). Students of *home economics* learn how to run a home *economically.* A Chinese student wrote of a project to dispose of food waste:

> We tried out different ways, such as washing the waste, using deodorizers and even a centrifuge, but still weren't able to find an economic solution to eliminate the smell.

She meant *economical.*

The *immune* and *economy* words families are just two of thousands in English. When a new word enters your vocabulary, check a dictionary to see what related forms may exist in other parts of speech. While reading, watching a movie or conversing with a native speaker, *keep your eyes and ears open* (that's an idiom meaning remain alert) for new forms of words you already know. Remember from Chapter 7 (see page 136) that as a word's part of speech changes, pronunciation and accent may change with it, following what may seem like no apparent rule: *e-CON-o-my* and *e-CON-o-mist*, but *e-co-NOM-ic* and *e-co-NOM-i-cal*; *NAY-tion* but *NAA-tional*; *de-VEL-op*, *de-VEL-op-er* and *de-VEL-op-ment*, but *de-vel-op-MEN-tal*. When in doubt, check a dictionary.

One final thought on the right word: be sure the word you type is the word you mean. In other words, proofread! Two Chinese students doing a news writing exercise on the 2010 plane crash that killed much of Poland's leadership wrote that the Katyn massacre during World War I had wiped out *more than 20,000 members of Poland's elite officer crops;* they meant *corps.* (Crops are what farmers grow.) For some reason known only to the gremlins that haunt newsrooms, two of the easiest typographical errors to make—and the most embarrassing if no editor catches them—are *crap* for *crab* and *pubic* for *public.* And if you think it's been easy typing CUNY correctly time and time again on an English QWERTY keyboard, think again. Spellcheck may not catch it, but proofreading should.

MARGOT MIFFLIN

FINDING YOUR VOICE

Co-director of the arts and culture reporting concentration, Margot Mifflin knows her beat cold. A contributor to *Entertainment Weekly* for its first 10 years, she has also covered the arts, pop culture and women's issues for publications including *Elle* magazine, *The Village Voice*, *The New Yorker* and Salon. As a freelance writer, she was a plaintiff in the landmark electronic copyright case Tasini v. *New York Times*. On her subspecialty—tattoos—she has published *Bodies of Subversion: A Secret History of Women and Tattoo* (powerHouse Books, 1997, 2013) and *The Blue Tattoo: The Life of Olive Oatman* (University of Nebraska Press, 2009).

What makes good writing?

Clarity, concision, control and style. If you diagram a good piece of criticism, you'll see that the lede says something specific and compelling that pulls the reader in. The piece flows from there, with topic sentences that move the argument along point by point; references to and descriptions of the work that support whatever critical assertions are made; and a satisfying kicker that relates to whatever theme was established at the outset, but doesn't repeat it.

The big step in transitioning from reporting to criticism is finding your voice: reporters who've been trained to remain neutral sometimes have difficulty expressing an opinion in writing. The best practice is doing it for a good while *without* using the first person—finding the language that articulates and supports the opinion rather than attaching "I think" or "I feel" to an unsubstantiated assertion.

What's different when you're covering a specialty?

When you're covering the arts, you need historical knowledge of the field you're covering. That includes terminology describing techniques (*chiaroscuro* in painting), genres (*noir* fiction), historical movements (Edwardian fashion) and theories (the *auteur* theory in cinema). And you'll need to read widely in the discipline or disciplines you're covering—not only in specialist and trade publications like *Billboard* or *Publishers Weekly*, but also in generalist publications that have strong arts coverage, like Slate.

How does a writer make the transition from general assignment into a field like the arts?

It depends a lot on what outlet you're writing for and how much mobility is encouraged or allowed there. Sometimes a staffer in one section may write freelance pieces for another, then switch. But arts reporting itself is not so different from other kinds of reporting beyond the required background knowledge and the particular story forms, like the walk-up (written before an awards ceremony) or the tie-in (a story making connections between cultural events). It's criticism that presents a whole different kind of writing challenge.

In your concentration, international students may be covering the arts in New York—a world arts capital—for the first time. What problems do you commonly see in their work, and what strengths?

The strengths are that they bring a global perspective to a city that, for all its diversity, is quite geocentric and self-reflexive. I've learned from international students about, for example, a world music festival that I didn't know existed, or Italians' views of American approaches to

Italian food. New York is such a melting pot that they aren't conspicuous as outsiders, and I'm always impressed by how quickly and fearlessly international students find their footing here and seize on whatever culture they're covering.

The problems I see are largely with grammar and pronunciation, which are best addressed through tons of reading (of any sort), and by listening to radio and podcasts: Shows like the Slate "Culture Gabfest" or NPR's "Pop Culture Happy Hour," where culture writers discuss issues every week, not only unpack what's happening, but also teach them correct pronunciations: how do you say Gabourey Sidibe or Sleater-Kinney or Colm Tóibín? Radio is also a great way to absorb the rhythms and idioms of the language.

CHAPTER 9

AMERICAN IDIOM

Journalists need to be able to think on their feet and hit the ground running, especially when they are boots on the ground. They can't afford to have that deer-in-the-headlights look on their faces when dealing with editors, who are probably stressed out these days from wearing too many hats. Reporters need to keep their eyes and ears open at all times, and avoid making knee-jerk assumptions about what a story is or what facts they'll uncover in reporting it Otherwise, they'll soon find themselves in hot water.

Sprinkled throughout this book is the phrase *that's an idiom meaning* . . . If you've been paying attention, the preceding paragraph will make perfect sense. It is written much the way Americans speak: in one idiom after another. In case you haven't been paying attention, here's the annotated version:

Journalists need to be able to *think on their feet* (react quickly to new or unexpected circumstances) and *hit the ground running* (start producing immediately), especially when they are *boots on the ground* (reporters on site, in the field). They can't afford to have that *deer-in-the-headlights look* on their faces (looking paralyzed with shock or fright) when dealing with their editors, who are probably *stressed out* (under too much pressure) these days from *wearing too many hats* (doing too many jobs). Reporters need to *keep their eyes and ears open* (remain alert) at all times, and avoid making *knee-jerk* (automatic) assumptions about what a story is or what the facts they'll uncover in their reporting are. Otherwise, they'll soon find themselves in *hot water* (trouble).

Merriam-Webster defines *idiom* as "an expression that cannot be understood from the meanings of its separate words but that has a separate *meaning* of its own." In other words, *the whole is greater than the sum of its parts.* That—you guessed it—is an idiom.

Every language has its idioms, but in English, almost everything is an idiom. While researching a paper on idioms during my teacher-training, I found a scholarly work on the subject with a list of idioms appended that was pages long, even without definitions. I was shocked at how many expressions I had never thought of as idioms actually were—phrases like *close call, second nature* and *come in handy.* Idioms make up a huge portion of American English, and for native speakers, using them is just a matter of *doin' what comes naturally.* (That's not exactly an idiom, but a song title from the 1946 Broadway musical *Annie Get Your Gun* that has become a common expression.) To those still learning the language, idioms can be baffling. When I told a Polish student I was going to give her a *pop quiz,* she said, "I know what *pop* is, and I know what a *quiz* is, but I don't know what they mean together." Exactly. (Translation: a quiz, or short test, not announced in advance.) You may know what each individual word in an idiom means, but the combination makes no sense.

Consider this passage from *Metropolis,* a novel by Elizabeth Gaffney (Random House, 2005) about immigrants in late 19th-century New York. The author had some fun with a newly arrived German's problems following American English. In one passage, he's at an employment agency when a clerk tells him:

> "*Anyway, you've had your beauty sleep, and I think I can tell from looking that you ain't got evening plans.*" **Beauty sleep?**

the stablemen wondered. **Evening plans?** . . . *He wasn't sure how he should respond . . . His English might have been better if only the few people who talked to him had made more sense.*

And later:

"You don't know how to give yourself a leg up, do you?"
A leg up? *Americans said much that he didn't understand.*

It's idioms, of course, that trip up the immigrant in the novel. (*Trip up* is an idiom, meaning to confuse or interfere.) *Beauty sleep* is a good night's sleep that will, theoretically, make you look better. *Evening plans* are pretty much what the phrase suggests—plans for the evening. But *a leg up?* Definitely an idiom, meaning an advantage or an early start—in another idiom, a *head start.*

In the media, it's crucial to master idioms. Sources will use them in interviews or e-mail, and reporters need to understand them clearly or risk errors. They will need to be able to quote those sources accurately—that is, idiomatically. When reporting in English, they will want to sound more fluent by using them in their writing or speaking. And that's where they may get into hot water. Understanding what an idiom means is one thing, an extension of vocabulary-building: you encounter a new phrase and memorize it. Using it is quite another: you have to get an idiom exactly right, or you will make no sense to your English-speaking audience. So how *do* you get them right? The same way you get to Carnegie Hall: practice. (That's an old New York joke that has become almost an idiom in itself. A tourist is asking directions: "Excuse, me, how do I get to Carnegie Hall?" "Practice!")

Luckily, idioms are fun. Most international students are eager to learn them so they can sound more like native speakers. (British variations on American idioms are noted in this chapter.) They also enjoy discovering parallels between English and their cultures. In English, we like to *kill two birds with one stone* (accomplish two goals with one action); the Polish equivalent translates as *roast two chickens on one fire.*

The Polish also say *not my pair of Wellingtons* (British for boots) for *not my cup of tea* (something I don't like) and *better fish than no dish* for *half a loaf is better than none* (it's better to have only part of what you want than nothing at all). Finally, idioms *open a window* onto English, allowing the learner to look through and at least glimpse the language's imagery and how its native speakers see the world. By knowing English idioms, you will begin to understand how native speakers think—an invaluable tool for anyone in the media.

The definitive list is the 470-page *Oxford Idioms Dictionary for Learners of English* (Oxford, 2006). (See page 302.) A number of excellent shorter lists, as well as interactive quizzes, are available online by using search terms like *ESL* and *idioms*. Rather than repeat what is available elsewhere, this chapter will focus on recognizing idioms and using them correctly.

MAKING SENSE OF IDIOMS

"Break a leg!" students cheerily wish one another whenever I teach a lesson on idioms. It's their favorite. Sound like a curse? Actually, it's the opposite: theater people's way of wishing someone good luck. As Mel Brooks put it in a song from his 2001 Broadway musical *The Producers*, "It's bad luck to say good luck on opening night," so actors do the opposite. The French have another way of saying it: *"Merde."* (Look it up.)

The idioms list I often share with students, from NationMaster .com, runs six printed pages, and it *doesn't scratch the surface* (an idiom meaning it is far from complete). Some examples that illustrate the range and richness of idioms:

As I often warn international applicants to CUNY, just living in New York *costs a fortune*—that is, it's very expensive. I could also say it costs *an arm and a leg* (in French, *ça coûte les yeux de la tête*—literally, *it costs the eyes from your head*), or that they'll *pay through the nose* for just about everything.

Graduate students and professional journalists alike must be prepared to *burn the midnight oil*—work long hours into the night, a holdover from the days of oil lamps. If they seem to be working all the time on too many assignments, or if they're partying too much on top of their work, we might say they're *burning the candle at both ends*—wearing themselves out, or *running themselves ragged* (pronounced *RAG-ged;* see page 142). To stay healthy and productive, they occasionally need to *turn in, hit they hay, take a cat nap* or simply *crash*— in other words, get some sleep. (*Hit the hay* conjures a hay-stuffed mattress, *cat nap* the many short sleeps a cat takes in the course of a day. *Crash* is more slang than idiom, as in *Can I crash at your place tonight?* Or *I need a place to crash in New York where I won't pay through the nose.*)

Given half a chance, journalists may *work themselves to death;* if they do, English has a wealth of idioms for death and dying to send them on their way: *kick the bucket* (which led to *bucket list,* the things you want to do before you die), *swims with the fishes* (Mafia slang popularized by the *Godfather* movies), *bought the farm, went south* and its offshoot, *took a Dixie. (Dixie* is a sentimental term for the American South. But to *sell someone south* or *down the river* means to betray or discard that person for personal gain. Those expressions originated in the days of slavery in America when, the farther south, the worse slaves were treated.) Other death-tinged idioms include *swan song,* a final appearance or dramatic farewell, from a legend that swans sing as they die; *fall on (one's) sword,* accept the blame for something that's gone wrong (from military tradition dating back to the Romans, and reminiscent of the Japanese *seppuku*), also expressed as *take the fall* or *take the rap*; and *dead as a doornail,* meaning "distinctly dead" or no longer under consideration, as in *Rubio's campaign is dead as a doornail.* Before modern times, NationMaster explains, a doornail was the one that held a knocker in place. "After it was driven through the door, the pointed end was bent over and buried in the door, to prevent movement. This nail was unrecoverable, so was considered dead."

An unsuccessful candidate may have started out as *a dark horse* (unexpected, and unexpectedly strong), but voters may have preferred not to *change horses in midstream*—change leadership in a time of crisis. Among other expressions from America's pre-automotive days, its language retains idioms like *closing the barn door after the horse gets out*—taking precautions when it's already too late.

Just as English is rich in death idioms, it is rich in expressions for craziness or eccentricity (though my personal favorite is the New York Yiddish term, *mishegas*). An apparently crazy person may be *not all there, not playing with a full deck* (from card games), *two bricks shy of a load* or just plain *nuts*. *"The lights are on,"* you may think, *"but no one's home."*

Journalists who *can't see the forest for the trees* may be overwhelmed with the details their reporting has uncovered but lost sight of *the big picture* (the main point that really matters, as opposed to details). If you can no longer *see your nose in front of your face* or *what's right in front of your nose*—what's obvious—it may be time to get off the story.

Get the picture? These are just a few examples of idioms you can expect to hear in everyday conversation with Americans. One more that may be useful to international journalists covering the United States is *herding cats*, which is next to impossible, as any cat-lover knows and accepts. Because Americans have an inbred sense of independence and individuality, getting them to agree and take joint action on just about anything is *like herding cats*. See Barry Blitt's *New Yorker* cover for the issue of Jan. 21, 2013, showing President Obama, constantly struggling with Congress, as a lonely figure holding a shepherd's crook amid a sea of cats (http://www.newyorker.com/culture/culture-desk/cover-story-herding-cats).

MAKING YOUR IDIOMS MAKE SENSE

Thanks for putting me up.
Thanks for putting up with me.

Which is correct? Both *put up* and *put up with* are American idioms—actually phrasal verbs (see page 219)—but the correct choice depends on what you are trying to say. *Put (someone) up* means allowing that person to sleep at your home, as in *Can you put me up this weekend?* *Put up with (someone or something)* means tolerating any difficulties or *mishegas* that person brings along. Remember that alleged Winston Churchill quote on prepositions at the end of a sentence: "This is nonsense *up with which I shall not put*." (See page 110.) And then there's *put up or shut up,* meaning "act on what you are saying or stop talking about it," according to the Free Dictionary (thefreedictionary.com), which can also be expressed as *put your money where your mouth is.*

An Indian student at CUNY, reporting on discount shopping in Brooklyn, wrote in a photo caption: *Jeans on sale at Mandee in Ridgewood, Brooklyn.* In the interest of clarity, I asked, "Do you mean *on sale* or *for sale?*" *On sale* means prices have been reduced, as in *everything goes on sale the day after Christmas,* and these jeans may well have been. But everything in a shop is *for sale*—available for purchase—so I double-checked.

No wonder idioms confuse so many people. Unfortunately, the best advice I can give journalists is this: memorize them, practice using them and learn from being edited when you make mistakes.

A Chinese student at CUNY was *so close and yet so far away* when she e-mailed me to postpone a coaching session, saying she was on deadline with a long-form story. "I think it is going to *make me full-handed* since Tuesday," she wrote. "You mean you'll *have your hands full,*" I replied. She also could have said *I think I'll have a lot on my plate* or *I think my plate is full.* Any of those three choices would have been idiomatic, but hers was not. (And she meant *until,* not *since.*)

Sometimes mistakes are not a matter of those funny phrases you don't understand, but trying to translate literally or mold English to the constructions of your native language. An Italian student was trying to be idiomatic when he wrote that someone *pointed the finger against* someone else, but in English the idiom is *point the finger at* (accuse). An Indian student wrote, "I think my mind comes to conclusions very soon"; she meant *jumps to conclusions.* The same student wrote that she had dialed 911 *in impulse* when the idiom is *on impulse,* and that "we take all possible efforts to keep our homes clean and safe." Americans *make an effort.*

Similarly, Americans *make a decision*, but the British *take a decision*. Idioms are one of the places where British and American English diverge, so make sure to choose the right idiom for your particular English-speaking audience. If you lose your job in the United States, you've been *fired*; in the U.K., you've been *sacked* or *given the sack*, or you *got the sack*, all of which mean terminated. In America, job losses due to reductions in the workforce are called *layoffs*, and the worker is *laid off* or *let go*; in Britain, he is *made redundant*, meaning superfluous or no longer needed. Americans say *different from* when speaking correctly and *different than* less formally; the British and Irish say *different to*. In repeating but shortening a verb, Americans drop the past participle, while the British tend to substitute a form of *do*. When I interviewed Reid Anderson, artistic director of the Stuttgart Ballet, in 2010 and asked, "Do you choreograph?" he answered, "I have, but I don't." The Canadian-born Anderson used the American short form, *I have*, rather than the British, *I have done*. (Canadians spell like Brits but tend to sound almost exactly like Americans and use American idioms.) Similarly, the British say *I will do, I could do, I might do* and so on, whereas Americans say simply *I will, I could, I might*.

IDIOM VERSUS SLANG

All slang is idiomatic, but not all idioms are slang. *Slang* refers to "very informal, sometimes offensive language that is used especially by people who belong to a particular group, such as young people or criminals," according to the Longman Dictionary of Contemporary English online. It may be part of a specific linguistic culture, like the rhyming slang of the London Cockneys, in which, to cite just one example, *trouble and strife* means *wife*. Professional jargon like the media terms in Chapter 2 are also a form of slang. As Longman notes, slang often originates with the young, perhaps as a way of distinguishing their culture from their parents', and thus changes quickly with the passage of time. (As the young grow older, they tend to keep using the slang of their own generation. When they try to sound hip by adopting their children's, they sound ridiculous. So can publications.)

Consider the evolution of slang for one simple adjective: wonderful. In the 1920s it was *the bee's knees* or *the cat's pajamas,* and those terms are still heard occasionally. In the 1930s it was *the greatest thing since sliced bread*—a loaf that could be bought pre-sliced by machine, which was an innovation then. By the 1950's, it was *neat* or *keen*—which sounded silly to Woody Allen's character when Diane Keaton's was still using them in the 1977 movie *Annie Hall.* In the 1960s *neat* gave way to *cool,* which in turn gave way to the psychedelic *groovy.* In the 1990s everything was suddenly *awesome,* except in British English, in which everything remains *brilliant* to this day. *Cool* resurfaced in the early 2000s, but as I write in 2015, I've noticed that these days everything seems to be *perfect.* You propose a time and place for an interview? "Perfect," the source responds. An usher directs you to a seat in the very last row of a theater? "Perfect," you say, even though it's not. When I coach one particular CUNY student from South America, she reacts to every change I make in her copy with "Perfect!" The word has become another way to say thank you and politely end an encounter, as *awesome* was before it. This, too, shall pass.

Since slang changes quickly, it also quickly becomes dated. Look no further than the works of Eugene O'Neill, America's greatest playwright to date. Writing in the first half of the 20th century and aiming to portray his characters in a naturalistic way, O'Neill filled their dialogue with the slang of the time. A century later, despite a lyricism that can border on the operatic, his plays sound incredibly dated, like this passage from *Anna Christie:*

> *I'm wise to what's in back of your nut, Dutchy. Yuh want to git rid o' me, huh?—now she's comin'. Gimme the bum's rush ashore, huh? Lemme tell yuh, Dutchy, there ain't a square-head workin' on a boat man enough to git away with that. Don't start nothin' yuh can't finish!*

Maybe all journalists secretly want to be the next O'Neill, but we can't afford to. Yes, we're writing for right now, but especially in the age of digital archives, we're also writing for an audience far into the future. Slang is also, by nature, informal in register (see page 116). While journalists today want to sound conversational rather than stuffy, they do want to achieve a register appropriate to the topic they are covering. So use slang sparingly: to capture a moment in time; to convey the flavor of a source's speech, as you would any quote (see page 92); or to make a point.

As when using idioms, you have to know what slang means and get it exactly right. And be careful. If you find yourself at a New York cocktail party, don't offer to *cut the cheese*, as a hapless out-of-towner did on an episode of "Mad Men." The phrase refers to an unintentional discharge of intestinal gas, which you don't want to be caught doing in polite company. Cockneys would call it a *raspberry tart*. Remember, it rhymes.

IDIOM'S EVIL TWIN: CLICHÉ

The *evil twin* is a plot device in movies and television, especially *soap operas*. (That's an idiom for the kind of melodramas originally broadcast to housewives on daytime radio and TV, named for the soap companies that sponsored them. Westerns are called *horse operas*—that is, the cowboy-and-Native Americans kind, as opposed to movies made in the Western Hemisphere.) A saintly, beloved character suddenly has a long-lost twin—perhaps the *black sheep* of the family, the member who's different from everyone else—who of course looks exactly like her (because she's played by the same actress) but has a *black heart*. Complications follow.

Idioms, too, have an evil twin, and its name is cliché. (The word comes straight from French and retains the pronunciation and accent mark.) It means "an idea or phrase that has been used so much that it is not effective or does not have any meaning any longer," according to the *Longman Dictionary*.

"Shakespeare sure used a lot of clichés," said a high school classmate of mine when we were studying *Hamlet*. Yes and no. When Shakespeare wrote phrases like *brevity is the soul of wit* and *the lady doth protest too much*, they were original—at least, as far as we know four centuries later. Repetition and overuse have made them clichés, until today even they sound tired and worn out.

Any idiom can all too easily turn into a cliché if it's used too often and too commonly. Journalism is full of clichés. any fatal fire, car wreck or murder is labeled a *tragedy* (see page 268); every dish mentioned in a restaurant review is *drizzled* with sauce or dressing; every new company in the business pages is *up and running*. Even sentence structures can become clichés if a publication uses them so often that they become predictable. "Backward ran sentences until reeled the mind," goes an old joke making fun of *Time* magazine's habit of inverting word order—an acceptable construction in English, an effective variation if used occasionally, but laughable if overused. Then there's *The New York Times's* habit of *putting the cart before the horse*—yes, that's an idiom—by letting pronouns precede (go before) their antecedents (the things that are supposed to go before. See page 194). So balance your eagerness to adopt English idioms by constantly striving for fresh language and imagery.

From a Danish student at CUNY writing on an election in which nine parties were contending:

> *On the right end of the left-wing parties you find the Social Democrats.*

And from an Italian student writing about the overnight ferry to Stromboli:

> *The passengers are still wrapped in their sleeping bags and entangled in their dreams when the words land on them like a bucket of icy water.*

Yes, that's a bit of a mixed metaphor (see page 258), but I think it works.

Finding your own way to express an idea is a big step toward finding your voice—that personal stamp that marks you, and you alone, as the creator of any given piece. It's what makes readers look forward to seeing your byline.

Break a leg.

GREG DAVID

THE BOTTOM LINE

The bottom line was originally an accounting term, referring to that all-important last line of a balance sheet that tells if a business has made or lost money. In everyday English, it has come to mean the end result. Greg David knows about bottom lines. As director of the business and economics reporting concentration, he is the CUNY Journalism School's go-to expert in the field. A member of the senior adjunct faculty, he also blogs and writes a weekly column for *Crain's New York Business*, which he edited for 25 years. He is a regular contributor to WNYC Radio and the author of *Modern New York: The Life and Economics of a City* (Palgrave McMillan, 2012).

What makes good writing?

The most important word to describe good writing is clarity. It has taken me a long time to learn that. And by clarity I mean clarity of thought and clarity in how you write. You must be precisely clear in your mind about what you want to say, and you must be able to say it clearly so everyone understands it.

How does a beginning writer in English accomplish that? How do you get to that point?

I think they would go with my second point. How you get to it is, you must get to the bottom line on everything you want to say. You need to get to the bottom line of what your journalism story is about: what is this story going to say? But then you want to get to the bottom line of what every paragraph is supposed to say. You think through all the complications, and you decide what *is* the essence of what you want to say, at each level—in the story, in the section, in the paragraph. And that will get you, I believe, to clarity. And that is, in my experience, what readers really prize.

The other crucial element in good writing is outlining. The people here at the J-school look at me, and I can just tell they're thinking, "I don't have time to outline." But the truth is, they don't have time *not* to outline, because the outline helps to force you to come to conclusions about what you're writing, and the outline helps to shape your clarity. And if you take the time to outline, *then* the other steps will come so much more easily.

What needs to be in a nut graf?

The nut graf *is* the bottom line on your story. It is what the story's about, often why it's timely, and what its importance is. Nut grafs should be only two sentences, three in the rarest cases, and if you write a good nut graf, you have done that; you have gotten to the bottom line on your story. It says, "This is what this story is about. This is why you should read it. This is why it's important."

What are the biggest problems you see in writing from our international students?

It actually ranges very widely, right? Some of these problems our American students have, especially getting to the bottom line on the story, working through the complications and writing with clarity. Everyone has those problems.

Idiom becomes a very big problem. Even if they've studied English extensively, the idiom's a problem. And also some foreign languages just have different constructions for where you put the verbs and where you put the nouns, and how long your sentences are, and I think those represent transition difficulties. So the basic problems of getting to the bottom line and writing with clarity are then made worse by the idiom issues.

I do a lot of radio . . . and they only want sound bites. So I can't just talk. I don't talk and then let them pick the sound bites. So I go into every interview having decided what sound bite I want and how I'm going to say it. I take the same approach with my column: what am I saying today, and how am I saying it?

CHAPTER 10

THE TOP 20 TROUBLE SPOTS

Four years of coaching at the CUNY journalism school have (or is it *has*?) brought an endless, and seemingly infinite, stream of problems and questions. Some are particular to a given student's native language, but many are *across the board*. (That's an idiom meaning they're common to students from many languages and cultures—including Americans.) When I started the English for Journalists blog (http://englishforjournalists.journalism.cuny.edu/) to focus on these troublesome grammar points, I received just three words of advice from faculty members: "lots of examples." As of mid-2016, the blog comprised nearly 60 entries and had been consulted more than 30,000 times not only by CUNY students, but also by readers around the world. When editing students, I frequently include in my comments links to the relevant posts so they may read and digest them off deadline.

A look back reveals 20 grammar points that come up again and again. Updated and in alphabetical order:

ACTIVE VERSUS PASSIVE VOICE

Small-town newspaper reports on church socials and other such gatherings often used to end with this sentence: *A good time was had by all.*

Today it makes us laugh—or should—because it's such a backwards way of saying what it means: *Everyone had a good time.* Written in passive voice, it sounds pretentious. It would sound far less so in active voice.

In grammatical terms, *voice* refers to the relationship between the subject of a sentence and the action of the verb. Translation: voice indicates whether the subject acts or is acted upon. If the subject performs an action, the sentence is in *active voice.* If the subject is acted upon—the recipient of the action—it's in *passive voice.* (Note how those last two sentences illustrate the very concepts they define.) In passive voice, the subject of the sentence is essentially the object of the verb.

Journalism at its best is an active form of writing: reporters tell their readers who did what, sometimes to whom. That's why so many headlines (though far from all) are written in active voice. In one day's news:

Obama Announces Health Pick
Warily, Jordan Assists Rebels in Syrian War
Tenants Near Harlem Gas Explosion File Suit Against City

Using active voice also tightens (see page 240) your writing, saving a couple of words per sentence—the auxiliary verb and *by*—to reduce your word count and thus make room for more facts. A few improvements on student work:

A recovery is expected in sectors such as retail sales, construction and transportation.

Who expects the recovery? That's an important fact that can give your report credibility. In active voice:

Economists expect a recovery in sectors such as retail sales, construction and transportation.

It was announced on Feb. 14 that the bill has been expanded.

A double passive. Who made the announcement? And who expanded the bill? Adding those key facts would strengthen the sentence. Rewrite it in active voice:

The sponsors announced on Feb. 14 that they had expanded the bill.

Houston was among the leading U.S. Metropolitan Statistical Areas exporters in 2011, when its housing market was ranked by AFIRE for the first time.

Instead, turn that subordinate clause around:

. . . when AFIRE ranked its housing market for the first time.

The writer headlined the story:

Houston's housing market fueled by foreign buyers

I suggested turning it around:

Foreign buyers fuel Houston's housing market

"Why not use active voice?" I asked. She moaned: "It's more active?" But that's precisely the point. In most cases, you want your writing to be as active as you can make it.

Not every headline needs to be written in active voice. From *The New York Times*: *Cuomo (Is) Caught Up in Rare Conflict With Prosecutor;* from the *New York Post* the same day: *Teens (are) killed when truck hits bus on college visit.* In headline writing, auxiliary verbs are generally dropped unless, of course, the writer needs to pad out the hed to fill the assigned space. (And why are all the words capitalized in one of those heds and not the other? The papers follow different styles.)

Sometimes writers (or speakers) have their reasons for using passive voice—for example, in this excuse popular among politicians, originally attributed to President Ulysses S. Grant (1869 to 1877) and repeated in recent decades by Nixon, Reagan, Clinton, Bush and Bush (http://www.msnbc.com/rachel-maddow-show/passive-voice-bush-family-tradition):

Mistakes were made.

By using passive voice, the writer or speaker avoids assigning blame—or even admitting to knowing who made statements assigning it.

Occasionally passive voice is simply the better choice. In an editing exercise, a student produced this lede:

> *The country chose Barack Hussein Obama, 47, a first-term Democratic senator from Illinois, as its first black chief executive, the 44th president of the United States on Tuesday.*

Here, active voice made the sentence sound artificial and stiff; clearly the writer was scrambling to find a noun to serve as the subject. Here's what *The New York Times* said on Nov. 5, 2008:

> *Barack Hussein Obama **was elected** the 44th president of the United States on Tuesday, sweeping away the last racial barrier in American politics with ease . . .*

ANTECEDENTS

In late 2012, Richard Mourdock was probably wishing he had paid more attention in his eighth-grade English class. Mourdock, then a Republican Senate candidate in Indiana, got into *hot water* (that's an idiom meaning trouble) by saying that when rape results in pregnancy, "it is something that God intended." What does English class have to do with it?

It would have been bad enough if Mourdock had said, as he apparently intended, that what God intended was the pregnancy. His implication that rape—a serious crime—might be God's will outraged many people. Where they see a political controversy, I see a grammar point: an unclear antecedent. Just what did he mean by "it"—rape or pregnancy? "What is *it*?" "Who is *they*?" I've written on any number of student stories. *It* and *they* are pronouns, and pronouns require antecedents— the nouns they replace, generally to avoid repetition. The grammatical term derives from Latin, *ante-* meaning before (not to be confused with *anti-*, meaning against) + *ced-*, from *cedere*, meaning to go (the root of many words, including *precede, proceed* and *succeed*). As a writer, you need to make sure your readers understand just what the antecedent is.

"Mark Owen" (the pen name of the Navy SEAL later identified as Matt Bissonnette), who wrote a book about the raid that killed Osama bin Laden, supplied another case in point during an interview on CBS' "60 Minutes." From the transcript:

> *Among the unfinished business was the crashed helicopter. It was a secret design, loaded with secret gear. They had to blow it up. A message was passed to their explosives expert—called the E.O.D. man—"prep it to blow," they said. But the "it" in the message was a little vague.*
> **Mark Owen**: *Well, the E.O.D. guy thinks he means prep the house to blow. So there we are in the middle of this. And he's, like, "OK, roger that, prep it to blow." So he's running around the first floor of the house, setting his charges, getting ready to blow up the house. And somebody looks over at him is like, "Dude, dude, what are you doing?" He's like, "Ah, I'm prepping it to blow." He's, like, "Not the house, the helicopter." Well, he hadn't got the word that there was a helicopter even down.*

Do antecedents matter? If you had been a Navy SEAL still in that house, they certainly would have mattered to you—and your survivors.

Be careful about using a pronoun to refer to a whole sentence, a phrase or an idea, as I did in the second graf of this section: *What does English class have to do with it?* In this case, I think it's clear that *it* refers to the situation described in the preceding sentence. But such may not always be the case, especially if there's a noun—i.e., a potential antecedent—nearby. *What does (noun) have to do with it?* is something of an idiom, as in the Tina Turner song "What's Love Got to Do With It." (A British variation: *What's that got to do with the price of eggs?*)

Remember that pronouns need to agree in number with their antecedents. From a piece by a student:

> *Once inside, any guest would be hard pressed to say that they weren't actually in a pocket-sized French cafe.*

They has no plural antecedent. Presumably *any guest* is the antecedent, but that's singular. Two possible fixes:

> *Any guest would be hard pressed to say that he wasn't actually in a pocket-sized French cafe.*

But that sentence courts accusations of sexism. You could say *he or she*, but that sounds clumsy. Often the easiest fix is to pluralize:

> *Guests would be hard pressed to say that they weren't actually in a pocket-sized French cafe.*

From another student, in a story about a neighborhood with a high number of sex offenders:

> *"We have cameras all the way across here, and alarms at every door," he said and pointed at the cameras hanging outside of the school.*
> *Inside, they have 50 cameras, and the entrance is guarded from 7 a.m. to 10 p.m. every day, he said.*

Who is *they*? The *we* in the preceding sentence is not enough of a plural antecedent. Instead:

Inside, the school has 50 cameras, and the entrance is guarded from 7 a.m. to 10 p.m. every day, he said.

Finally, remember that *antecedent* means *ante* + *cedent*—that is, going *before* the pronoun. Some publications can be a little sloppy on that point. At *The New York Times*, this construction is now used so often it seems practically *knee-jerk* (that's an idiom meaning automatic), especially in anecdotal ledes:

As he compiled images for his book, the photographer Arthur Grace found countless pictures that he didn't remember taking.

This one is easy to fix:

As the photographer Arthur Grace compiled images for his book, he found countless pictures that he didn't remember taking.

Or:

(While) Compiling images for a book, the photographer Arthur Grace found countless pictures that he didn't remember taking.

A variation on the theme:

Putting her Jimmy Choo years behind her, Tamara Mellon has plans, no doubt involving fashion.

In this case the pronoun *her* is a possessive, referring to Mellon, who isn't introduced until later in the sentence. Better:

As Tamara Mellon puts her Jimmy Choo years behind her, she has plans, no doubt involving fashion.

In summary, remember these three simple rules for using a pronoun:

- Put the antecedent before the pronoun.
- Make sure they agree. (For more on the subject, see page 227.)
- And above all, make sure the antecedent is clear.

ARTICLES

You know what articles are: those three little words, *a, an* and *the*, that precede nouns. You know how to use them, at least in theory. But you may have trouble getting them just right or, if your native language has no articles, remembering to use them at all.

Articles come naturally to native speakers of English, and they are crucial to speaking and writing. Without them, English sounds harsh, brusque and incomplete, like (forgive me, Russian alumnae!) Boris and Natasha in the old "Rocky & Bullwinkle" cartoons. If you've never seen them, check YouTube (https://www.youtube.com/watch?v=yHqy-chPMnM).

A brief refresher:

The refers to a specific (noun), *a* or *an* to any (noun). In general, use *a* if the word that follows begins with a consonant sound, *an* if it begins with a vowel sound. *The* can be used for singular or plural, but *a* and *an* are always singular. The plural of *a* or *an* is no article at all.

So:

Someone sent me a fruit basket!
Would you like an apple? (There's more than one in the basket.)
I'd rather have the banana. (There's only one.)
Did you buy bananas?
Where did you put the bananas you bought last night?

Note that I said "consonant *sound*" and "vowel *sound*." Sometimes we use *a* before a vowel—for example, *a usual procedure, a uniform*—when the vowel begins with a consonant sound. (*Usual* sounds like *you-sual*, not *ooh-sual*.) We also use *an* before a consonant that is silent, as in *an honor*. (The British will talk about *an historic event*, even though the *h* is not silent.) Ease in speaking should be your guide: if it's hard to say, it's probably wrong. That's why we say *an apple*, not *a apple*. Similarly, *the* is normally pronounced *thuh* but may become *thee* before a vowel sound, as in *the event*. (See page 139.)

Not every noun requires an article. Nouns that can't be counted never take *a* or *an*, though you can use *the* if talking about something specific. An example: *English is not my cup of the tea*. First, *not my cup of tea* is an idiom, describing something you dislike or would prefer to avoid. Second, *tea* requires no article unless you're referring to specific tea: *Would you like a cup of the tea I bought today?*

Articles are used idiomatically in other ways—for example, *in bed*, as in *I was sick in bed all day* (not *in the bed*). Americans say *in school* and *out of school*: *Will the kids be in school on Monday?* Or: *I've been out of school for years* (meaning I graduated or otherwise completed my education). In a general sense, kids *go to school* and my students are *in graduate school*, but they attend *the CUNY journalism school*. When Americans are sick, they go *to the hospital*; the British simply go *to hospital*. Similarly, British undergraduates go *to university*; after they graduate, they may reminisce, *"When I was at university . . ."* As undergrads, Americans go *to college* or are *in college*, even if they attend *a university* (not *an*).

Students in the CUNY J-School's business concentration sometimes write about companies that are *in the red*—not *in red*, as one wrote—or *in the black*. (On accounting ledgers, black ink signifies profit; red means loss.) But sometimes a company will turn a profit *in time* to avoid bankruptcy—maybe because its employees come to work *on time*. Another student wrote about *"the* U.S. trade relations." No article needed there.

There are also specialized or local usages. Among the five boroughs of New York City, only *the Bronx* takes an article (as a noun, but as an adjective, *Bronx residents* unless you mean specific ones). Neighborhoods within boroughs are a little trickier. In Manhattan, we have *Lower*

Manhattan, Greenwich Village, Chelsea, Harlem, Washington Heights and *Inwood,* among others, but *the Lower East Side, the Upper West Side, the East Side.* Washington Heights is *the Heights* for short, much like *the Village.* And it's always *Central Park,* never *the Central Park.*

DANGLERS

Dangle means "to hang loosely," according to merriamwebster.com. In English, a dangling modifier—dangler for short—is an adjective or a phrase that hangs loosely on a sentence, generally because it's misplaced. Remember the entry on antecedents and pronouns (see page 194), which stressed that the link between them must always be clear? The same applies to modifiers and what they modify.

As you become more comfortable with English, you'll find yourself writing more complex sentences using subordinate or dependent clauses—the ones beginning with words like *that, which, who, whose, when, where,* etc. that add definitions or descriptions. (See page 233.) Complex sentences are especially prone to becoming danglers, as many students have shown.

Here's a relatively simple example:

By buying high and selling low, the company's finances took a serious hit.

The finances didn't buy and sell; the company did. Better:

By buying high and selling low, the company took a serious financial hit.

While dining at restaurants in and around the city, beautiful Hispanic women or young enthusiastic men might have served us many times.

The writer meant the beautiful women and enthusiastic men were the servers, not her dining companions. Better:

While we were dining at restaurants in and around the city, beautiful Hispanic women or young enthusiastic men might have served us and many times.

Or, tighter:

At restaurants in and around the city, beautiful Hispanic women or young enthusiastic men might have served us and many times.
On a small folding table against a wall in the dining room, she placed two hats whose brims were attached with hair, one in red and another in beige.

What was red and beige, the hats or the hair? Move the descriptive phrase closer to what it modifies:

*On a small folding table against a wall in the dining room, she placed **two hats, one in red and another in beige**, whose brims were attached with hair.*

Or even tighter:

On a small folding table against a wall in the dining room, she placed two hats, one red and one beige, whose brims were attached with hair.

The next example is a quote:

"After working for Ixia since 2004 and having been promoted to CEO last year, the board saw fit to fire Mr. Alston for

*misstating age and academic credentials," Robison said in his
report.*

Robison didn't mean the board had worked for Ixia and been promoted; he meant Alston had. A journalist might not reword a quote (see page 89), but it's a shame no one seems to have edited Robison's report. Here's what he might have written:

> *After Mr. Alston had worked for Ixia since 2004 and been promoted to CEO last year, the board saw fit to fire him for misstating age and academic credentials.*

Similarly:

> *While expanding in domestic and international markets, Landson said AirTran created a solid foundation for Southwest to build upon when it comes to international operations.*

Landson did that expansion all by himself while he was talking? Probably not. In this case, a simple comma setting off the attribution solves the problem:

> *While expanding in domestic and international markets, Landson said, AirTran created a solid foundation for Southwest to build upon when it comes to international operations.*

The more complex the sentence, the more likely danglers will sneak in:

> *Starting operation as an HIV/AIDS service organization, God's Love has evolved into a provider of meals and nutritional advice for patients living with more than 200 severe*

diseases, in which its volunteers cook and home deliver the food.

Let's do a dangler check. *Starting operation as an HIV/AIDS service organization, God's Love has evolved . . . ?* Did the group God's Love (We Deliver) start as an HIV/AIDS organization? Yes, so that's fine. How about *. . . nutritional advice for patients living with more than 200 severe diseases, in which its volunteers cook and home deliver the food?* Do the volunteers cook and deliver the food in the diseases? I think not. Correct (and with a little editing):

> **Having started** as an HIV/AIDS service organization, God's Love has evolved into a provider of meals and nutritional advice. Its volunteers cook and home-deliver the food **to** patients living with more than 200 severe diseases.

Copy editors love to spot danglers, which make them laugh.

> *After meeting with City Councilwoman Rosie Mendez several times, Mendez decided to do a $300,000 capital funding project for the park in the spring.*

That sentence has Mendez meeting with herself. Instead:

> *After meeting with City Councilwoman Rosie Mendez several times, (whatever governing body) decided to do a $300,000 capital funding project for the park in the spring.*

> *The brides Da Na and Bu Xiu posed for photographers holding bouquets in white dresses in the heart of Beijing.*

The photographers were probably holding cameras, not bouquets, which were probably not wearing white dresses. Instead:

*Holding bouquets and wearing white dresses, the brides Da
Na and Bu Xiu posed for photographers in the heart of Beijing.*

Even the pros get it wrong—often. A sentence in *The New
York Times Magazine's* 2014 feature "The Lives They Lived," an
annual issue celebrating people who have died in the year just past,
read:

*Less than five years after graduating from Black Mountain
College, in North Carolina, Ruth Asawa's industrial-wire
sculptures were getting notice in the national press.*

It was Asawa, not her sculptures, who had graduated. Instead:

*Less than five years after Ruth Asawa graduated from Black
Mountain College, in North Carolina, her industrial-wire
sculptures were getting notice in the national press.*

Finally, a shining example of correctness from Cariba Party, CUNY
class of 2015, who got it exactly right (and which I nearly ruined through
too-fast, knee-jerk editing):

Now that he's almost 60, his eccentricities are not fading away.

I'd have been right to edit if it had read as I misread it in haste:
Now almost 60, his eccentricities are not fading away. But it didn't.
Congratulations, Cari.

As Mariana Marcaletti from Argentina, CUNY class of 2014, so
charmingly put it when we talked about danglers, "The connection is not
properly done." That is correct: the connection between modifier and
what it modifies is not made properly. When you write, make sure it is.
Pick your sentences apart; read them aloud to see if the meaning is clear.
If they make you laugh, rewrite.

ELEGANT VARIATIONS

Surely you've been taught to avoid repeating the same word over and over again when writing in English. But some writers take that advice to the extreme, *bending over backwards* (that's an idiom for trying much too hard) to avoid repetition when, really, it doesn't matter. That's how the phrase *elongated yellow fruit* entered the language. It is an elegant variation—an unnecessary, usually longer synonym—for a simple, concise word. Journalism is rarely about elegance; it's about simplicity and clarity. An elongated yellow fruit is just a fancy word for banana, so say *banana*. The same goes for *fluffy white stuff* when you mean snow.

One CUNY journalism student came dangerously close to elongated yellow fruit syndrome when she wrote:

> *The morning after President Obama addressed the nation about the conflict over chemical weapons in Syria, Melrose residents observed the anniversary of the Sept. 11 attacks by expressing deep reservations about possible U.S. military action in the Middle Eastern country.*

Here *the Middle Eastern country* is just the writer's attempt not to repeat *Syria*. Instead of either, how about:

> *. . . by expressing deep reservations about possible U.S. military action* **there***.*

The chances of confusion would seem to be minimal. The only other place mentioned in the sentence is Melrose, and the U.S. is unlikely to take military action against the Bronx. *There* saves four words.

A frequent victim of elegant variation is *said*. Beginning journalists chafe at repeating *said* time after time after time; they prefer to substitute words like *stated, explained, declared, opined.* Resist temptation. Use *stated* for a quote from, say, a written or official statement. Save *explained* for a quote that actually explains what precedes it. Avoid *declared*; forget *opined* altogether. As an old saying in journalism goes: "We don't print the truth; we print what people tell us." *Tell* means *say to.* Use *said.*

FRAGMENTS

If, like the Chinese artist Ai Weiwei, you pick up a ceramic vase and drop it onto a hard floor, it will probably break into pieces, or *fragments.* (A word more specific to pottery and glass: *shards.*) Writing, too, can contain fragments—incomplete sentences that seem to express a thought but lack a crucial element, most often a verb. That sentence in which I introduced *shards* is an example.

Reporting on a film festival, a CUNY student from Italy wrote:

Great participation also in the various afternoon screenings of films, documentaries, short films and video clips.

This is a fragment because it has no verb. To make it a complete sentence, add one:

There was also great participation in the various afternoon screenings of films, documentaries, short films and video clips.

Better still, eliminate the *there was* construction (see page 236) and be more specific about the meaning of *great participation*, which implies a judgment that the participation was good:

Attendance exceeded expectations in the various afternoon screenings of films, documentaries, short films and video clips.

From the same story:

"We have recounted, through the cinema and the work of African artists, a side of Africa almost unknown in Italy," said

Gianfranco Belgrano, administrator of Internationalia and co-organizer of the festival. "A reality of a continent that is growing from an economic point of view, from a demographic point of view and from a cultural point of view."

Here the fragment is the second sentence of the quote. Should you change the quote to eliminate the fragment? That depends on your publication's policy. (See page 89.) In this case, the quote was translated from Italian, so it would be perfectly acceptable to render it more like this:

"The reality is, the continent is growing from an economic point of view, from a demographic point of view and from a cultural point of view."

Or:

"In reality, the continent is growing from an economic point of view, from a demographic point of view and from a cultural point of view."

That said, experienced writers who know how to write a complete sentence often choose to use fragments for emphasis, effect or brevity, as I have, I hope judiciously, throughout this book. And TV newscasters often introduce stories with fragments. A TV anchor on a local New York newscast introduced a story by saying:

A mystery on Long Island: a man is shot twice in a barbershop early this morning.

The sentence is a technically a fragment: even though the part after the colon is a full clause with a subject and a predicate, the part before the colon is not. As I write in mid-2105, it seems fashionable for newscasters to introduce stories using verbs in present continuous tense: *Vice President Biden, tonight considering a run for the White House.* This construction may have evolved from the conventions of headline writing for print, in which the present continuous lends immediacy. But use it sparingly.

GENDER AND PRONOUNS

When a child is whining at the dinner table for a gadget or quietly asking for a touchscreen because the toddler is bored, he doesn't need an iPad. He needs you.

"Should it be *he or she*?" the writer, a Russian, asked as we were going over his or her piece.

Good question.

In the distant past—up to the early 1970s—the masculine pronouns *he, him* and *his,* were assumed to be universal, representing male and female alike (much like *man* for all of humankind), as in:

He who laughs last laughs best.
Let him who is without sin cast the first stone.

Then the second wave of American feminism came along, and anything with so much as a whiff of sexism about it had to go. We girls who expected to be called *women* the minute we turned 18 also started demanding *he or she* instead of assuming one pronoun fits all if it happened to be masculine. (And *coed* as a noun? Don't get me started.)

He or she may be nonsexist, but it's also clumsy: *Let him or her who is without sin cast the first stone.* Just look at the way I worded that sentence in the second paragraph: *going over his or her piece,* in this case to avoid suggesting the writer's identity. Repetition aggravates the problem:

He or she doesn't need an iPad. He or she needs you.

How can you make your point cleanly while avoiding sexism? Often, the easiest fix is to pluralize the whole sentence:

When children are whining at the dinner table . . . they don't need iPads. They need you.

AP Style suggests another way, when applicable:

Q. Does AP prefer "he or she" or just "she" or "he" when referring to a singular pronoun? For example, If he or she makes $10,000 more, his or her refund is reduced by $2,100.—from Georgia on Sun, Aug 31, 2008

> *A. Better to avoid two pronouns: If **the person** makes $10,000 or more, **the refund is reduced**, etc.*

A third possibility: make some examples male, some female, as I have done in this book. In the children-and-technology piece, the writer led with an anecdote about a little girl, then later switched to boys.

Whichever fix you choose—pluralizing, recasting the sentence, citing examples from both sexes—be sure it doesn't make the sentence more clumsy than *he or she* would. If it does, revert. On no account use *they* with a singular antecedent, as in:

Whatever the sex of the candidate, they deserve serious consideration.

Better:

All candidates deserve serious consideration regardless of their sex.

Personally, I rather like *s/he*, but most stylebooks do not. Don't use it.

In a similar attempt to wipe out sexism, the '70s also brought gender-neutral words like *chairperson*. (A Doonesbury comic strip of the period lampooned the fad, depicting a newly elected legislator who introduced himself as a "freshperson Congressperson.") Four decades later, it is once again safe to call someone a *chairman* or *chairwoman*, as per AP Style, but please, not *chair*. And instead of *congressperson*, try *U.S. representative*.

GERUNDS AND INFINITIVES

English is a fluid language. Nouns sometimes morph into verbs—*transition, access* and *impac*t, in common usage over recent years. (Not that your publication's style necessarily approves. When in doubt, check.) And verbs can be nouns in two of their forms: infinitives and gerunds.

An infinitive is *to* plus the base form of the verb—*to be, to have, to go, to stay,* etc. It is used as a noun: *She loves to swim.* (What does she love? *To swim.* The infinitive is the direct object, and objects are nouns or pronouns.)

A gerund is essentially the verb's present participle—*base + -ing*—used as a noun: *She loves swimming.*

In that case, where *love* is the verb in both sentences, the two forms are interchangeable and equally correct. That's not always the case; some verbs demand to be followed by an infinitive, some by a gerund, as in this example from student work:

> *Shoe repair shops tend **to gather** in big cities like New York because people who live there can afford **buying** expensive footwear or **spend** money on extra protective or orthopedic work.*

Tend takes the infinitive; you always *tend to do* something. *Afford,* on the other hand, could go either way, although *afford to buy* is more common. But notice that yet another verb follows: *spend.* Because it's of equal weight in the sentence to *buy,* it needs to be parallel to it—the same form:

*. . . people who live there can afford **buying** expensive foot-wear or **spending** money on extra protective or orthopedic work.*

Or:

*. . . people who live there can afford **to buy** expensive footwear or **(to) spend** money on extra protective or orthopedic work.*

In the case of *spend,* the *to* is optional. The form is easily understood from context to be an infinitive because it is parallel to *to buy* (see page 216), so it's safe to drop it. The same is true in another student's sentence:

This experience helps people (to) understand the blind world.

After *help,* you generally don't need *to* unless the sentence sounds awkward without it.

Another example:

Jason Hansman, senior program manager at IAVA, said veterans' major challenge is to learn how to promote themselves.

To learn or *learning?* In this case, either is correct:

Hansman said veterans' major challenge is learning how to promote themselves.

But:

*She suggested **to look** at the company's website called "The Exceptional Cranberry" to know more about the healthfulness of cranberries.*

No. *Suggest* requires the gerund, so here it needs to be *looking.*

How do you know which verbs take infinitives, which take gerunds and which take either? Listen to the way people talk; pay attention when you're reading; and consult lists like this one on TestYourEnglish.net (http://www.testyourenglish.net/english-online/subjects/gerinflist.html) or this one on EngVid.com (http://www.engvid.com/english-resource/verbs-followed-by-gerunds-and-infinitives/), which includes an interactive quiz.

After some verbs, the choice of gerund or infinitive depends on the meaning. *I stopped to buy newspapers,* for example, means you stopped for that purpose; *I stopped buying newspapers when I got an iPad* means you no longer buy them.

Since gerunds function as nouns, any nouns directly preceding them need to be possessive. Not:

> *The idea of* **customers** *actually going to the store for returns appeals to him.*

Instead:

> *The idea of* **customers'** *actually going to the store for returns appeals to him.*

Theoretically, Shakespeare (or whoever he really was) could have used either the infinitive *(to be)* or the gerund *(being)* in the opening line of Hamlet's soliloquy: *To be or not to be, that is the question.* He made his choice and, in doing so, gave us the greatest use of the infinitive in the English language. Whichever choice he made, he knew the power of parallelism.

INDEFINITE NOUNS

> *My makeup made a wow-effect with my girlfriends who knew I had been practicing makeup at home but never had a chance to see me in one.*

After freelancing in England for a couple of months and Paris for one year, he came to New York in 2009.

Last night I went to see some photo exhibition on the East Side of Manhattan.

These sentences sound just slightly off. Their meaning is clear enough, but something about them suggest they didn't come from a native speaker. The problem stems from their use of indefinite nouns, and the articles, adjectives or pronouns that go with them.

An indefinite noun is one that is not specific—in these cases, *makeup* (no particular makeup), *year* (what year?) and *photo exhibition* (which one?). Like the definite article, *the,* and the indefinite ones, *a* and *an,* indefinite nouns need to work with pronouns and adjectives. That's where complications begin.

In the first sentence—where the *girlfriends knew I had been practicing makeup at home but never had a chance to see me in one*—the problem is *one.* Here the point is not just whether the noun is definite or indefinite, but also whether it's countable or uncountable. Can you count makeup? No. Makeup is a collective noun that includes foundation, blush, lipstick, mascara and so on. You can't count *one makeup, two makeups, three makeups.* You could use *some,* as in *never had a chance to see me in some.* But *some* usually indicates a positive context; for negative, *any* is better. So: the girlfriends *never had a chance to see me in any.* (In such cases, *some* and *any* function as pronouns.)

In *After freelancing in England for couple of months and Paris for one year . . , . one* is a little too precise—especially after a vague phrase like *a couple of months.* Instead, most Americans would say *for a year.*

In *some photo exhibition on the East Side of Manhattan,* you want the indefinite article *a* rather than *some.* To Americans, *some* in this context implies vagueness. *Some photo exhibition* suggests you don't remember what the exhibition was, who the photographer was or where the gallery was, and you don't really care. It was just *some exhibition.*

Similarly, from a Japanese student

I would like to set up some system to connect readers and writers. A *system* would be better. *Some system* sounds as if the writer has no idea what that system might be.

When I start up some project . . . Also vague. Instead, start up *a project.* Better yet, tighten up and *start a project.*

I should gather comments from the public through a blog or some people that I know.

In this case, *some* adds nothing and you can drop it completely: *through a blog or people I know.* Notice that the writer didn't say *I should gather some comments . . .* The comments are indefinite; the people are indefinite, and *some* is implied. So neither clause needs it.

One more example:

Michael Wolf, an economist at Wells Fargo Securities Economics Group, said increasing mortgage rates have slowed down some demands in the market.

Unless "some demands" means some specific demands and not others, you don't need "some." A simple "demands" works better. Or possibly *demand* if you mean desire to buy.

LIKE VERSUS AS

In ninth grade I was publicly humiliated by a strict old-lady English teacher for using *like* when I meant *as.* I don't remember what I said; it was a *long* time ago. But perhaps I was influenced by a catchphrase of the time: *Tell it like it is.* It is, of course, ungrammatical. (Or so that English teacher would say.) Why?

That sentence consists of two clauses: *tell it* and *it is.* To join two clauses, you need a *conjunction,* a part of speech whose name comes from the Latin roots *con-* (with) and *junct-* (join). Strictly speaking, *like* is not a conjunction; it's a preposition. (To quote Madonna, *"Like a Virgin."* Or the movie title *Like Water for Chocolate.*) So technically the catchphrase *should* have been *Tell is as it is.* But it was the '60s; who but English teachers cared about grammar?

Some examples of *like/as* confusion from student work:

> *But like Edmunds noted, Qiu finds himself stuck with a circle of Chinese friends despite his desire to make more American friends.*

This one is easy: two clauses are being connected. It should read: *But as Edmunds noted.* Similarly:

> *Dialog in the Dark is a special exhibition that represents an opportunity to rediscover the city like a blind person does.*

A blind person does is a clause. So it needs *as*.

On the other hand:

> *Those people can still enjoy life as everybody else.*

Everybody else is not a clause (no verb); it's the object of a preposition, which *as* is not. So *like everybody else* is correct.

Sometimes sentence construction makes the question trickier:

> *This feeling when you're applying mascara and your eyes suddenly look like you're 20 can't be described.*

Technically, it should be *as if you're 20.* But in this case, correctness makes the sentence sound awkward. So you might try rewriting. One possibility:

This feeling when you're applying mascara and your eyes suddenly look 20 can't be described.

Or:

This feeling when you're applying mascara and your eyes suddenly make you look 20 can't be described.

The distinction between *like* and *as* is blurring as more and more authoritative sources accept *like* as a conjunction. In *The New York Times*, a music critic wrote:

> *She was standing in an aisle in the Met's auditorium during a rehearsal break one recent Friday, staring up at the stage **like** it was a gifted child having trouble fulfilling its potential.*

He meant *as if.*

And after a coaching session, a student e-mailed me: *Like always, it's fun and rewarding talking to you.* She meant *As always.* But I hope so.

PARALLEL STRUCTURE

If you studied geometry before taking up journalism, you know the definition of *parallel*: "being an equal distance apart everywhere," as the Free Online Dictionary puts it. The word applies to grammar, too, though the same source's definition is a bigger mouthful: "Having identical or equivalent syntactic constructions in corresponding clauses or phrases."

Translation: in writing English, words or phrases with equal functions in the sentence must be structured equally. Equal = parallel.

Here's a near-perfect example of parallel structure from a CUNY J-school student: *I shoot video and stills, record audio, edit in Final*

Cut Pro, Photoshop and produce interactive projects in Tumult Hype.
One subject—*I*—with four or five parallel predicates (verb + object), depending on whether you accept *Photoshop* as a verb. (That's where the "near-perfect" comes in). If not, it's a noun and the sentence should read: *I shoot video and stills, record audio, edit in Final Cut Pro **and** Photoshop, and produce interactive projects in Tumult Hype.*
From another student:

> *Being entrepreneur is such a solitude and hard-working.*

Other problems aside, *solitude* and *hard-working* serve parallel functions in the predicate. But *solitude* is a noun, and *hard-working* is an adjective. They need to match. Some possible fixes:

> *An entrepreneur is solitary and hard-working.* Here they're both adjectives modifying *entrepreneur*, so you don't need *being*. (And don't forget the article.)

> *Being an entrepreneur requires solitude and hard work.* In this case they're both nouns.

Here's a more complex example:

> *Overall imports like consumer goods, capital goods and higher import of autos were again at $229.9 billion in February, the same number as in January.*

Does this mean auto imports are part of the overall imports? If so, the sentence should read: *Overall imports like consumer goods, capital goods and autos, were . . .* Or does it mean autos are in separate category? In that case, it should say: *Overall imports like consumer goods and capital goods and higher import of autos . . .* Of course, that *and . . . and* construction makes the sentence a little hard to read. You could insert a pair of commas (*consumer goods and capital goods, and higher import of autos, . . .*) or reword the sentence something like this: *Overall imports like consumer goods and capital goods, combined with higher auto imports, were again at $229.9 billion . . .* (The author said the first solution was correct.)

> *They wanted to know how this union would affect their income. How would Russians benefit from teaming up with a country on the brink of default? Will Belarusians become richer? And why would both countries have to pay more for European cars?*

Here the flaw in parallelism is in the verb tenses: *would benefit, will become, would have to pay.* All three questions are examples of *how this union would affect their income,* so they need to be parallel. Since the union in question was still under discussion and not an accomplished fact, *will* is premature. So change it to: *Would Belarusians become richer?*

> *. . . by answering the questions Russians really cared about, I could get my readers involved in business and economic life, both in Russia and the outside world.*

Both requires what follows it to be parallel. Here it's followed by a prepositional phrase and a noun—definitely not parallel. Two possible fixes:

> *. . . both in Russia and **in** the outside world.* Two prepositional phrases.

> *. . . in both Russia and the outside world.* Moving *in* before *both* means it's followed by two nouns, and that makes it parallel.

Is the following sentence parallel or not?

> *He is not married, he has no kids, he is a young professional who prefers to keep his options open and doesn't rush into binding himself to any type of long-term responsibility.*

It's correct. It contains three clauses that are parallel, even though one uses a different verb and one has a compound predicate. My criticisms are (a) that clauses should be joined by semicolons, not commas, and (b) that even with semicolons, it's a little long for one sentence. Break it up and tighten:

> *He is not married; he has no kids. He is a young professional who prefers to keep his options open and doesn't rush into any long-term responsibility.*

PREPOSITIONS AND PHRASALS

The CUNY Graduate School of Journalism is *at* 219 West 40th Street, but *on* 40th Street. It's *in* Manhattan, but *on* the West Side or *in* Midtown. Students live *in* apartments in whatever neighborhood they can afford. *In* Manhattan, they live *in* the Village, SoHo or TriBeCa; *on* the Upper East Side or Upper West Side; *in* Morningside Heights, Harlem, Washington Heights or maybe even Inwood. Some live *in* Brooklyn, Queens or the Bronx, a few *on* Staten Island.

For many of the new students who arrive each August, apartment-hunting is not only exhausting but also a lesson in prepositions. Like articles—and who doesn't need to review those?—prepositions are (mostly) little words that mean a lot in English.

A preposition, according to Merriam-Webster online, is "a word or group of words that is used with a noun, pronoun, or noun phrase to show direction, location, or time, or to introduce an object." Note that last word: *object*. Prepositions always come in phrases, and every preposition has an object. That object has to be a noun or something masquerading as one—a pronoun, a gerund, a clause. Some examples from literature:

> *For Whom the Bell Tolls*
> *Into the Wild*

On the Road
To the Lighthouse

If a word you know as a preposition has no object, it's probably being used as an adverb, as in phrasal verbs. (See below.)

Prepositions tend to be specific to their uses, as in my lede: you live *in* a building, *at* an address, *in* a neighborhood (unless it's a Side), *in* a borough (unless it's an island). Why *in* rather than *on* Manhattan? Because Manhattan refers to the borough, which includes a few smaller islands like Roosevelt, plus Marble Hill on the mainland, which was part of Manhattan Island until the Harlem River was rerouted a century ago.

For a general guide to which prepositions go with which words— and which words take none at all—here's a good list: http://esl2000 .com/writing/corrections/preplist.html. The list isn't searchable, so just scroll. Again, it's just a guide. Choosing the "right" preposition is sometimes a judgment call that depends on how the phrase sounds to a native speaker's ear.

Some issues from student work, with prepositional phrases in bold:

*U.S. home prices nationwide dropped slightly **in the end / of** 2013.*

Not quite. Prices may have dropped *in 2013* or even *in December 2013*, but they dropped *at the end* of the year. An event happens *on* a date *(Christmas is on Dec. 25)*, *in* a week *(It's in the last week of December)*, *in* a month *(It's in December)* and *at* the beginning or end of something *(It comes at the end of the year)*.

In addition / to poor weather conditions,** the 13.2 percent drop **of new orders** last month was another likely reason **of the dramatic decrease.

This sentence contains four prepositional phrases. In the first two, the prepositions are correct: *in addition* is a common phrase, and something is always *in addition to* something else. But: a drop *in* new orders, and always a reason *for* a result.

In the '50s, *productions* **from abroad** *were imitated, and Argentine television borrowed expressive elements* **to pre-existing forms / of communication / like theatre or radio.**

This one has five, and only one error: *to pre-existing forms.* The clue here is *borrow*; you cannot *borrow* something *to* someone. (That's *lend.*) You can only borrow *from.*

For his campaign / in 2012, *the International Longshoremen's Association conducted a boycott aimed* **at trade / with the Soviet Union / during periods / of crisis / like the Soviet invasion / of Afghanistan / in the 1980s.**

This one has nine, and again only one choice of preposition is incorrect: the first. *For his campaign* sounds like a purpose, as if the union took this action specifically to help the candidate in question. Instead: *During his campaign . . .* To avoid two *during* phrases in the same sentence, change *during periods* to *in periods.* (Two *in*'s are less obtrusive than two *during*'s.)

The same story included this sentence:

As a well-known advocate **of Jewish issues,** *Nadler seems to care more* **about the Middle East** *than Eurasia.*

Advocate of or *advocate for?* It depends on what follows. An *advocate of* something supports that position: *He is an advocate of stricter gun control laws.* (Tighter: *He advocates stricter gun control laws.*) But an issue is not a position, so Nadler is an advocate *for,* or possibly *on,* Jewish issues.

"When they are trying to put children **to daycare,** *you can see the long line," Gonzalez said.*

Actually, you put children *in* or *into* daycare. But this is a quote. Should you clean it up? When in doubt, ask your editor. (See page 90.)

The wrong preposition can make a sentence amusing or turn its meaning completely around:

*The reward is that you're doing something **to the community** that you love and **to the place** that you call "home."*

Doing something *to* something has a negative connotation: *"What have you done to my story?"* *the reporter screamed when he saw the edited copy.* This writer here meant *do for*: to help someone. So: *The reward is that you're doing something **for** the community that you love and **for** the place that you call "home."*

Remember that the objects of prepositions are always nouns or noun-substitutes. If you're using a verb, it needs to be a noun form of the verb. To review: the noun forms are gerunds or infinitives. (See page 210.) But an infinitive cannot be the object of a proposition. *After to go to the store, she put the groceries away?* No, *after going.*

If a word you know to be a preposition has no object, chances are it's being used as an adverb, especially in a *phrasal verb*. A phrasal is a combination of a verb and an adverb or preposition that has an idiomatic meaning.

*He threw the trash **down the chute**.* Here *down* is a preposition. Where did he throw it? *Down the chute.* But in the sentence *She sat down,* it's an adverb, part of the phrasal *sat down.*

You probably already know dozens of English phrasals. My favorite interactive quiz is at Activities for ESL Students, http://a4esl.org/q/j/ck/fb-phrasalverbs.html. Take it as fast as you can, repeating it until you get all the questions right. You want your choices to become automatic.

One last word on prepositions: as previously noted on page 110, some old-fashioned English teachers would tell you, *"A preposition is nothing to end a sentence with."* They would rather you say, *"A preposition is nothing with which to end a sentence."* In real life—and in the media—people commonly end sentences with prepositions, and nobody is much the worse for it. My advice: when writing, if you can find a graceful way not to split a preposition from its object, please do. But if being technically correct will make your sentence awkward or clumsy, don't bother.

PUNCTUATION

"Recorded announcement!" begins the comment I put on student work so often I should save it on a function key. "In English, periods and commas go INSIDE quotation marks. PLEASE LEARN THIS. It drives us crazy."

The differences between punctuation in English and other languages are small and subtle, but they matter. If your professors or editors see you making the same punctuation errors over and over again, they'll think you either can't learn or can't be bothered. General guidelines on punctuation appear throughout this book, but here are some of the problems most common among international students:

Periods and commas go INSIDE quotation marks.

Not:

At this square in Buenos Aires, the mothers of the "desaparecidos", the political opponents who went missing during Videla's regime, have marched every Thursday since 1977 to claim justice for their sons.

Instead, this is correct:

At this square in Buenos Aires, the mothers of the "desaparecidos," the political opponents who went missing during Videla's regime, . . .

"I didn't even know Agatha Christie was the name of a writer. It seems it was the universe that gave her this name".

Write it this way:

*"I didn't even know Agatha Christie was the name of a writer.
It seems it was the universe that gave her this name."*

In attribution after a quote:

*"I remember the impact that his iconography produced on
me, those simplified little men and his earthy palette"*, he told
Galería Magazine.

Instead:

*"I remember the impact that his iconography produced on
me, those simplified little men and his earthy palette,"* he told
Galería Magazine.

But semicolons and colons go outside quotation marks.

**The actual quotation marks should be " and " instead of <<
and >>** as many languages render them. Others use dashes to indicate
the beginnings of quotes; in English we do not.

**Use commas in large numbers and points (periods) in deci-
mals**—the opposite of standard practice in most of Europe. If you mean
three hundred fifty-two thousand, write *352,000,* not *352.000.* If you
report that a new highway is projected to cost *$6.8 billion,* write it that
way, not *$6,8 billion.* (If you're a TV reporter, say it *six point eight billion
dollars, not six billion eight hundred million dollars.*) If you're writing
about the slogan for Ivory Soap—*ninety-nine and forty-four one-hun-
dredths percent pure*—write *99.44,* not *99,44.* If you're reviewing restaurants, write that the entrée seemed overpriced at $24.95, not $24,95, as
a European waiter might write it on the check.

If your native language is set as the default on your computer, reset
it to the appropriate form of English for your publication, which should
change punctuations marks to its standard—for example, eliminating the

upside-down question marks in Spanish. Grammar check should then flag you on possible errors, and spellcheck should stop flagging almost every word as a misspelling. Otherwise, your copy will drive your editors crazy.

RUN-ONS

A student working on two stories simultaneously was quoting a lot of sources but having trouble rendering those quotes correctly. Three examples:

> *"It is not the responsibility of the city to enforce an immigration policy, that is the responsibility of the federal government."*

> *"But drugs will always be an issue, there is a poor community here that always needs attention."*

> *"Even for the businesses here, they have to start paying the minimum wage, people have to understand that people have to live with minimum wage," Infante said.*

As written, each of these quotes is a *run-on*—that is, a sentence containing multiple independent clauses that could (and should) be separate sentences. Run-ons are so named because they breathlessly run on from one thought to the next to the next without proper punctuation, making it hard for the reader come up for air. Ideally, a sentence should express one complete thought. Yes, complex sentences (see page 21) have dependent clauses, but they are part of a single sentence. Never connect two clauses with a comma, and preferably not with a dash; that's how run-ons are created.

The easiest way to fix a run-on is usually to break it into two sentences:

> *"It is not the responsibility of the city to enforce an immigration policy. That is the responsibility of the federal government."*

> *"But drugs will always be an issue. There is a poor community here that always needs attention."*

"Even for the businesses here, they have to start paying the minimum wage. People have to understand that people have to live with minimum wage."

Or, with better placement of the attribution:

"Even for the businesses here, they have to start paying the minimum wage," Infante said. "People have to understand that people have to live with minimum wage."

From another student:

"We track them, wherever they protest, we counterprotest to stop this campaign of lies and misinformation," says Shylene Mejia, Secretary at the Dominican Advocacy Coalition.

Instead:

"We track them, wherever they protest," says Shylene Mejia, secretary at the Dominican Advocacy Coalition. "We counterprotest to stop this campaign of lies and misinformation."

Semicolons and colons may join two clauses to highlight their relationship. A case could be made for a semicolon in this example:

Usually I associate the Woodbridge station with joy, it signals a kind of homecoming after a long and tiring day in the city.

Better:

Usually I associate the Woodbridge station with joy; it signals a kind of homecoming after a long and tiring day in the city.

A colon between two clauses indicates that the second follows from the first:

Maria de Fátima and Nisete have a lot in common: both are from northeast Brazil and have migrated along with millions aiming to escape their jobless, drought-prone region since the 1970s.

"We are in our bubble, and nothing affects us because we think it's not going to happen to us. But it is already happening: when they touched the 43, they touched us all."

We don't use punctuation when we speak, so speech may sometimes sound like run-ons. But we don't have to write it that way. So a student may have heard this:

"I definitely think that Cuban art is undervalued, I see a huge potential for a rise in prices for Cuban artists."

But she should have written:

"I definitely think that Cuban art is undervalued. I see a huge potential for a rise in prices for Cuban artists."

SUBJECT/VERB AGREEMENT

"The heat and humidity is back," a local New York newscaster said during the *dog days* of August. (That's an idiom for hot, sultry summer weather that leaves dogs, and humans, barely able to move.) She was stating the obvious, but also raising a grammar point: subject/verb agreement.

In English, nouns and their verbs need to agree in number. That is to say, singular nouns require the singular form of a verb; plural requires plural. Heat and humidity are two different things—a compound subject joined by *and*—and therefore the subject is plural. The newscaster may have been thinking of *heat-and-humidity* as a single unpleasant weather condition, but grammatically she was wrong. She should have said *The heat and humidity are back.*

Non-native English-speakers are often confused about which form is which, especially among state-of-being and auxiliary verbs. A quick review:

Singular		Plural	
I	am/have/do	we	are/have/do
you	are/have/do	you	are/have/do
he, she, it	is/has/does	they	are/have/do

Notice a pattern? Except for *I am*, the only variation is in the third person singular: *he, she, it.* Similarly, in present tense the base forms are used for most verbs except when the subject is *he, she* or *it,* in which case an *s* is added.

Remember that the subject determines whether the verb is singular or plural. A relatively simple example:

Brazil shows how the fall in oil prices affect different countries.

The subject of the dependent (*how*) clause is *fall,* which is singular, not *oil prices.* (The noun closest to a given verb is not necessarily its subject.) So the verb should be *affects.*

He expects growth in both top and bottom lines in 2015, and expectations for sales in the shoe division is particularly high.

Although *shoe division* is closest to the verb, the subject of the sentence is *expectations,* which is plural. So the verb needs to be *are* to match it in number.

But organizations like the South East Bronx Community Organization has preserved low-income housing in the area and is working toward providing affordable housing for the residents of the area.

This sentence has a compound verb, and the subject of both is *organizations*—not *South East Bronx Community Organization.* So the verbs should be *have preserved* and *are working.*

In subject/verb agreement, one of the trickiest cases is sentences like this one. Many writers would say the verb in that sentence should be *are*, since *cases* precedes it. But they'd be wrong. In fact the subject is *one*, modified by the prepositional phrase *of the trickiest cases,* so the verb needs to be singular as written.

Sometimes, though, the verb could be either, depending on meaning. From The New Yorker:

> *One of the studio's programmers who was with Murray backstage recalls. . .*

As published, this sentence says one particular programmer was with Murray backstage, not that he was a one of many programmers who were there. In that case, the verb would be *were.* The writer could have set off the clause off with commas and made it nonessential: *One of the studio's programmers, who was with Murray backstage, recalls . . .* But that's not true of every dependent clause.

Pronouns like *someone, everyone, everybody* and *no one* are singular and take singular verbs. (In casual conversation, though, Americans are constantly confusing their pronouns and saying things like *Did everybody bring their laptop?* Or they may be trying to be non-sexist, in which case *Did everybody bring a laptop?* or *Did you all bring your laptops?* would be more graceful than *his or her laptop.*) *None* is also singular, meaning *not one,* but phrases like *none of the (plural noun) . . .* take plural verbs in at least two styles, AP and *The New York Times.* When in doubt, check your publication's style guide.

Any compound subject containing *and* is automatically plural. If the conjunction is *or,* however, the verb agrees with the noun closer to it. And in a case like this, posed to me many years ago by a friend's daughter?

> *No man and no woman is/are . . .*

I'm still pondering but leaning toward *is*. Yes, the subject is compound, but each of the pronouns is negative, and that sounds a lot like *no one* to me.

TENSES

Just before Election Day 2012, a student asked why his Craft professor had made the following edit in one of his stories:

> *"The turnout will be seriously affected," said Russell C. Gallo, the Republican candidate in the 45th district for the State Assembly, who* ~~runs~~ **is running** *against veteran Democratic member of the New York Assembly Steven H. Cymbrowitz.*

You might think this clause calls for the simple present, *runs,* since the reporter is referring to something that is happening as he writes. But you'd be wrong. Notice the tense I used in that sentence: *is referring* and *is happening,* both present progressive, also known as present continuous: auxiliary + present participle (*-ing* form).

In English, the correct use of those present tenses is counterintuitive—that is, the opposite of what you'd expect. If something is happening right now, you might expect it to take the simple present: *he runs.* But in fact we use present continuous: *he is running.* Simple present is used for actions that take place customarily, or routinely, or habitually:

> *How many newspapers do you read (every day,* or *regularly)?*
> *I read three or four before class—online, of course. I also monitor several newscasts.*

But:

> *Which paper are you reading (right now)?*
> *I'm reading The Post.*

In past tense, the continuous can be a little more complicated.

In 2012 Mitt Romney ran against President Obama.

It's history, so simple past. But what about this?

That election season President Obama ran for re-election.

Or:

That election season, President Obama was running for re-election.

On Monday many candidates were running for office. (By Wednesday, half of them were also-rans, or losers.) President Obama was running for re-election. He was running against Mitt Romney.

These uses of the continuous verb are correct because, even though you're talking about the past, you've pinpointed a moment in time. It's as if you've specified a "right now" in the past.

In this case, either is correct. Yes, election season is over, but if you're talking about it as a span of time, *was running* is also acceptable. In some contexts, you might choose it to give your piece a greater sense of immediacy.

Then there are the *perfect* tenses. Even the most advanced student of English has trouble mastering our tenses; so do some native speakers. (In eastern Pennsylvania, where I grew up, people often use past perfect—*I had gone*—when they mean simple past—*I went*.) Simple present (*I go*), simple past (*I went*), simple future (*I will go*) really are simple, mostly. The ones labeled "perfect" are another story.

Perfect, in relation to tenses, refers to time—the past, time completed or "perfected" (from Latin). Somewhere in the sentence, an action takes place in the past, even if the tense is future perfect. In its simplest form, a verb in a perfect tense consists of a past participle plus an auxiliary:

Present perfect: *I have gone*
Past perfect: *I had gone*

(Let's stick with those for now; future perfect is not often used.)

Past perfect   *Simple past*   **Present perfect**   *Present continuous*

Past   A past moment   NOW   Future

Simple past indicates that something happened at a particular moment in the past: *I came to New York in August to enroll in journalism school.*

Present perfect means that something *has taken place* over a span of time, from a point in the past up to and including the present: *I have come to New York to become a great journalist.* That's what you wanted when you came; that's what you still want, and you're still in the process.

Past perfect is used for an action that took place before another action in the past; therefore the sentence needs to contain two verbs, one simple past, one past perfect: *I had never thought about going to journalism school until I heard about CUNY's program.* You *heard about* CUNY at a particular moment in the past; before that, you *had never thought* about J-school.

Some words serve as clues to what tense you need. *Before, until* and *by the time,* for example, usually indicate a specific point in time, therefore simple past: *Before I came here . . .* or *Until I came here . . .* They suggest that the verb in the other clause should be past perfect: *Before I came to CUNY, I had not written much in English.*

On the other hand, *since* referring to time (as opposed to *since* meaning *because;* see page 250) implies a span of time and calls for present perfect: *Since he received his TOEFL scores, he has worked much harder on his English.* He received his scores at a specific moment in time; *has worked* refers to his activities in a time span from then to now. But: *Since* (because) *his TOEFL scores were good, he was admitted to the program.* Simple past in both clauses.

In both present perfect and past perfect, verbs may be continuous or progressive (referring to actions in progress)—in other words, the *-ing* form. I could just as easily have written: *Since he received his TOEFL scores, he has been working much harder on his English.* Or: *Before she came to CUNY, she had been writing mostly in French.*

As for future perfect, it indicates an action that *will have happened* by some future date. Think of the learning outcomes section of a syllabus: *By the end of this course, students will have learned how to . . .* You *haven't learned* it yet, but during the course, you *will.* When the course is over, you *will have learned.*

And then there's conditional perfect: *I would have passed if I had studied.* In this case *had studied* is not past perfect, but an obviously contrary-to-fact conditional.

And "(Now, a *pop quiz* (see page 176): is the following sentence correct or incorrect?)"

The word 'refusenik' has entered English after the 1970s move-ment of Russian Jews protested anti-Semitism and were denied permission to emigrate abroad.

(Pause to think.)

It's incorrect. *After* denotes a point in time, so the verb should be *entered.* Or: . . . **has** *entered English* **since** *the 1970s movement . . .*

THAT VERSUS WHICH

Relative clauses—those subordinate clauses that add information to sentences—can be confusing, even to native speakers of English. They can help you avoid monotony and achieve that variety in sentence structure prized in English writing.

Some relative clauses serve as giant adjectives or adverbs. For example:

You'll find the mailboxes in the corridor where my locker is.
The *where* clause acts as an adjective modifying *corridor.*

I didn't check my messages last night, when I went to the theater. The *when* clause acts as an adverb modifying *last night,* itself an adverbial phrase.

Those are the easy ones. *Where* deals with place, *when* with time. But then there are the tricky ones: *that* and *which.* They're pretty much the same, right?

Well, yes, in the sense that they're relative pronouns that lead you into the clause and connect it to the rest of the sentence. And no. The difference is how they're used.

That is used in essential clauses—those that define or limit the nouns they modify. They are, in fact, essential to the structure and meaning of the sentence; if you take them out, the sentence falls apart. It's a little like the article *the*: if you're talking about a specific (noun), use *that.*

Which is used in non-essential clauses—the ones that add information, such as a description, that isn't 100 percent necessary to the meaning of the sentence. Here's an easy test: If you can lift out the clause and the sentence still makes sense, it's a non-essential clause and takes *which.* If you can't, it's essential and requires *that.*

One more thing: *which* clauses are set off by commas. *That* never take commas.

That's the theory. Now, some practical examples from student work.

In 2011 the Office of the Inspector General, which controls the Department of Veterans' Affairs, investigated the hospital after a patient died because staff members did not notice his heart monitor was disconnected.

The clause gives added information about the Office of the Inspector General that is useful to know but is not essential to the meaning of the sentence. So *which* is correct.

> *They claimed rapid escalation of marijuana arrests in New York City in migrant communities and communities of color, which are the most vulnerable populations.*

Again, *which* is correct. You could put a period after *color,* and the sentence would still make sense. You could also tighten the sentence by changing the clause into an appositive, a noun phrase that renames or further identifies it. . . . *migrant communities and communities of color, ~~which are~~ the most vulnerable populations.*

> *One small fish can be sliced into four fillets, which are then used as bait to catch bluefish.*

Same here. The sentence could end after *fillets.*

> *"Children are reinforcing their heritage," said Gerard Lohrdal, open-space greening director of GrowNYC, a nonprofit that aims at improving New York's quality of life through environmental programs.*

The final clause defines the nonprofit, so *that* is correct.
Sometimes, if the meaning is clear, you don't even have to say *that*; it's understood:

> *In the Flatbush Food Co-op, customers can find almost everything (that) they need.*

But!

> *"The garden can also be a bridge between the school and parents," she explained, speaking of parents that aren't fluent in English.*

When referring to people, use *who* instead of *that* or *which*. That said, it's becoming more and more common in casual conversation to use *that* for people. Let register (see page 116) be your guide.

He has a faithful corps of students who are following his approach: "No pain, no gain."

Correct.

And don't substitute *what* for *that* or *which*. And don't substitute *what* for *that* or *which*. *What* actually means *that which*: *I don't understand what you're saying.*

THERE IS/ARE/WAS/WERE/WILL BE

Technically, there is nothing wrong with using *there is* and its other tenses to indicate that something exists; I did it in this very sentence, as I have throughout this book. But as a journalist, you want your writing to be as active and powerful as it can be. *There is* constructions tend to be relatively weak, and they add a word or two that could be tightened away. (See page 240.)

When tempted to use this construction, search for a stronger way to say what you mean, as in these examples from student work:

There have been talks among employees about thousands of jobs to be cut in the U.S., but IBM has not confirmed any specific layoff scheme.

Here *there have been* is not only weak but also vague. Are rumors flying? Have the employees been talking among themselves about layoffs? Have they formed protest groups? Has the company held information sessions? The writer needs to decide and rephrase accordingly:

Employees have been talking about thousands of jobs to be cut in the U.S., but IBM has not confirmed any specific layoff scheme.

Or:

Among employees, rumors are spreading about thousands of jobs to be cut in the U.S., but IBM has not confirmed any specific layoff scheme.

Or:

Employees have been attending information sessions on the thousands of jobs to be cut in the U.S., but IBM has not confirmed any specific layoff scheme.

(And *plan* would be a better word than *scheme*; see page 264.)

That said, sometimes it would needlessly complicate a sentence to use a different construction, as in the first paragraph of this book:

There is no more underappreciated component of a news operation than the copy desk. . . . And there is no better place to polish your English.

I could have written:

No component of a news operation is more underappreciated than the copy desk. . . . And none is a better place to polish your English.

But I honestly don't think it would be an improvement.

When you do choose *there is/are* constructions, remember that the subject is not *there* (an adverb, preceding the verb) but the noun that follows. So to be correct, your brain needs to jump ahead and make the verb agree with that noun in number. In conversation, you can get away with saying *There's been some studies*, but in writing be correct and say *there've*. Always go back over a written piece to make sure the subjects and verbs agree.

WHO AND WHOM

> *Knock, knock.*
> *Who's there?*
> *To.*
> *To who?*

You mean to WHOM. Knock-knock jokes are practically an art form in English, and when I heard this one from Fred Kaimann, syndication manager at Advance Digital, I roared. These two relative pronouns seem so difficult for so many people, even native English speakers. Many don't know the difference but think *whom* just sounds more correct, so they tend to use it when they're trying to sound educated. Nine times out of 10, they're wrong.

So what's the difference? It's very simple. *Who* is the subjective, or nominative, case; use it for the subject of a sentence or clause. (In *Who's there?* it's the subject of *'s*, or *is*. Note that it's not spelled *whose;* that's the possessive form of *who.*) *Whom* is objective—that is, used as the object of a verb or a preposition. That's why it should be *to whom*—*to* is a preposition—rather than *to who*. If whatever the pronoun stands for is performing the action of the verb, use *who*. If it is being acted upon or is the object of a preposition, use *whom*.

Is this example from student work correct or incorrect?

Windsor Terrace has turned into the residence of young urban professionals, who the natives call yuppies.

Incorrect. Yes, *who* is connecting its subordinate clause of the sentence, but it's the direct object of that clause. If this sentence were written as two, it would look like this: *Windsor Terrace has turned into the residence of young urban professionals. The natives call them yuppies.* It's smoother to connect the two clauses into one complex sentence, which *whom* does while standing in for *them.*

Remember that New York TV anchor who introduced a story with a sentence fragment? (See page 207.) She—or perhaps her teleprompter writer—also said:

> *A mystery on Long Island: a man is shot twice in a barbershop early this morning. Whom fired the gun?*

Here it should be *who* because the pronoun is the subject of its clause.

You wouldn't say *Whom moved my cheese?*—or at least Spencer Johnson, author of the book *Who Moved My Cheese?* would hope not. There, *who* is clearly the subject.

That much is simple. Often, the tricky part is figuring out whether the pronoun is a subject or an object. As relative pronouns, *who* and *whom* connect clauses and need to match the pronoun's function in the sentence.

Another example from a student:

> *We have to pay attention to whom the media gave the news.*

In this case *whom* is correct. Not because the whole clause *whom the media gave the news* is the object of the preposition *to*, but rather because it's the indirect object of the verb *gave*. (*The media gave them the news*.)

I said it was tricky. Even the noted American stage director Michael Kahn was either confused or misquoted when he said incorrectly in an interview for the book *Upstaged* by Anne Nicholson Weber:

> "Their heroes are *whomever* is the major movie star of the moment."

It should be *whoever*. *Whoever* and *whomever* follow the same rules as *who* and *whom*. In this case, the pronoun is the subject of a clause: *whoever is the major movie star of the moment*. The entire clause is a predicate nominative, equivalent to the subject of the sentence, *their heroes*.

Granted, Kahn was speaking, not writing, and speech tends to be less precise. In a *New Yorker* cartoon (http://www.condenaststore .com/-sp/It-s-She-s-driving-me-crazy-and-I-m-not-sure-whom-to-turn-to-New-Yorker-Cartoon-Prints_i8904654_.htm), a woman looks over a man's shoulder and corrects his e-mail: "It's 'She's driving me crazy and I'm not sure <u>whom</u> to turn to.' " Technically it's wrong to end a sentence with a preposition, but that's the way people talk. And in casual conversation, most people would find nothing wrong with the *who*. Writing tends to be more formal and correct, although in journalism you don't want to sound stuffy.

WORDINESS AND TIGHTENING

This concept of tightening is a shining illustration of the English expression *last but not least*. One of the first, and most important, pieces of advice I received as a very junior reporter for my college paper at age 17 was "Write tight!" Throughout high school, I had been encouraged to show off how much I knew whenever possible by writing long, complex sentences using big words, and plenty of them. That's fine if you're Henry James, or an academic.

But you're a journalist. You need to convey maximum information in a limited word count or, on Twitter, 140 characters. If you're not a native English-speaker, the job is even harder: you may not know exactly how to express your thoughts, so you use more words.

Tight writing is writing that says what it means in as few words as possible. No, let me rephrase that: Tight writing says what it means as briefly as possible.

An example from student work:

> *For the objectionists to gun control laws, one major argument that always comes into play is that there is no need for new legislation to reduce violence.*

Instead, how about:

*Objectors to gun control laws always argue that new legislation
is not needed to reduce violence.*

That's 16 words instead of 27—enough for a whole new sentence. In contrast, the sentence that followed—*The authorities, they say, can do that by simply keeping firearms from the wrong people*—was exactly right. From the same piece:

*This seems to be the case for the bill introduced last Tuesday by
a group of four House lawmakers.*

Here are two ways to tighten:

. . . the bill introduced Tuesday by four House lawmakers.

Four implies a group. And cut *last,* as per AP style: "The word last is not necessary to convey the notion of most recent when the name of a month or day is used. Preferred: It happened Wednesday. It happened in April. Correct, but redundant: It happened last Wednesday." So that's another word you can save.

Similarly, you can often save two in the phrase *in order to . . .,* as in:

*In order to avoid the sequester, Obama has been talking with
members of Congress.*

The infinitive (*to* + verb) implies that's the purpose. Just say: *To avoid the sequester . . .* Occasionally you'll need those two words for clarity; when in doubt, read the sentence aloud to see if it makes sense without them.

Sometimes prepositional phrases produce wordiness. From another student:

The media team of Twitter is made up of 30 people.

Better:

Twitter's media team has 30 people. Six words instead of 11.

As the number of users of Twitter increases . . .

Better:

As Twitter users increase. (But not: *as Twitter users grow.* Their number may *grow,* but users must *increase,* unless you mean they're getting taller.)

Do a few words here and there really make a difference? Ask any print journalist who's ever trimmed *widows*—those pesky little lines of type with a single word or syllable—to make a story fit. Tightening your writing lets you pack more facts, and more ideas, into the same number of words. (Editing an academic paper recently, I trimmed 1,000 of the 5,800 on first reading just by tightening.) Copy editors are masters of the art; if you have a chance to work with a good one, you'll learn a lot about writing tight.

DEBORAH STEAD

NO PERFECT DRAFTS

After 25 years in journalism—including postings to London and Moscow—as an editor at *The New York Times, BusinessWeek* and Oxygen Media, Stead joined the CUNY journalism school as director of Career Services. In 2012 she "retired," which in her case meant cutting down to two days a week as a writing coach. As the J-school's resident grammar nerd, she administers the grammar quizzes that periodically terrorize Craft students.

What makes good writing?

For me—and I'm going to draw a lot from journalism when I talk about this—it's a combination of knowing clearly the breadth and limits of the subject you're covering, and then executing on that. So I would say good writing for me has to do with muscular sentences; that is, I prefer a strong verb to a verb with an adverb, so I'd rather say that somebody "raced to the next destination" rather than saying "went quickly."

Along with that, just concision generally. Not a lot of extra words. Not "on a daily basis" if you can say "every day." Not "general consensus" if you can say "consensus." Concision, and along with that, specificity. So I don't want to read a sentence about how something went without seeing an example or something vivid. In terms of vivid writing, I would say what adds to that for me is the absence of cliché, so fresh metaphors that work. If it's a matter of setting a scene, I really want to taste and smell and see in the most specific way possible. It goes without saying that I also like the active voice versus the passive voice, although occasionally the passive voice is right.

I like sentences to have a certain rhythm: a long sentence, then a punchy, short sentence. Not very long, Latinate sentences where I get lost in the middle.

Backtrack a little and talk about concision and tightening. I tend to be a very wordy writer, but then I go back as an editor, and then, oh, this can go, that can go. What advice would you give in making writing concise?

What you've described is probably what works for most people. I even heard Joyce Carol Oates, at a lecture about her writing, say, "I need to get everything down and then cut. I can't do it straight from my mind." So I would say—and this probably goes to good writing, too—do not expect your first draft to be perfect. In journalism, and writin g in general . . . you have to have the confidence to see something mediocre, not quite so good on the page, then, with a fresh eye when you're the reader, not the writer. So a couple of hours could go by, if you can manage it; you come back, and you look at it as a reader, and you'll see it. I think it's impossible to write a polished—I would say "a polished draft," but that's an oxymoron.

It's impossible to write in a polished style straight out of your brain, I think. I can't do it. I don't know anyone who can, but maybe someone can. All that will happen then is paralysis. I think we do see that sometimes with students. If they don't have the confidence to see an ordinary piece of writing on the page and know that it will get better, then I think what we have to do is tell them that all writers have terrible first drafts, or at least drafts that can be improved.

When Dean Bartlett (see page 43) **was asked what advice she would give international students or international journalists, among the things she said was, "Grammar, grammar, grammar." What do you have to say on that subject?**

I agree that grammar and structure and usage all are incredibly important in good writing. My own experience with international students is . . . that's not something they struggle with, when they move to English, as much as American-educated students do these days. I'm not sure why. It could just be the education systems.

Certainly international students occasionally have trouble with word choice or idioms or prepositions, but when it comes to the muscle and bone of a sentence, they understand it a little better than the people with problems. If there are students with problems in this area, they tend to be American-educated students, and not the international students. Even on the quizzes I give, I would say the international students, on average, do a bit better.

I would agree that proper usage, learning the idioms and the idiosyncrasies of American punctuation versus, say, British—yes, all that's important. . . . It's word choice, pretty typical . . . And idioms. And perhaps tone.

Another thing about good writing is flow. Certainly journalism has enough tricks up its sleeve that we have a million transitional phrases. . . . Look, it's a formula. You can pick from a lot of transitional phrases, and so let's try not to make it so choppy.

Another particularly American thing is the anecdotal lede or the narrative through a story, a leisurely way of going through a story, our notion of what we call a *nut graf* (see page 36)—that is, you introduce, you draw a reader in, and then . . . you tell why you're telling the story. I'm not sure that goes on in foreign journalism as well.

One thing I do run up against when I'm coaching international students is something I would call a kind of polite style that maybe is not an American style, that I have to talk to them about because sometimes it will border on editorializing. They'll want to compliment someone, or they'll say that someone is "esteemed" or an important person. If they come from a country where there's not a free press, I can understand it; it's an old habit. Maybe they worry about getting into trouble, but sometimes it's just across the board. It's a little more polite. . . .

The American ideal, whether we hit it or not, is for every newspaper to be objective, so we never say, for the most part, with the mainstream press, "Well, this is a liberal paper, and so you should also read a conservative one." We do save that for our editorial, op-ed pages, but in the reporting we strive for objectivity. Sometimes you do have to guard against that, I think. American-style journalism is founded on a principle of objectivity, and that's not always true of press around the world.

CHAPTER 11

SOME FINER POINTS

Using English like a native is a matter of mastering details, one after another after another. A career copy editor may spend a lifetime mulling whether *day lily* should be one word or two, or puzzling out whether a writer really means *affect* or *effect*. The more attention non-native English-speakers pay to details like these, the more precise their English will eventually become. And the more their editors will respect them.

This selective, alphabetical guide is a mere sampling of some finer points of English usage that commonly crop up both in professional media and, especially, among CUNY journalism students. It is by no means complete; for a far more comprehensive guide, see a dictionary or a stylebook. In fact, many of these points, and hundreds more, are covered—and sometimes contradicted—in the style guides particular publications have adopted. As always, when in doubt, follow the style of the one for which you are working.

aboard, abroad These words are very close in spelling, and spell-check won't catch errors like this one from a Chinese student: "It didn't mention any review of the media at home and aboard." *Aboard* means *on board* a plane, train, ship, etc., as in this report from the Canadian Broadcasting Corporation: "A Canadian was among 298 people *aboard* Malaysia Airlines Flight MH17, which crashed in Eastern Ukraine, officials in Amsterdam said." The student intended to say *abroad*—in other countries.

adjectives used as nouns In English, some work and some don't. In stories about disasters or wars, for example, it's fine to talk about *the dead, the wounded, the missing*; all those adjectives, which are really participles, are also recognized as nouns. But *the disappeared*—translated literally from the Spanish *desaparecidos*, the victims who "disappeared," and are presumed dead, during South American dictatorships—does not sound idiomatic in English except in that particular meaning. When in doubt, check a dictionary to see if the adjective in question is accepted as a noun.

affect, effect In English, one little letter can make a big difference. Perhaps the most commonly confused homophones (see page 157) are *affect* and *effect*. *"I think that had a big **affect** on my ability and desire to lead people as a group and do things together,"* one CUNY student wrote in a quote; another wrote, *"Maybe these pictures will have some **affects** on the people who view them."* Both meant *effect*. The two words sound exactly alike in normal speech (unless an English teacher is exaggerating the pronunciation, stressing the first syllable to make a point). It's not a simple matter of one's being a noun and one's being a verb; either can be either, as this chart shows.

	Verb	Noun
affect	To change, influence or have an effect on To move someone emotionally The shocking news did not seem to *affect* him.	An emotional response, expressed or observed Despite the shocking news, his *affect* remained unchanged. (Pronunciation exception: this one is *AF-fect*.)
effect	To bring about or make happen The new policy *effected* change.	Result or consequence Mental or emotional impression Purpose or intention The new policy had the desired *effect*.

(Definitions from dictionary.com)

aggravate, irritate *Aggravate* means to make something worse or more serious: *Air pollution can aggravate breathing problems.* *Aggravated assault* is a criminal charge that means the assault was made more serious by purposely or recklessly inflicting bodily harm, without regard for human life. When tempted to say that a situation was *aggravating*—in an English idiom, *got on your nerves*—use *irritating*, which means to cause discomfort or inflammation: *Pollution can irritate the eyes, throat and respiratory system.* The noun forms (*aggravation, irritation*) and adjectives (*aggravating, irritating*) follow suit.

alleged, allegedly Under American law, people charged with committing crimes are innocent until proven guilty in a court of law. Many journalists think they can safely describe those accused of crimes with phrases like *the alleged murderer, the accused killer, the suspected embezzler.* But in fact you are only adding an adjective and still calling the accused a murderer, killer or embezzler. Nor are the journalists protected from potential libel suits if those charged are not convicted. Instead, specify the legal charges or accusation, or say who is doing the accusing:

> *He had been charged with first-degree murder.*
> *He is accused of killing . . .*
> *Federal investigators say he embezzled . . .*

Similarly, saying someone was *arrested for* a crime also assumes guilt. Instead, say *arrested on charges of . . .* or, more simply, just *charged with.* So when a CUNY student from Denmark wrote:

> *She was arrested for arranging or attending demonstrations against President Bashar al-Assad and "spreading false news."*

A safer way of way of saying it would have been:

> *She was accused of (or charged with) arranging or attending demonstrations . . .*

alternate, alternative Easily confused. As a verb, *alternate* means to go back and forth repeatedly between two options (*He alternates between two jobs*); as a noun, a substitute (*an alternate on a jury*); as an adjective, every other (*on alternate days*). *Alternative* implies a choice: as a noun, *we have no alternative*; as an adjective, *passengers on the disabled train sought alternative transportation.* Seen on the *New York Times* home page (nytimes.com), the headline, "As Trump and Cruz Spar, G.O.P. Looks for an Alternate." The headline writer meant alternative.

anecdote, antidote Often confused because they sound so much alike, but not even close in meaning. An *anecdote* is a short narrative or vignette; journalists often write *anecdotal ledes* (see page 245), starting stories by using one particular source's experience to illustrate a larger point, which is then spelled out in the *nut graf.* An *antidote* is a substance that counteracts the harmful effects of poisons or toxins.

as, since, for Preceded by a comma, these three conjunctions mean *because.* When a CUNY student wrote that an internship "is supposed to be demanding as we are supposed to work hard, make mistakes and then learn from them," she needed a comma after *demanding.* The comma is important to prevent confusion, for *as* and *since* can also indicate time: *The radio is on as I am writing. Since* can mean *after* as well as *because: The problem has been solved since I complained* means it has been solved in the time after the complaint, while *the problem has been solved, since I complained* means it was solved as a result of the complaint. *Because* is generally not preceded by a comma.

collaborate, cooperate Non-native English speakers tend to use *cooperate* as an all-purpose word for working together. They may not know the word *collaborate,* or especially if they are Europeans, the word may be tainted by its meaning during World War II: collaboration with the Nazis by people whose countries they invaded. But to American ears, *cooperate* often sounds slightly off.

Both words mean working together; the difference between them is a matter of nuance. Consider this sentence: *The entire team cooperated on the election coverage.* A native English-speaker would be more likely to say *collaborated,* in the sense of actively working on a project or toward a goal. *Cooperate* tends to indicate compliance: *The man was arrested and charged with drunk driving after he refused to cooperate with a highway patrolman.*

When pronouncing *collaborate,* speakers of languages like Japanese that have no *l* sound, or in which it hard to distinguish from *r,* need to be especially careful. Otherwise, it may come out sounding like another word frequently used in journalism: *corroborate* (confirm, verify).

compose, comprise Americans tend to think they sound educated if they use *comprise,* but more often than not they get it wrong. Derived from the French *compris,* past participle of *conprendre* (which can mean *include* as well as *understand*), it means *include.* The whole *comprises* its parts: *Most concertos comprise three movements.* So it makes no sense to put it in passive voice, saying something is *comprised of* something else, as in this sentence from *The New York Times: The Royal Ballet has brought us a season comprised almost entirely of British choreography.* Instead: *The Royal Ballet has brought us a season comprising almost entirely British choreography.*

A CUNY student got it backwards: *There are three distinct disorders, NF1, NF2 and Schwannomatosis, that comprise neurofibromatosis, all affecting the nervous system with varying degrees of intensity.* Instead: *Neurofibromatosis comprises three distinct disorders, NF1, NF2 and Schwannomatosis, all affecting . . .*

compounds When two words are joined with a hyphen, as in *singer-songwriter* and *actor-director,* they are called *compounds.* Those examples are compound nouns, in which the two parts are of equal weight, indicating that the artist in question is both. In compound adjectives, one of the hyphenated words modifies, or describes, the other, and together they modify a noun, as in *best-kept secret.*

Whether or not the phrase is hyphenated can change its meaning. If you are reporting on a company's *10th-anniversary celebration*, it means the company is 10 years old. But *10th anniversary celebration* means its 10th celebration, no matter how old the company is.

Ages and lengths of time are among the most common errors in compounds. If a source mentions her *3-year-old son*, write it that way, with hyphens but no *s*, if the age precedes the noun. But her son *is 3 years old*. Similarly, a CUNY student from Brazil wrote, "I came to Rio de Janeiro with both of them, by bus on a three days trip." She meant *a three-day trip*.

Adverbs ending in *-ly*, which does the same job as a hyphen, are an exception to the rule. An *often-cited case* needs a hyphen; a *frequently cited case* doesn't. And an exception to the exception: words like *friendly, likely, lively* or *kindly* when it's an adjective. Despite the *-ly*, they're adjectives. So someone who looks friendly is *friendly-looking;* someone with a kindly face is *kindly-looking*.

convince, persuade *Persuade* means to get someone to think in a certain way or do something through reasoning or perhaps by reporting the facts—in short, to change that person's mind. Someone who already strongly thinks that way is *convinced* and needs no further *persuasion*. So when an entrepreneurial journalism student wrote, "I tried to con-vince my boss to build a magazine app," she meant *persuade*.

different from, than, to When making comparisons, to be technically correct in American English, say something is *different from* something else. In casual conversation, however, Americans commonly say *different than,* a phrase that is becoming more and more widely accepted in the media. The British, Irish and others who follow British usage will often say *different to,* as in *This is different to that.*

double negatives Some languages require two components to express a negative; French, for example, requires both *ne* and *pas* (*Ce n'est pas le mot juste,* for *That is not the right word*) or *ne* and another negative (*Ça ne fait rien,* an idiom meaning *That means nothing* or *It doesn't matter*). English calls for just one negative per thought; double negatives like *I didn't do nothing* sound uneducated. (Even so, Americans from some regions or ethnic groups routinely use double negatives informally for emphasis.) So avoid double negatives in speaking and especially writing. An entrepreneurial journalism student wrote, "I'm trying to create a platform to aggregate voices from places that are not on the radar, *neither* in the interest of mainstream media but are extremely important for our country." Better: *. . . places that are **not** on the radar **or** in the interest of mainstream media, but are extremely important for our country.* Or, using a *neither/nor* construction, *. . . places that are **neither** on the radar **nor** in the interest of mainstream media, but are extremely important for our country.*

due to, because of *Due to circumstances beyond our control* is a commonly heard phrase, but that doesn't mean it's correct. *Due* is an adjective, not an adverb or a conjunction—which is how it's generally (mis)used. Think of *due* in its original sense as something owed, like an assignment on deadline. So, for example: *The Yankees game was canceled due to rain.* Wrong. Here *due to* is trying to be an adverb modifying the clause before it. Correct: *The game was canceled because of rain.* And *The game was canceled due to it was raining?* Very wrong. Here it's trying to be a conjunction linking two clauses. Instead: *The game was canceled because it was raining.* But: *The cancellation was due to rain?* Right, because here *due* is a predicate adjective, modifying the subject of the sentence (the cancellation).

economic, economical *Economic* means having to do with the economy: *an economic meltdown, an economic miracle. Economical* means inexpensive or a good value: *Buying in bulk can be more economical.* A CUNY international student wrote, "To break stories that challenge the powerful, the political and economical forces that rule our world must remain the core activity for us." She meant *economic.*

-ed, -ing adjectives Participles are verb forms that, among other uses, may serve as adjectives. Present participles end in *-ing*, past participles in *-ed*. Non-native English-speakers often confuse them, saying *I am exciting* when they mean *I am excited* or, worse, *I am boring* instead of *I am bored*. Use the *-ing* form to describe what makes an effect and the *-ed* form to describe the person who feels that effect: *The media need to be interesting to keep their audience interested.*

estimate, expect, predict All three words have to do with the future, but they require different constructions. When students in CUNY's business concentration were gearing up for a monthly federal jobs report with blog posts about the likely news, they used these words, but not always correctly. It wasn't the meaning that was off, but rather the constructions:

> *Economists surveyed by Bloomberg estimate personal income to increase 0.4 percent in March.*

You don't *estimate* something *to grow;* you estimate *that it will grow.* Three possible fixes:

> *Economists surveyed by Bloomberg* **estimate** *personal income* **will** *increase 0.4 percent in March.*

> *Economists surveyed by Bloomberg* **expect** *personal income* **to** *increase 0.4 percent in March.*

> *Economists surveyed by Bloomberg* **expect** *(that) personal income* **will** *increase 0.4 percent in March.*

In other words, there are two possible constructions using *expect*, but only one for *estimate*.

> *Predict works more like estimate than expect. Vitner predicted home prices to change their growing pace in the second part of*

the year? No, *Vitner predicted that* home prices *would* change their pace, *estimated that* they *would,* or *expected* them *to.*

every day, everyday One word or two? It depends on the meaning. *Every day,* two words, is an adverb meaning daily: *Many New Yorkers ride the subway every day. Everyday,* one word, is an adjective meaning ordinary, habitual, routine, nothing special: *an everyday occurrence, everyday clothes.*

Confusion on this point is widespread. A CUNY international student wrote, "I took brisk steps and reached the station, a place that gave me immense joy everyday once I stepped down from the train"; she meant *every day.*

That space may not be crucial to the reader's comprehension, but it is to your precision as a writer. Consider this passage from a Hillary Clinton campaign story in *The New York Times,* where someone apparently still knows the difference:

> *When she visited a high school in Las Vegas last week to talk about immigration, she found the students had welcomed her with a handmade sign with her campaign slogan. They had botched the punctuation—and a bit of the meaning, though perhaps it still resonated. "Everyday, Americans need a champion," it read.*

In pronunciation, *every day* takes equal stress on both words unless the speaker intends to emphasize *every: I do this EVERY day.* In everyday, the accent tends to be on the last syllable, except in the 1968 song "Everyday People" by Sly and the Family Stone.

fewer, less Use *fewer* for things that can be counted, *less* for things that can't. When a student wrote, "These are all sound reasons why less and less Chinese would give birth to a second child," she technically should have said *fewer and fewer.* "Technically" because Americans frequently disregard this grammar rule—for example, in supermarkets, where signs over checkout lines usually say "10 items or less" when *fewer* would be correct. But in writing, which tends to be more formal, it is better to be technically correct. Similarly, use *many* for things that can be counted, *much* for things that can't: *too many tourists, too much coffee.*

get The most overused word in the English language. Look it up in any dictionary, and you'll probably find at least two pages of possible meanings and uses. *Get lunch, get a job, get paid, get a promotion, get married, get pregnant, get a passport, get registered*—the list goes on and on. In casual conversation, no one will mind, or probably even notice. But peppering your professional writing or speaking with *get* makes your vocabulary seem limited. Whenever it is possible or graceful, substitute another, more vivid word or a different construction. Use some of those synonyms in the dictionary, or rework the sentence; sometimes even passive voice is preferable. So *have, eat* or *buy lunch; find a job; be paid; earn a promotion; marry; become pregnant; obtain a passport;* and *register.*

historic, historical *Historic* refers to something that made history: *the Supreme Court's historic decision recognizing same-sex marriage. Historical* refers to something that happened in history, or is connected to it: *the historical record, a historical landmark, the Historical Society.*

home, house, housing *Housing* is the collective term for the places where people live. Business writers spend a lot of time reporting on the *housing market.* A *housing crisis* usually refers to a crisis in the availability or affordability of places to live. In the media, the mortgage crisis that triggered the 2008 recession is often called a *housing crisis.*

Home refers not just to the physical space, but often to the dweller's emotional attachment to that space. ("Home is where the heart is.") A home is generally a *house* or an *apartment* (which the British would call a *flat*). A *house* usually refers to a freestanding dwelling, as in *a single-family house.* A *townhouse* can mean a single-family house in the city, for those who can afford one, or more likely a multi-floor row house anywhere.

An apartment can be a *rental*, a *co-op* or a *condo*. In *co-op* (short for *cooperative*, and not *coop*, a home for chickens) buildings, more common in New York than elsewhere, the homeowner doesn't own the actual space, but rather a share in the building proportional to that space. In a *condo* (short for *condominium*) building, the *homeowner* buys the physical unit. Whether you own a house, a condo or a co-op, you're a *homeowner*.

From CUNY students:

New home sales were flat in March. For single-family houses, sales slumped to 384,000, according to U.S. Department of Commerce's latest report. Correct. *New home sales* refer to sales of all new homes, be they houses, condos or co-ops. And *single-family houses* describes a category precisely.

After Hurricane Sandy hit New York City on October 29 in 2012, 650,000 homes were damaged or destroyed, according to the Department of Housing and Urban Development. Correct, since those *650,000 homes* could have taken any of the forms mentioned above. Also note the name of the federal department: *Housing* and Urban Development. (But the writer should have checked style for rendering dates.)

Today, empty houses are a common sight on Staten Island. Correct, since the writer was reporting specifically on houses.

The pace of the house market's recovery is slowing down. Incorrect. This story was about all forms of housing. It should have said *housing market*.

in order to This phrase, beloved among academic writers, can almost always lose the *in order* in journalism, with rare exceptions for clarity. Those two words indicate purpose, which the infinitive (*to +* verb) can do on its own. A CUNY student wrote: "In order to continue to play such an important role, journalists need to deeply understand the new media rules." *To continue* would have done the job just as well and tightened the sentence by two words (and *to continue playing* by one more).

masterful, masterly Like *historic* and *historical*, these related words are often confused. *Masterful* means acting like a master, someone who holds power over others: *To the frightened young woman, Mr. Rochester seemed a masterful figure.* *Masterly* means unusually skillful, like someone who has mastered an art: *a masterly job, a masterly painter.* Note that *masterly*, despite its *-ly* ending, is an adjective, not an adverb. So it is impossible to perform a task *masterly*, but rather, *in a masterly way*.

media This word is, always has been and always shall be plural. No matter how many TV anchors report what *the media is saying*, or how many publications now accept the word as singular, they are wrong. Treating *media* as singular simply makes no sense; it has been the plural of *medium* since the Romans began using the word more than 2,000 years ago. Moreover, lumping together *the media*—news outlets as diverse as *The New York Times*, Fox News, *People* magazine, *People's Daily* and countless others—as a single bloc makes even less sense, especially in this era of more, and ever more diverse, media.

mental health terms Journalists and civilians alike commonly— and mistakenly—use *schizophrenic* to mean divided, paradoxical or contradictory. The inaccuracy stems from a decades-old misunder- standing of the term as denoting a split or multiple personality. In fact, *schizophrenia* is a severe neurological disorder that may involve delu- sions, hallucinations, and other severely dysfunctional thought patterns and actions. Mental health professionals or their clients are certain to complain about any misuse by the media.

Similarly, be careful using terms like *retarded;* today, terms like *developmentally disabled* or *challenged* are more accepted. Better yet, be specific about the nature of the disorder: *He has Down syndrome; he has autism.* (The latter has come to be preferred over *he is autistic,* on the reasoning that this wording does not define the person by the disorder.)

mixed metaphors A *metaphor* is a word or phrase—a verbal image, if you will—used as a symbol for what the writer really means.

(A *simile* makes a comparison using *like* or *as*; a metaphor stands on its own.) Metaphors are fine when used sparingly; mixing them is not. A mixed metaphor "combines different images or ideas in a way that is foolish or illogical," according to merriam-webster.com. It results in laughter—on the copy desk if you're lucky, in public if you're not. (See *The New Yorker's* column-fillers headlined "Block That Metaphor!") Some examples from CUNY international students:

With buybacks' momentum cooling down in the third quarter of 2014 . . . Momentum is a force in physics, a moving object's mass multiplied by its speed, while *cooling down* refers to temperature. Momentum does not cool down, but rather *slows down* (better yet, just *slows*).

The American company has been tailoring Chinese consumers' palates. Actually, if it was tailoring anything, it was *tailoring* its product *to* Chinese palates. (*Tailoring palates* = changing tastes.) But *tailor,* noun or verb, refers to making clothes, not food. While Merriam-Webster does recognize a second definition—"to make or change (something) so that it meets a special need or purpose"—the use of *tailor* here comes dangerously close to mixed metaphor. The writer could have chosen a more all-purpose word: *The American company has been **adapting** to Chinese consumers' palates.*

Tow-Knight fellows in entrepreneurial journalism spend a lot of time studying the "media ecosystem" and seem especially prone to mixing in other metaphors:

The Guardian has already built strong, solid pillars in the digital and multimedia ecosystem.

The Hispanic audience is a time bomb for the America media ecosystem.

Yes, *ecosystem* can mean an interconnected network, but it still brings environmental images to mind—not so much architectural ones or weaponry. (And it's not clear how the Hispanic audience is likely to explode—in population, perhaps, but would that be destructive, like a time bomb?) So maybe *The Guardian* has *established a strong, solid presence* in the ecosystem, and maybe the Hispanic audience is *an important factor.*

When a student from Spain, reporting on murders linked to Mexico's drug trade, wrote about "the hell of violence Mexico is immersed in," she was mixing an image of hell with a water image, *immersion.* That word means being covered with a liquid like water—which would presumably put out the fires of hell. The writer could have solved the problem by saying simply *Mexico's hell of violence.*

premier, premiere A German friend e-mailed to ask: "Why do they write this with an *e*? *Friday evening I was at the Premiere of Hello, Dolly!*" English has two similar words, *premier* and *premiere*, both derived from the Latin and later French words for *first. Premiere* is a noun meaning the first time a show, film, etc. is presented. *Premier* can be a noun (as in a nation's *premier,* a top-ranking official, the meaning my friend was most familiar with) or an adjective, meaning best or most important (*the city's premier theater*).

presently, at present Most adjectives form their adverbs by adding *-ly.* So if *current* becomes *currently,* its close cousin *present* becomes *presently,* right? Wrong. *Presently* is a rather formal or old-fashioned way of saying *soon,* not *now: The mayor will see you presently.* If you must, say *at present,* short for *at the present time.* Or just use the simpler *now.*

real estate agent, Realtor Realtor, with a capital R, is a trademark referring to a member of the National Association of Real Estate Boards, or one of its constituents, and follows its Code of Ethics, according to the association's website. Do not use realtor, lowercase, as a generic term for anyone in the business; like the mental-health professionals cited above, Realtors are sure to complain. Instead, say *real estate agent.*

recreation, re-creation Most American publications have dropped diacritical marks like hyphens when they are not needed for clarity, or between double vowels in words like *cooperate* (though *The New Yorker* still uses an dieresis, or two dots, over the second vowel in *cooperate, preeminent, reenact,* and so on). But some words absolutely demand that hyphen to avoid confusion. *Recreation* (pronounced with a short *e*: *rec-reation*) means leisure-time activity and its beneficial effects, but about something that has been created again or anew, use *re-creation* (pronounced *ree*). In that meaning, the verb *recreate* takes no hyphen.

reflexives A reflexive is a pronoun containing the syllable *-self* or *-selves*: *myself, yourself, himself, herself, itself, ourselves, yourselves, themselves, oneself.* (Never *hisself* and *theirselves,* which sound uneducated. A Brazilian student wrote: "On Facebook, he asked for collaborators, and several people answered saying that they had relatives from that region or that they theirselves were from there." She meant *themselves.*) A reflexive refers back to the subject of the sentence, clause or phrase; as merriam-webster.com puts it, "the action in a sentence or clause happens to the person or thing that does the action." In other words, he does it to *himself.*

It can be used for emphasis, as in *I'll do it myself,* meaning personally. But be careful: *by myself* (or any other reflexive) is an idiom meaning *alone.* If you wrote a story *yourself,* you did it without help. (If you're ever accused of plagiarism—falsely, we at CUNY fervently hope—the appropriate response is, "Of course I wrote it myself!") If you wrote it *by yourself,* you were alone when you wrote it.

A member of CUNY's class of 2016 wrote:

> *But the final "Yes" came after Glenn D. Lowry, Director of MOMA, saw by himself a big exhibition organized by the Torres García Museum in Porto Alegre, Brazil.*

Unless Lowry was alone when he saw the exhibition, she meant *Lowry himself* saw it.

Some examples of good usage from international students:

His sisters, mother and Cabrera himself don't give identical versions of his story. Correct because *himself* is used for emphasis.

A quote from a profile: *"I'd much rather help someone be great than be doing great things myself," she said.* Another matter of emphasis.

From a cover letter by a student applying for an internship: *I am attending classes including "Introduction to Documentary Film," taught by Yoruba Richen, a documentarian herself.* Again, the reflexive is used to emphasize Richen's qualifications to teach the course.

She doesn't see herself coding all her life. Correct because the reflexive is the direct object; she is performing the action (*doesn't see*) on the direct object (*herself*). Similarly: *She certainly considers herself an adult.*

From a Tow-Knight fellow's blog post: *I've always led the definition of our mobile products . . . . building all the mobile wireframes of our apps myself.* Meaning she did it personally.

Don't use a reflexive if a regular pronoun will do. A Pennsylvania State University student, speaking on TV about his lawsuit charging that the administration ignored fraternity hazing, spoke of "the abuse that myself and others were repeatedly experiencing." Granted, he was under stress (and not writing for *The Daily Collegian*), so lapses in grammar are understandable. But he should have said *I and others*.

reign, rein In a Letter to the Editor in *The New York Times*, Laura Quayle of Lynn, Mass., asked: "Would Mrs. Clinton rein in Wall Street, or would she reign in Wall Street?" Quayle (or whoever copy-edited her letter) demonstrated that she understood something many writers do not: the difference between *reign* and *rein*. *Reign* means to hold a royal position as head of state: *The Queen of England reigns, but she does not rule. Reins* are the leather straps used to control a horse, and that is the spelling in the phrasal verb *rein in*, which means to limit, control or slow.

resume, résumé Without the accent marks, from French, *resume* (pronounced ruh-ZOOM) means to start again: *The United States has* *resumed bombing in Afghanistan.* With them (and pronounced REH-zoo-may in English), it means that all-important document journalists need to keep up to date at all times: the one that details their education, experience, skills, etc. for prospective employers. In academia, it is called a *C.V.,* for *curriculum vitae.*

Speaking of résumés, outside the United States they commonly include photos as well as personal information such as age, marital status and family, citizenship, personal interests, even class of driver's license. If you are submitting a résumé to an American company or publication, delete all such information. American law prohibits discrimination in hiring on many grounds. To prevent lawsuits, many companies will look no further at an applicant who has put that information on a résumé. So keep two versions of your résumé on your computer: one for your own country, one for the States.

road, street In general, *road* refers to thoroughfares in the country, *street* in a city. When a CUNY student from India wrote, "On the roads in New York City, we often see tall buildings being built or repaired." *Streets* would have been better. When she wrote, "Jorge Mineola, a 36-year-old construction worker, felt his life had come to a standstill last year when the police arrested him for getting drunk and creating a scene on the road," she was asked where the incident had happened. It was in the Bronx, she said, so once again *street* was correct. Even so, Road (capitalized) is sometimes part of the proper name of a street, even in a city, and should not be changed. *On the road* is an idiom for traveling or being in transit (*I've been on the road all day*), while *on the street* means out in public (*word on the street*) or along the city sidewalks (*I bought it on the street*).

say, tell, talk, speak These verbs are all about communication. The differences are subtle, and non-native English-speakers often confuse them. Since they're so often used with quotations, it's especially important for journalists to get them right. Which one to use in a particular sentence depends on its syntax—the way words are put together to express a thought. More specifically, it depends on whether the verb has a direct object, an indirect object, both, or none at all.

Transitive verbs take objects; intransitive verbs do not. *Say* is transitive. You can't just *say;* you have to *say something*. In a sentence using a quote, whether direct or indirect, that entire quote often functions as the direct object. A French student at CUNY wrote: *"New York-based jazz musician Zayn Mohammed, 28, said **the highly commercialized recording industry leaves little room for artists to follow their own muse."** This indirect quote is the direct object of *said*. What did he say? *That the highly commercialized . . .*

In another passage from that story: *Saxophonist Jon Gordon said he feels the same. "My hope is that it will help us to move the scene forward to whatever it's going to become," he said.* What did Gordon say? First, that *he feels the same;* second, the direct quote.

A Chinese student at CUNY wrote: *"It's just immoral, frankly," Nadler said, explaining why he voted against the Farm Bill.* Same here. But, also from that story: *"They just want people to starve, and it's disgusting," Nadler **told** photojournalists. Tell* is transitive but requires an indirect object, as in *Tell me a story.* You *say something **to** someone*, but you *tell someone something.*

Talk and *speak* are intransitive, taking neither direct nor indirect objects, though you can talk or speak *to* someone. (*She talks to us **about** grammar all the time. Last week she spoke **for** an hour!*) Is this sentence correct or incorrect? *He sighed and talked me, "I know the Japanese media."* Incorrect. It has an indirect object *(me)* and a direct object (the quote), so *talked* is wrong on two counts. Instead: *He sighed and told me, "I know the Japanese media."* Or: *He sighed and said **to** me, "I know the Japanese media."*

You can't *talk someone* or *talk something,* except in an idiom like *He talks a good game,* meaning that someone sounds good but can't or doesn't produce. (But you can talk to someone or, as Hamlet advises the players, speak the speech.)

scheme In British English, *scheme* refers to any kind of plan—*a* *new railway scheme, the government's social welfare scheme.* But to Americans, the word has a negative connotation, suggesting a plan to cheat or defraud. So when a CUNY student from Vietnam wrote, "IBM has not confirmed any specific layoff scheme," she would have been better off, for her audience, saying *any specific layoff plan.*

singular and plural While this topic didn't even make the list of CUNY students' top 20 problems (see Chapter 10), it is far and away the most-consulted entry on the English for Journalists blog. The most common way to form plurals in English is simply to add *-s* to a noun: *one reporter, two reporters; one desk, two desks; one laptop, two laptops.* So does that mean any noun that ends in *-s* is automatically plural?

Not necessarily. Let's start with an old newsroom joke, attributed to various journalists going back as far as Horace Greeley (1811–1872), editor of *The New York Tribune*:

> *"Are there any news?"*
> *"Not a single new."*

It sounds ridiculous. *News* is the aggregate of all the reports of the day; therefore it's uncountable, singular. Merriam-Webster online describes the word as "noun plural but singular in construction." So it takes verbs in singular form: *Is there any news?*

Politics? Another "noun plural but singular or plural in construction." When it's used to mean a single topic—*Politics is my favorite beat*—it's singular. But when referring to a person's political opinions or a set of relations, it's plural:

> *David's politics are very conservative.*
> *Office politics were driving me crazy, so I quit.*

Economics? The same. Referring to a social science, it's singular; referring to a set of conditions, it's plural:

Economics is often called "the dismal science."
The economics of the project make it impossible to proceed.

Ethics is also singular for a field of study, plural for a person's moral standards:

Ethics is a field that requires critical thinking skills.
It takes strong ethics for a journalist to remain credible.

And *the Olympics?* Plural, according to Ask the Editor at apstylebook.com:

> *Q. The Olympics is, or the Olympics are? Thanks —from*
> *Charlotte on Mon, Oct 08, 2007*
> *A. The Olympics are . . .*
> (It's short for *the Olympic Games.)*

Collective nouns are treated as singular in American English: *My class is covering the election tomorrow. The company is no longer turning a profit.* But here's a significant difference between British and American English. In British usage, words like *government* and *corporation* (or the name of one) are treated as plural:

The government have decided to raise taxes.
Barclays have reported record profits for the third quarter.

In America, they're singular:

The government has decided . . .
Barclays has reported . . .

Sports teams are treated much the same, at least in Britain. The British will say *Manchester United have won again*—an apparently singular subject, the name of a team, but a plural verb. In the United States, most names of sports teams are plural anyway—the New York Yankees, the Chicago Cubs, the Boston Red Sox (yes, Sox is plural, a variation on *socks*)—so they naturally take plural verbs.

What about *number,* as in this concert review: *At Thursday night's performance in Symphony Hall, there were a visibly uncomfortable number of empty seats.* Shouldn't that be *there was a number,* since *number* is singular? Again, from AP's Ask the Editor:

> *Q. Should "a number of " phrase be followed by a singular or plural noun? For example, "A number of options is/are available." —from Bend, Ore. on Sat, Mar 22, 2008*
>
> *A. A number of options are available, based on this guidance in Fowler's Modern English Usage: When the word number is itself the subject, it is a safe rule to treat it as singular when it has a definite article, and as plural when it has an indefinite.*

I prefer to think of it this way: *a number of* has become an idiom meaning more than one. So I vote that *there were a number* is permissible.

Finally, *none.* The word means *not one,* so in theory it should be singular. Under AP style: *When used in this sense, it always takes singular verbs and pronouns: None of the seats was in the right place. Use a plural verb only if the sense is no two or no amount: None of the consultants agree on the same approach. None of the taxes have been paid.* But at *The New York Times, none* is considered plural: *None of the seats were in the right place.* The moral of the story: check style for your publication.

split infinitives It was once considered a grammatical crime to place an adverb between *to* and the verb in an infinitive, as in the "Star Trek" tagline *to boldly go where no man has gone before.* The rules have relaxed, but it is better to not split an infinitive—I mean, *not to split an infinitive*—if you can do it gracefully, without making the sentence sound clumsy.

tragedy Perhaps the second most overused word in English—at least in the media, which label almost any bad news this way. A house fire kills six children? It's a tragedy. A tornado wipes out a small town in the Midwest? Tragedy. Thousands of refugees flee Syria for Europe? You guessed it. Classically, *tragedy* means a drama in which a noble or high-ranking figure is brought down by his own character flaws. The Greeks wrote tragedies; Shakespeare wrote tragedies. In that sense Richard Nixon's loss of the presidency over the Watergate scandal might be considered a tragedy. But however sad, most news is not, strictly speaking, tragedy.

After Malaysian Airlines Flight 370 vanished in 2015, a Chinese student wrote, "In order to avoid the tragedy from happening again, the ITU (International Telecommunication Union) adopted a decision in WRC on Nov 12th, 2015 that there will be a typical radio frequency for satellite to track the aircraft wiring." Better (and with a little further editing): *To prevent such an incident from happening again . . .*

who's, whose Like *it's* and *its, who's* is a contraction (for *who is*) and *whose* is the possessive. When a French-speaking CUNY student wrote, "The voice of one more expert, a lawyer who's client experienced something similar, will be needed to get a better grasp of the issue," she meant *whose.*

CHAPTER 12

NEW MEDIA, NEW VOCABULARY

Not so long ago—1999, in fact—*The Daily Prophet* in J.K. Rowling's Harry Potter novels seemed like, well, fantasy. A newspaper with pictures that moved? Only in the world of witches and wizards. Yet that's essentially what we have today, except that the news"paper" is no longer printed on paper for a large percentage of its audience. Instead, we read our news on laptops and tablets and phones on which the pictures do move, in the form of streaming video and GIFs. Consider the rocking ship to which readers of nytimes.com woke up on July 17, 2015, illustrating a story on the home page about the lack of legal oversight on the high seas (http://www.nytimes.com/2015/07/28/world/a-renegade-trawler-hunted-for-10000-miles-by-vigilantes.html). Newspapers also talk, not only in the videos but also in audio clips and podcasts.

The job titles that defined 20th-century newsroom hierarchies still exist, but supplemented by a wealth of new ones unknown a generation ago. Restless American journalists used to look for jobs in the classified ads of *Editor & Publisher*, the weekly trade magazine that went monthly in 2004; its very name defined many of the jobs advertised, along with a few others like reporter, photographer and production manager. (Even more quaint: if you were sending out resumes *cold*—with no introduction to the management—you would look up a publication's address and the name of the relevant editor in a reference book published annually.)

Today, the job titles advertised on the E&P website, Poynter.org and journalismjobs.com—blogger, web developer, engagement editor, data journalist, content and social marketing manager, social media editor, real-time curator, manager of newsroom practice change and mass spread—hint at a media world where the possibilities for innovation will be endless and print may soon be dead.

In the late 2000s, I used give an occasional talk titled "The Changing Media," but the media changed so fast that within a few years it had become obsolete. Case in point: *The Roanoke Times,* where I had a summer internship in 1975 and my first job after college, was a morning newspaper in my day—print and nothing but. In 2007, when the Virginia Tech campus shootings took place in Blacksburg, part of the paper's circulation area, *The Times* reported events as they unfolded via live blog. Today, no doubt, its reporters would be live-tweeting their coverage from the first word of gunshots on campus. After all, in 2011, many of the first reports on the Arab Spring reached the rest of the world via Twitter.

As the media become increasingly digital in nature, the way they use English is also changing. Now, journalists for whom words are still their stock in trade talk about *text* rather than *print.* Editors still write headlines, but often one for print and a different one for the web to more attract *hits* through S.E.O., or *search engine optimization* (see below). Old-timers wince, but *access* has become widely accepted as a verb. As newsrooms face increased pressure to help make money, firewalls are crumbling and hybrids like *native advertising* are becoming part of the media landscape.

Some journalists *scrape the web* in search of data suggesting trends they can turn into stories. They produce *interactive* features and *moderate* comments from readers that can turn news into a conversation. As of late 2015, *coding* is the hot new skill every young journalist wants to learn. Not long after Google Glass was introduced, CUNY's ever-visionary Professor Jeff Jarvis asked his entrepreneurial journalism students to imagine going out to report a story and live-streaming what they saw through the glasses: "Wouldn't that be great?" Google Glass may have gone the way of the Edsel by now (Google it), but CUNY students have been known to use bodycams as reporting equipment and may check out GoPros from the equipment room. Those producing more traditional video are using it to illustrate text stories or producing stand-alone features. Look no further than "Muslim Image-Makers, Made in Moscow," produced by Natalia V. Osipova, CUNY class of 2012, for *The New York Times* (http://www.nytimes.com/2015/07/28/world/europe/muslims-in-moscow-work-to-break-a-stereotype.html?hp&action=click&pgtype=Homepage&module=photo-spot-region&region=top-news&WT.nav=top-news).

For 21st-century professionals, new media bring a whole new vocabulary of jargon—half journalistic, half techie. As technology spreads, so do the English terms that go with it. Many computer-related terms originated in English, and as electronic devices have taken over the world, users in some other countries have simply adopted the English words that go with them. (The French still call computers *ordinateurs,* as they did when personal computers became widespread in the early 1980s, but in Poland computer stores sell *laptopy,* grafting the Polish plural form -*y* onto an English word.) If you're already digitally savvy, you may already know many of the terms below, which are among the most common as of early 2016; expect to be hearing new ones by the time you read this book. If you're a more traditional journalist making the transition to digital, they may be your bridge to a 21st-century career.

One word of warning: don't go too far—as some *digital natives* have been known to do—by, for example, using text-message abbreviations in their copy. Unless directed otherwise or making a point, write in standard English.

aggregator A website that *aggregates,* or collects, stories from other websites, often on particular themes, and republishes them in full or summarized with links. The Huffington Post is largely a general-interest aggregator, though it produces original content as well. The Media Wire page of poynter.org (http://www.poynter.org/category/mediawire/), website of the Poynter Institute for journalists, is one of a number of sites aggregating news about the media that are useful in keeping up with the industry.

app Short for *application*, a specific task that a digital device may be programmed to do. The almost infinite number of apps available today for mobile devices like tablets and smartphones can do everything from taking pictures to recording interviews to calling a cab to ordering food for delivery. News apps—those that exist for conveying news to its consumers—range from those of newspapers and television stations to messaging and calling apps like WeChat, through which many digital natives get their news.

archive Like archives for paper documents (the National Archives in Washington stores important historical ones like the Declaration of Independence and the Constitution), a digital archive stores text, photos, video and other components of online journalism for posterity. Some publications charge for access to their archives; some offer them free to subscribers, some to anyone. *Archive* may be used as a noun or a verb. News sites *archive* material when it is no longer current; it is then stored in the *archive*. (A tip to journalists: don't depend on digital archives to store your work forever; web pages often disappear without warning. Make sure to keep hard copies— printouts, photocopies or PDFs—for future reference and your portfolio.)

audio Recorded sound that supplements text or comes with a *video* (see below). The Latin word *audio* literally translates as *I hear* and is the root of other English words including *audible* (able to be heard), *auditor* (a student who does not formally enroll in a class but attends to listen) and *auditorium* (a place to hear concerts, speeches, etc.).

blog Short for *weblog*, and now universally used in its place. As a noun, a website on which a journalist or publication publishes running news reports or commentary, with the most recent entries, or *posts,* at the top. As a verb, to write and post material on a blog; a journalist who does so is a *blogger.* Popular blogging platforms for professionals and amateurs alike include Wordpress, Typepad and Blogspot. A video blog is called a *vlog,* pronounced just as it's spelled, not V-*log.*

bot A computer program intended to do a repetitive task, freeing the user for other tasks that require use of the human brain.

browse, browser In an old-fashioned bookstore or library, browsing meant looking through its wares without seeking any specific title. Online, *browse* means to search for information, sometimes a very specific piece, by using a *browser,* or *search engine.* Google, Bing and Yahoo are leading browsers in the United States and many other parts of the world. But some countries have their own official browsers—notably China's Baidu, which substitutes for Google there, especially since the government blocked Google in 2009.

broadcast Widely disseminate information, especially audio or video. For decades, *broadcasting* meant signals transmitted through the air and picked up by receivers like radios or television sets. Cable TV replaced those over-the-air signals (now renamed *analog*) with information transmitted directly through a cable to the set, and satellite TV with signals from a dish connected to the set. Smart TVs that connect through wifi may soon make those technologies obsolete, but just as we still "dial" phone numbers, we still call those forms of journalism *broadcast* or *broadcasting.*

clickbait Online content primarily intended to attract as many *clicks* or *hits* as possible through sensationalist presentation. Clickbait is often suggestive rather than accurate (such as "5 Foods You Should Never Eat," or a 2015–16 series suggesting the actresses Judi Dench and Meryl Streep had died) and is often financed by advertisers—a fact not always mentioned prominently.

click or **click-through rate** The number of users who reach a web page via a specific link. The click rate is one of the metrics used to evaluate the effectiveness of publicity tools like e-mail blasts, online advertising campaigns, etc.

clip To *clip* means to cut off small pieces—for example, or hair or nails. To print journalists, *clips* are stories cut out and filed in the *morgue,* or library, or the samples of their work they send out with job applications. In audio or video, a clip is a short segment inserted into a larger report. For example, movie reviews on TV or online often include *film clips* showing a brief scene to illustrate the review.

cloud A remote shared server on which files may be stored and retrieved via the Internet, as opposed to storing the information only within devices like laptops or tablets. The many cloud storage services available include Google Drive, Apple's iCloud and Carbonite.

code, coding The formatting of digital information in ways that allow the creation of web pages, apps, operating systems and other forms of software using established computer languages such as HTML.

comments Responses from readers, often published online with a story. As journalists increasingly strive to engage readers and make their reporting a conversation rather than a one-way transmission of information, they encourage readers to comment on their work, or on the news in general, with user-friendly online forms. They also mine comments for story ideas and potential sources. Comments may or may not be *moderated* (see below).

computer-assisted reporting Any use of digital technology in the pursuit of journalism. It may be as relatively simple as browsing the web for ideas and sources, or as complex as *web-scraping* or analyzing databases to look for information that suggests trends, and thus trend stories.

content (*not* contents!) Any material—text, audio, video—produced for publication. Note that, as a general term (*content on the site*), it is singular. *Contents*, plural, means what is contained inside something: *the contents of the bag*; a book's *table of contents*.

content management system (CMS) A centralized computer system dedicated to the creation, editing, presentation and eventual archiving of content. In short, a system that enables journalists to publish and preserve their work.

crowdsourcing, crowdfunding Drawing information (*crowdsourcing*) or financial support (*crowdfunding*) from a large number of sources, especially online, as opposed to one or two traditional ones. News organizations now routinely use crowdsourcing to obtain information from the public. Some have even turned to crowdfunding to raise money for special projects or investigations. For example, since Miyuki Inoue, a 2014 Tow-Knight Fellow in the entrepreneurial journalism program at CUNY, returned to her job at Asahi Shimbun in Tokyo, she has been working on A-port, its crowdfunding project in "solution journalism." Websites like Kickstarter originated crowdfunding in the early 2000s as a nontraditional way to finance artistic and other projects.

database A digitized collection of information, or data, organized for easy access by both its administrators (who manage it) and users like journalists (who go to it for information).

data journalism/visualization *Data journalism* is rooted in data and statistics, as opposed to interviews, the reporter's direct observation, etc. The journalist may use tools as common as an Excel spreadsheet or a wide range of software dedicated to journalistic purposes. *Data visualization* means presenting data in any visual format that will help the audience digest it more easily than sheer numbers.

digital Related to electronic media or content, in which all information is *digitized*—that is, converted into sequences of the digits 0 and 1 for storage and retrieval. *Digital media* publish or broadcast in digital form, i.e., electronically, as opposed to print or analog broadcasting (see above).

digital native A member of the generation(s) born from about 1990 on who grew up using digital media such as computers, cellphones, text messaging, social media, etc. and considers them the normal, standard way of communicating rather than newfangled inventions. As *legacy* (pre-digital) media continue to reinvent themselves for the digital age, digital natives—i.e., younger employees—are highly sought after, often leading to tensions with newsroom veterans.

download As a verb, to transfer information from the Internet to a device like a laptop, a smartphone, an e-book, etc., or from a larger device to a smaller one; for example, songs may be *downloaded* from iTunes to a listening device. As a noun, content that is downloaded: *Let me see if it's in my downloads.* The opposite is *upload*: photos may be uploaded to social media, files to cloud storage, etc.

embed To place content directly into other content. Examples: information may be embedded in the body of e-mail rather than sent as an attachment; video may be embedded in a website, on Facebook or in a blog post.

engagement editor A journalist whose job is to *engage,* or involve, a publication's audience in its operation by using such tools as comments, interactive features, social media, surveys, etc.

feed A frequently updated stream of information such as headlines with links, news summaries, new blog posts, etc., sent to online subscribers via e-mail or apps. *RSS feeds* use the common Rich Site Summary format (also called Really Simple Syndication).

forum An online discussion similar to *comments* but intended to take the form of a running conversation.

GIF (pronounced *jif*, like the American peanut butter) Short for *graphics interchange format*, an image format that allows the creation of animation to illustrate online journalism.

graphics Visual content other than photography that a print or online publication uses to supplement text, contributing to the overall design. Graphics or *infographics*—those that convey information—may include graphs and charts, maps, timelines, and now GIFs and *word clouds*. In journalism, all graphics should ideally be infographics.

hashtag The symbol #, once called the "number sign" (or "pound sign" on phones) but reinvented in the Twitter age as the symbol that enables users to link their tweets to others on the same subject, initiating and joining conversations. The hashtags of 2015, for example, progressed from *#JeSuisCharlie* in January to *#YouAintNoMuslimBruv* in December, with liberal doses of *#kardashian* throughout the year.

hits Slang for page views, or how many people click call up a web page. Hits are the rough equivalent of a print publication's circulation figures. The more hits a website receives, the more it can charge for advertising.

hyperlocal Covering a very small geographical area in depth, rather than trying to cover all the national and international news its readers can get elsewhere. A hyperlocal website may cover a city, like Philadelphia's BillyPenn (billypenn.com); a neighborhood, like Corner Media Group's eight sites covering Brooklyn, N.Y. (cornermediagroup.com); or as little as a few blocks.

image The digital-era word for *photo, picture* or any other visual element. Today's photo editors talk in terms of images rather than pictures.

interactive Allowing, or even requiring, the audience to interact with the journalism to make it fully effective. Interactive features may be as simple as a short survey or as complex as a multimedia report that allows the consumer to help determine how the story unfolds.

legacy media Media companies such as newspapers or radio or TV stations that were established before the digital age began. They are now struggling to keep up with digital media and adapt to competition from them.

links, linking A link is a URL (Uniform Resource Locator, or more simply web address), embedded in online text on which users may click to call up related content. Journalists may link from current stories to past or related stories, relevant websites, source material or any other online material that will serve the audience. As they strive to provide as complete a report as possible, linking has become an essential tool and skill. Journalists who do not provide links can expect to lose their audiences to those who do.

live-blog To report a story online as it develops by posting short updates online rather than waiting to write and publish a complete story as production deadlines permit, as in print. Journalists live-blog many news events, from the Paris terror attacks to Oscar night, though Twitter's brevity and speed have made it perhaps more attractive.

metrics (also called *analytics*) Statistics on use of web pages that meter, or measure, how many views a page is receiving, how long users stay on the page, where they are geographically, how they reached the page, what search terms they used, etc. Instead of deciding for the reader what is and is not news, media professionals now routinely use metrics as a major factor in deciding what content their audiences want, how to cover it, how to play it, etc. In fact, metrics now largely determine what *is* news.

microblog In languages like Chinese or Japanese, a single character can represent an entire word or concept (as opposed to a single sound, like a letter in English). So platforms like China's Weibo have been nick-named *microblogs*—something between tweets and blogs. Microblogs allow writers to say a good deal more in 140 characters than English-language journalists can on Twitter.

mobile From the Latin root for *move*, this word—originally simply an adjective meaning able to move—has become the name of a whole new communications field. Mobile devices like cellphones and tablets allow users to make calls, check e-mail, surf the web and take advantage of apps without being tethered to a cord or a desk—in short, on the move. As a result, new forms of journalism have been developed for the smaller screens of these devices. Pronunciation note: the British say *MO-byle* (and use that as a noun to mean their phones, as in *I'll ring you on my mobile*; Americans pronounce the word more like *MO-buhl* but make calls on their *cells*).

moderate, moderator Brave is the publication that posts reader comments without *moderating* them. Online, a *moderator* is an editor who reads and approves comments, or not, applying the publication's standards of language and civility. In broadcast journalism, a *moderator* is the host and chief questioner on a panel discussion, a debate among political candidates, etc.

multimedia Multi (Latin for *many*) + media. A multimedia report or feature uses more than one medium—text, video, audio, interactive, etc.—in combination to tell a particular story. Multimedia journalists are adept at working in more than one medium and understanding how they fit together.

narrated, non-narrated The verb *narrate* means, essentially, to tell a story; a *narrative* is the story itself. In video storytelling, a narrated report is one that uses a *narrator,* often in voiceover, to tell the story, guiding the viewer through the on-camera interviews, B-roll, other video clips and graphics. A *non-narrated* video uses no narrator, telling the story solely through the video and its editing.

native advertising A newly recognized form of content in which advertising is presented looking very much like editorial content; it may carry a label like "from our advertisers," "sponsored content," "branded content" or "sponsored post." While native advertising represents a crumbling of the traditional firewall between the newsroom and the business side, struggling media companies, especially legacy media, have come to accept it for a simple reason: they need the money. Old-time print journalists may consider native advertising the end of civilization as they know it, but the fact is, newspapers and magazines have long accepted "advertorials," ads that look only slightly different from editorial context—for example, pages of destination "features" in travel magazines, or large, text-heavy newspaper ads from corporations or countries that are only minimally marked as advertising. (And television has had its "infomercials," extended commercials that purport to be giving information about the products they sell.) According to the American Press Institute's definition, sponsored content "is generally understood to be content that takes the same form and qualities of a publisher's original content" and "usually serves useful or entertaining information as a way of favorably influencing the perception of the sponsor brand."

pagination In print media, *pagination* refers to the process (a long time in coming, and now long since accomplished) of producing pages entirely on computers rather than mechanically in a composing room. In the digital age, the word refers to the practice of breaking up one story into multiple pages to make room for more advertising, and to tally more clicks as readers move through the story.

platform A computer system that allows the user to perform desired tasks, or applications. The operating system is the platform that allows the computer to run at all. Wordpress is a blogging platform; Facebook and Twitter are social media platforms.

post To publish online—for example, on a blog, as in *Have you posted yet today?* Also a noun meaning an item posted: *Have you read my latest post?*

podcast An audio feature that may be downloaded and listened to offline. Thousands of podcasts in English are now available, often free, from radio networks like NPR, news websites, iTunes and many other sources. Podcasts are an excellent tool for keeping up with the news and exploring new forms of journalism while improving your English listening comprehension (see page 305).

push notifications Messages from news apps that activate mobile devices and alert their users to updates.

S.E.O. Short for *search engine optimization*, or making the best use of Internet search tools to attract readers to your content. S.E.O. demands that writers and editors figure out which words readers are most likely to search for online, then use them in copy and headlines. The more search terms you can match when a reader Googles those words, the more hits your page is likely to get, and its link will move higher in the Google results, attracting even more hits. In traditional print media, headline writing was an art form in which cleverness and subtlety were prized as a sophisticated way to draw the reader's attention, as in a 1988 classic from *The New York Times*: "How Many Nails Does a New House Take? Ten, Well Bitten." That's fine for print, but S.E.O. would reward something more like "Building New Home Causes Stress."

slideshow, audio slide show A series of images—generally still, but more and more likely to contain animations like GIFs—collected and arranged to tell a story or make a presentation. PowerPoint is a common slideshow tool for presentations, but slideshows are also frequently used to illustrate online journalism. An audio slide show adds sound, generally as a voiceover narration.

social media/networks Platforms such as Facebook, Twitter, Instagram, WeChat and many others that allow users to connect as a community, share information, update their status and perform other networking tasks.

sound bite An audio *clip* (see above) intended to summarize an idea, a position, etc., as briefly and memorably as possible in the hopes of receiving wide exposure in the limited time of an audio or video report. In fact, sound bites may be used so often in the media that they quickly become clichés. American politicians are often accused of talking in sound bites rather than addressing issues in depth.

S.O.T. Short for *sound on tape*, any piece of recorded sound, but often a short piece of audio inserted into a report. For just one example, a news anchor's reporting of an accident, a crime or a police investigation may include S.O.T. from a 911 emergency call.

sponsored content See *native advertising*.

still A photograph that does not move and thus captures a moment in time, as opposed to video.

streaming The transmission of audio or video from the Internet to a computer, smartphone, tablet, smart TV, etc., for one-time consumption without being *downloaded*, or stored in the device. Many websites routinely stream all kinds of content, and for some, like Netflix for movies and Spotify for music, it is their core business.

text Writing. Even veteran print journalists now talk about working in "text" rather than print because it covers writing posted online as well. A text message is one sent on a phone in written characters, not by voice; also called **SMS**, for Short Messaging Service.

timeline A visual chronology showing how a news event, historical trend or just about anything else unfolded over time.

Twitter, tweet, retweet *Twitter* is the social medium introduced in 2006 by Jack Dorsey that allows users to express their thoughts online in 140 characters or fewer. It is named for the conversation-like sounds made by a flock of birds; hence Twitter's blue bird logo. *Tweet* (named for a single bird sound) can be either a noun or a verb: when you *tweet* from a news event, the messages you send out are *tweets;* when you repost someone else's tweet, you *retweet* it. (Non-digital-natives often date themselves by mistakenly saying *I'm going to Twitter that* or *I just got a Twitter.*) Twitter may be the only place in the English language where *favorite* is recognized as a verb (*So-and-so just favorited your tweet!*). Let's hope it doesn't spread.

unique user/visitor An identifiably distinct user calling up a web page. No matter how many times the user visits that page, he is counted as one user. As a metric, the number of unique users more accurately measures how many people a page is reaching than the number of *hits.*

vertical A website that reports on, and caters to, every aspect of a specific topic, sometimes breaking through the traditional firewall between news and advertising. For example, a real estate vertical would not only report on real estate news, sales, trends, prices, etc., but also include a listings search to connect brokers and potential clients.

video Recorded moving images, generally with sound, that supplement text or stand on their own for television or online. Just as *audio* comes from the Latin word for *I hear, video* literally means *I see* (the root of other English words related to seeing, like *visible* and *view*).

videographer Video + photographer—that is, someone who shoots video for the media.

voiceover Narration superimposed on (placed "over") a video, in which the speaker is not shown on camera.

web-scraping Mining the World Wide Web, now more commonly called the Internet, for information like data that can suggest story ideas or supply facts to support those already in progress. As Sandeep Junnarkar, director of CUNY's interactive journalism program, described scraping in his online course on the subject, "It is simply the use of programming to grab information like numbers, images, addresses, URLs, phone numbers and just about anything else you can think of from the Internet, and transferring that data into a structured format like a database or spreadsheet, where it can be compared and analyzed. In other words, scraping allows you to create your own data sets (and to get ahead of your competition)."

widget A mini-app that can be embedded into a web page to perform a specific function. The dozens of optional widgets available on the blogging platform Wordpress.com, to cite just one example, include a monthly archive, a calendar of posts, author contact information, social media plug-ins and subscription options.

word cloud A graphic on a given subject using words as visual elements. Word clouds have been used for such purposes as illustrating by relative size and typeface how often particular words have been used in text or as search terms, or creating images—for example, word cloud portraits of people using words from their professions.

CARRIE BROWN

JOINING THE CONVERSATION

She may have started out at the *Eau Claire Leader-Telegram* in her
native Wisconsin, but Carrie Brown, director of the master's degree
program in social media, has become an indisputable pioneer of new
media. Previously an associate professor of journalism at the University
of Memphis in Tennessee, she developed courses in social media and
founded a graduate certificate program in entrepreneurial journalism.
She is a member of the American Press Institute's research advisory
board and, as manager of the Traveling Curriculum Program of the
Committee of Concerned Journalists, has visited more than 50 newspapers nationwide to help them adapt to the new media landscape.

**In the digital age, in the social media age, what makes good
communication?**

Good writing is, in some ways, the same as it ever was, but maybe
with a special emphasis on tightness—you know, brevity, being concise,
being able to convey a lot of meaning in a relatively short time. Because
you have a lot of people who are constantly being bombarded by information and therefore don't have a whole lot of time. It's not that things
are vastly different in terms of having good grammar, being a good sto-
ryteller, being able to communicate clearly, being able to get meaning
across very quickly, and helping people understand why they should

care. Why they should pay attention to this in particular, in a very fragmented media landscape, is a particularly important aspect of writing for digital or writing for social.

Online—maybe even more so than in traditional media—you have to know your audience, and therefore be able to better understand what's really going to resonate with them. There've been some studies that seem to indicate that online, with headlines and such, being too clever, but in a way that doesn't convey "Here's what this story is about," can be problematic. People aren't getting some of the other contextual clues that tell them, "Here's what this is."

So old-time teaser headlines don't work online. They certainly work less well for search engines.

Definitely for search engines. If you're trying to get people to click on something and they have a million different options, sometimes the first thing they're looking for is just relevance: What is this story about? Is it going to mean something to me? I don't think that ever means you can never use the clever headline under any circumstances. Sometimes people get a little too black-and-white about these things, but I do think that is something to keep in mind.

Do you see differences in social media between the international students and the American students? Are people in some countries less advanced?

For the most part, I've found that most students from other countries are fairly similar in terms of their digital and social media use to American students. Obviously whenever you're trying to communicate in a language that's not your first, no matter what format it is, there are some challenges. In certain countries, certain social media tools are more or less popular. In Memphis, I had many German students, for example, and there people were using Facebook but no one was using Twitter—not in the media sphere, not in anything else. But that's even started to change in the last couple of years. Everyone has homogenized, to a point, especially people who work in this media business. But the students I have now, coming from Brazil and France—they're definitely used to using these tools in a somewhat similar way. And other countries, obviously, are using social media in terms of protest. So journalists are accustomed to the idea that news is sometimes breaking on these sites, and therefore they need to understand them.

What should international journalists work on, in terms of their English for social media?

It's, in many ways, almost more important to be really sure you've got your grammar down. For social media in particular, if you have less space, having something very clear and quickly readable is maybe even more important. . . . It becomes even more important to tighten up your skills as much as possible and really practice it and get good at doing it.

Any particular advice for international journalists, whether they're experts or just starting to use social media in their work?

I would just jump in and start using it. You don't really get good at anything until you practice it, and one of the advantages of today's world is that there are a million different ways to practice. Try different things—experiment with new media, start running your own blog in which you can share some of your reporting, use all of these different sites.

Some of my students participated in some online courses before coming to CUNY, and I think that really helped. They got some background—not just in writing. These are great resources. If you take advantage of them, you can really sharpen yourself up.

Is breaking into English-language social media any different from just writing in English?

Other than the fact that you're communicating in a different language, I don't think there are too many fundamental massive differences in terms of the way people need to conceptualize. The way you're practicing journalism is essentially still the same—the same set of core values. As long as you come from a press tradition in which you're not just pumping out propaganda all the time, you should be able to translate your journalism online in similar ways.

Just start engaging with other people you are finding online who clearly share similar interests with you. It happens kind of slowly, but when you do that, gradually you start to become more known, and you start to find all the people you maybe didn't even know about, doing work you're interested in. That can be cool.

CHAPTER 13

JOURNALISM AND PUBLIC RELATIONS

When I was an assigning editor and my college friend Gina had her own public relations business, we used to call each other Hack and Flack. "*Hack!*" she would hiss at me, using the word for a workmanlike writer with no real talent or originality, the kind widely rumored to end up in newsrooms. "*Flack!*" I would hiss back, using less-than-complimentary slang for publicist. We were teasing, of course. Being called a flack didn't stop Gina from pushing for me or any other journalist to cover her clients. Nor did her calling me a hack stop me from relying on press agents, including her, for tips, story ideas, contact information, interviews or, when legitimate, press tickets.

Journalists and publicists may sometimes see each other as parasites, but their relationship is symbiotic: one could not function nearly so effectively without the other. Journalists supply what publicists need if they're going to keep their jobs and clients: publicity. While journalists don't want to be seen as mouthpieces for publicists, they would find their jobs much harder without them.

Not everyone who picks up this book will be a journalist, but many will need to work with them. *Publicists*—sometimes called *press agents,* especially in fields like entertainment and sports—work in *public relations*, "a strategic communication process that builds mutually beneficial relationships between organizations and their publics," according to the official definition adopted in 2011–12 by the Public Relations Society of America. (Note that phrase *strategic communication*, the current buzzword for the field.) Their job is to draw public attention to their clients, preferably for positive reasons; otherwise, they may be in the unenviable position of doing *damage control*, making their clients look as good as possible in unfavorable or embarrassing situations, often of their own making. Those who handle the press for government agencies, universities, foundations, non-governmental organizations or other such institutions may hold a more dignified-sounding title like *press officer* or *press secretary* (generically, *spokesman* or *spokeswoman*), even though the work is often much the same. One difference between American and British practice: in the American press, attributions to publicists or press officers are normally made by name; in the British press they are not, on the reasoning that the spokesman is speaking for the body he represents, and therefore his name is irrelevant. *Marketing* professionals help their companies find strategies to market, or sell, their products—anything from cars to low-fat cookies to nonprofit theater subscriptions to a college education. Those in *advertising* directly devise media campaigns for that purpose.

If any of those job titles describes you, you need to understand how journalists think, especially those in English-language media, and what they need from you to give you what you need from them, when they can. Like all media work, this is a matter of building and maintaining relationships, which cultural differences may affect. Public relations professionals often begin their careers in journalism, though it is less common to move in the opposite direction. They may have switched in search of a better fit for their personalities or goals, a somewhat more stable lifestyle or more money. Since the 2008 recession and the downsizing of many newspaper staffs, P.R. has become an even more attractive option than before.

Journalism and public relations have many similarities and require many of the same skills. Good communication is the foundation of both. P.R. needs to be just as clean, clear and concise as journalism. Press releases, a basic tool of the trade, are written in the same format as inverted-pyramid news stories, so someone trained as a journalist already *knows the drill*. (That's an idiom meaning to understand the process.) Just as reporters *pitch* story ideas to editors (see pages 37 and 49), publicists pitch ideas for coverage to journalists. The biggest difference is mission. Publicists work on behalf of their clients; journalists work only for their publications, at least theoretically, in service to truth and the public.

In that mission, American journalists in particular see themselves as highly independent. Remember that American journalism is adversarial in nature (see page 24): journalists don't take orders from the government, advertisers or their sources. Nor are they publicists; it is not their job to help the government promote a policy or help a struggling concert promoter sell tickets. Publicists cannot dictate, but they can try to influence. How can journalists be sure of getting the truth from publicists? Journalists are skeptical by nature and further trained not to believe everything they hear or read on a press release. Good ones scrutinize what publicists say, and what they don't. Then they do the reporting.

There is, of course, a wide range of public relations professionals, from the president's press secretary to the publicity chairman for a community group. Whatever the level or field, publicists' relationship with the media is a constant negotiation. They should understand that journalists don't like to look, or feel, as if they are working for the publicists. Press releases are meant to be a starting point for news stories, not printed *verbatim* (as written, word for word). Editors don't like to hear that a story idea came from a press agent; instead, they prefer to think of a press agent's good idea as the kernel of a story that is all their own.

The best advice I can give any publicist—the point I cannot stress enough—is to think things through from the publication's point of view. Think of its needs, not your own or your client's. Here are some basic suggestions for working effectively with English-language media.

KNOW THE PUBLICATION

When I was assigning for *The New York Times*'s Weekend section— which covered arts, culture and spare-time activities—it annoyed me when publicists would call pitching their enormously talented clients who designed spectacular fashion or jewelry. It was obvious those publicists had simply found my name, title and phone number in a directory and probably never read the section. Any publicist who had done the homework should have known to call the Style department, which covered those fields, along with society, parties, engagements and weddings, and lifestyle trends.

Before making a pitch, a publicist needs to be sure he's pitching to the right medium, the right department, and the right editor, reporter or producer. If you're promoting a client in the international tour business, contact the travel section, not the foreign news desk, which is sure to be overworked just covering the news. If you're pitching a cutting-edge gallery show for review, pitch to the critic who covers contemporary art, not the expert in classical Tibetan religious art. Pitching to the wrong place or person will not only waste your time but also make you look bad to the journalist, who may be less receptive to your next pitch when he *is* the right person.

KNOW THE JOURNALIST'S JOB

As arts editor for *The Times* Sunday New Jersey section, I was once asked to speak at a gathering of publicists from local arts organizations. "I am now going to give you the single most important piece of advice you need to work with me," I announced. "Ready?" Pens hovered over notebooks. "Don't ever call me on a Thursday." Laughter followed, but I was entirely serious. Why? Because Thursday was production day, when all the careful planning, writing and editing of the past week exploded into a frantic, labor-intensive, detail-oriented race to *close* (finish) the section by deadline. The last thing I needed on Thursday was phone calls from publicists seeking future coverage when I could think no further than 6 p.m. Any distraction was likely to prejudice me against the publicist in the future. The same was true when I moved on to the Friday Weekend section, which also closed on Thursdays. But the Sunday Arts & Leisure section, a midweek preprint for what was then a giant Sunday paper, went to press in the early-morning hours of Wednesday, making Tuesday the no-call day. Similarly, e-mail pitches, now far more widely used than faxes or hard copy, that land on deadline day are likely to be ignored as new ones pile up on top of them.

It's crucial for publicists to understand not only the journalist's deadlines, but also who in a department does what and, most important, who makes the decisions. They also need to understand *lead times* (see page 123), which may be a matter of hours on a daily newspaper, a TV news program or a website, but months on as glossy magazine with its time-consuming production processes. Pitch to an editor at the beginning of the production cycle—early in the day for a morning newspaper, which closes in the evening; the day after production day for a weekly section or a monthly magazine. On a day when major news is breaking, even if it seems to have nothing to do with the department in question, it's better not to pitch at all, since editors there may face early deadlines to give the news desks more breathing room.

Yes, it's work getting to know journalists and their work lives, their needs and their schedules, especially if you may need to pitch to many of them. But it's a good investment of time and energy, and not making that investment will eventually cost you.

KNOW THAT NEWS IS SEASONAL

What's the toughest day of the year to fill a New York arts section? The Tuesday after Labor Day, America's unofficial end of summer in early September. First, in summer the arts scene shifts from the city to festivals and regional theaters around the country; Broadway openings are few and far between, the blockbuster movies opened in June and the gallery scene all but shuts down. Second, everybody who is anybody in New York publishing takes all of August off, leaving a skeleton crew to publish whatever stories it can get its hands on. By Labor Day, all the copy that has been sitting in the computer for months, even years, has been used, leaving the editors scrambling. Second toughest edition: Jan. 2, for similar reasons after the Christmas holidays.

This is just one example of how seasonal news can be, in New York or anywhere. Good publicists will know the seasons and use them to their advantage. Pitching a feature on the relaunch of a long-dormant arts organization? Aim for late summer, when editors will thank you for it. A behind-the-scenes look at some of the quirks in the way Congress operates? Time it to a recess period, not when Congress is debating a finance bill whose failure to pass could shut down the government.

But don't wait for a slow season if you have a strong *news peg* (see page 36). It makes sense to wait for late summer if that resurging arts group is the Art Deco Society, for example, and the Rainbow Room, a New York Deco landmark, is reopening in early fall. But if you represent a struggling charter school that has won International Baccalaureate accreditation in June, pitch immediately—not just before the school year opens, when you'll be competing with dozens of other education stories for coverage.

KNOW THE BASIC TOOLS

Publicists use all kinds of tools to promote their clients' interests—more every day with the rise of social media (which makes digital natives increasingly attractive associates to veterans who haven't mastered Facebook, Twitter and Instagram). Still, the publicist's two most important tools remain the *press release* and the *press kit*. (In this case, *press* means all media, not just print. Instead of *press release*, some publicists now use terms like *news release* or *media alert*.) Whatever you call them, both releases and kits should be posted on the "news" or "media" page of any website associated with your client to make them available anytime a journalist might need them, even after hours.

A release is, basically, a news story written on behalf of the client whose work you are promoting, and therefore follows the same two principles of the classic news story: the *inverted pyramid* and *the 5W's*. (See Chapter 3.) Remember that the inverted pyramid is based on the assumption that a reader may not make it all the way through the story. A journalist who even looks at your release—and that journalist is likely to receive dozens in a day, hundreds in a week—is unlikely to read past the first paragraph, or maybe past the headline. So the most important information, the information that will make the journalist think your pitch might be worth a story, has to be right there at the top. So does the other information crucial to the release: the contact information. Who can schedule an interview? Where are press photos available online? Is advance registration required? All that information needs to be prominent on the first page of any release.

Above all, be very, very sure that all information on any release, especially name spellings, is 100 percent correct. Reporters will consult releases for basic facts as they write; a good copy desk will use them in the editing to fact-check spellings, dates, addresses, plotlines, etc. Make sure the release contains no error you can catch in advance, however small, that would require a correction if published. Editors hate having to run corrections, and sloppy releases will only prejudice them against you in the future.

More complete, and sometimes highly elaborate, is the *press kit,* a collection of reference materials for the press. Today it is just as likely to be the "Press" or "Media" button at the top of a web page as a folder handed out at an event, but it is useful to have both ready. A press kit usually contains both timely material, often with a news peg, and background information giving a more rounded picture of the client.

Components of a relatively simple press kit I devised as a volunteer project for that struggling charter school included:

- A press release announcing the news, the achievement of International Baccalaureate status.
- A 5W's fact sheet on the school.
- Its mission statement.
- Mini-profiles of teachers, students and others associated with the school.
- A calendar of events.
- Press clips on the school for the hard-copy press kit; links for the website.

- A three-minute video introducing the school, to be posted online or put on DVD for the press kit.
- Still photos that could be downloaded from the website.
- A simple double-sided card with basic information on the school.

Will every journalist covering the school use every piece of this information? Of course not. But for those who need it, it should be readily at hand.

At the other end of the spectrum—the most beautiful media kit I have ever seen—is the one produced by the Australian Ballet for its 50th-anniversary season in 2012. That season, which included the company's first tour to New York in 13 years, was very important to the company and occasioned a major push for publicity. This 24-page, full-color kit—so elaborate it required a table of contents—included:

- Excerpts from press reviews around the world.
- A quotable statement from the artistic director, David McAllister.
- Photos of dancers, in costume and in performance.
- Full-page descriptions of the works to be performed on the tour.
- Biographical information on the company's leadership, choreographers and principal artists, along with photos of the rest of the dancers.
- A world map pinpointing cities on five continents where the company had appeared for quick visual reference.
- "Getting to New York," a backstage look at the tour logistics.
- A brief history of the company.
- A full page of contact information, from publicists in Australia and New York to the company's official blog, Facebook page and Twitter feed.

Sound impressive? It was meant to be. The combination of text, visuals and readily available facts tells the company's story. Rarely does a publicist have the occasion or the budget to produce a kit like this one, but let it serve as an inspiration of what can be done. (The company's somewhat less elaborate 2016 media kit is at http://0b17240a51f735b169c4-a154deafd7909fc8152d3f3c001ec9cf.r67 .cf1.rackcdn.com/TAB_Media_Kit_Single_Pages_OCT13.pdf)

One unfortunate result of media downsizing in recent years has been the rise of what I call "the warm body school of journalism," as in "We need someone to cover (insert name of beat). How about you?" More and more, reporters are expected to report and editors to supervise coverage on fields outside their education, expertise or comfort zones, simply because there is no one else to do it. (On the other hand, the content producers at narrowly focused websites may know more about the field than you do.) So public relations professionals may find themselves knowing far more about their fields than the journalists covering them, especially when representing clients in homelands that have received little or sporadic press coverage. If so, seize the opportunity to educate the English-speaking world by making full use of those basic tools: the press release, the press kit and, not least, yourself as a contact point. Present yourself as a resource; never become a pest. It is a fine line, but one that needs to be consciously observed.

While cordial, relationships between journalists and publicists should never completely lose that adversarial edge. Journalists try not to become too chummy with publicists, which can lead to *conflicts of interest* (see page 24). (One longtime editor, now retired, said she steered clear of forming friendships with freelance writers for similar reasons until she was no longer commissioning them.) Publicists shouldn't seek to be journalists' friends, but rather facilitators who provide information and access. The most effective publicist is one who makes the journalist's job easy.

CHAPTER 14

ON YOUR OWN

Bad news: the work of learning a foreign language and improving your proficiency never ends. "Use it or lose it," as we say in English, and while that expression applies to many skills, it's especially true of languages. Many people study foreign languages in school, only to discover years later that they can't successfully buy shoes in Paris or make a simple phone call in Japanese. Without practice and advancement, our language skills lie dormant in our brains, or disappear altogether. Journalists need to *hit the ground running*. (That's an idiom meaning to start producing immediately.) So if you dream of being a correspondent in New York or London, don't wait until you're posted there to work on your English.

Maybe your school days are over and you have few resources—or think you do. If you're lucky, you may find classes, cultural centers, conversation groups, private teachers or other native English-speakers who can help. Foreign correspondents posted to your country are almost sure to be overworked (and untrained as teachers), but they are also eager to meet locals, especially journalists. They make excellent contacts who can introduce you to their publications, possibly leading to work as a *stringer* (see page 42), so try to make friends without being a pest. If you have access to *any* native speaker, not necessarily an English teacher or journalist, ask for feedback.

But you may live in a country or area where native English-speakers, never mind teachers, are *few and far between*. (That's an idiom meaning you don't meet them very often.) You may even live in a place where it would be socially suspicious, or politically dangerous, to make friends with English-speakers. Not to worry; there are plenty of other ways to improve your English if you're willing to work at it. Here are some resources and techniques you can pursue on your own.

BOOKS

"Do you know a good book on writing?" students ask every now and then. Writers love books about writing; we all have shelves of them. Here's some of what's on mine:

Three dictionaries. One is the *Longman Dictionary of American English* (Pearson, 4th edition, 2008), an intermediate-level learner's dictionary. You may start out using one that translates your native language to English, and vice versa, which is fine—up to a point. As you advance, switch to an all-English learner's dictionary like *Longman's* and eventually to a standard dictionary like *Merriam-Webster* so that you're not just translating words, but also seeing the definitions (and synonyms—new vocabulary words!) in English. Many dictionaries now come with CD-ROMs, are available as e-books or have free, word-by-word online versions—especially useful for their audio that lets you hear how unfamiliar words are pronounced.

A style guide. One of a journalist's most important tools is her publication's style guide, which establishes its rules on spelling, usage, punctuation and typography. A stylebook tells you things like how to render dates; which states or months may be abbreviated and which may not; whether to use courtesy titles like Mr. and Ms., etc. Each publication adopts a style for many reasons, among them consistency, conciseness and the all-important clarity.

The stylebook can teach you a lot about the English language. Confused about possessives? The stylebook has a long list addressing various cases. Unsure if you're using terms like *bipolar* or *schizophrenic* correctly? See the entry on mental illness. Wondering whether punctuation marks go inside or outside quotation marks? It's in the stylebook.

You don't have to memorize your stylebook (though much of it will seep into your brain with repeated use); it's a reference. And don't take the *-book* part too literally. An online version is actually preferable because it's constantly being updated and, in this digital age, it's always at your fingertips on laptop or mobile. As a subscriber, you'll get the updates by e-mail. In 2012, for example, AP compiled and circulated a very helpful primer of U.S. election terminology.

There are many stylebooks—some for journalists, like *The Associated Press Stylebook*, which the CUNY Journalism School uses (as do most small and medium-size newspapers in the United States); some for academics and book writers, like the *Chicago Manual of Style*; some for specialized fields, like the *APA Publication Manual* in psychology or the *CSE Manual* for scientists. In my own career, I've learned and used the *AP Stylebook*, *The Boston Globe Stylebook* (which I helped rewrite, as chairman of the F through O committee), and two editions of *The New York Times* stylebook. Why have I capped some of those titles and not others, and put none of them in quotation marks? Ask the stylebook.

And note that nasty word "rules." Too many reporters dislike rules and so never bother to learn the stylebook; "the copy desk will fix it," they sniff. That attitude is shortsighted. Any copy desk exists to make writers look good, and you want the people on it to be your friends. If copy editors spend too much of their time fixing your style, they'll have less time—and patience—to read for accuracy and clarity. If your copy shows you know and care about style, they'll love you.

The Elements of Style, by William Strunk Jr. and E.B. White. (Longman, 4th edition, 1999). This classic, also on my e-reader, was first published in 1920 and remains the most concise writing guide in the American canon. White (the revered *New Yorker* writer, as well as author of the children's books *Charlotte's Web* and *Stuart Little*) rediscovered his onetime professor's style guide in 1957 and was later commissioned to update it. Now almost universally known as "Strunk & White," it contains in a mere 57 pages eight "elementary rules of usage," ten "elementary principles of composition," and lists of words commonly misused and misspelled. If you have limited experience writing in English, this book is an ideal starting point.

Oxford Idioms Dictionary for Learners of English

(Oxford, 2006). As noted in Chapter 9, English-speakers are addicted to and depend on idioms. This 470-page book, organized alphabetically by keywords, supplies thousands of them, along with study pages on origins, structure and language, as well as exercises. An invaluable guide to decoding the way people actually use English.

Word Histories and Mysteries: From Abracadabra to Zeus

(Houghton Mifflin, 2004). Speaking of origins: for those who (like me) enjoy knowing where words come from, the editors of the American Heritage Dictionaries have collected hundreds. Each word has its own short chapter covering its origins, evolution and related idioms. *Hamburger*, for example, comes from *Hamburg steak*, a term that came to America with German immigrants. The adjective *hamburger* evolved into a noun and was eventually shortened to the now-universal *burger*. Each entry is not only enlightening but fun to read.

Eats, Shoots and Leaves: *The Zero Tolerance Approach to Punctuation,* by Lynn Truss (Gotham Books, 2006). The subtitle pretty much says it all. If you're bored or confused by your style guide's entries on punctuation, Truss conveys many of the same points with grace and humor.

Sister Bernadette's Barking Dog: *The Quirky History and Lost Art of Diagramming Sentences,* by Kitty Burns Florey (Melville House, 2007). American schoolchildren used to be driven nearly mad by

the seemingly endless diagramming of sentences in their English classes. As much as they may have hated the exercise, diagramming taught them structure visually by breaking down sentences into subjects, predicates, prepositional phrases and dependent clauses on frameworks that ran down the page like long division (another obsolete skill; we have calculators now). Florey's book is part homage, part refresher course in a technique that still works.

A Writer's Coach, by Jack Hart (Pantheon, 2006). If I had to choose a single, comprehensive book that covered everything CUNY J-school students need to know, it would be this one. A former managing editor and writing coach at *The Oregonian*, Hart edited two Pulitzer Prize winners and two other finalists, so he knows what he's talking about. The 12 chapters cover grand themes, from "Method" to "Mastery," but they're filled with very specific pieces of advice. "Humanity" may be an abstraction, but Hart teaches writers how to inject the human element into their stories through anecdotes and quotations. In "Clarity" he devotes almost three pages to avoiding danglers (see page 200). Hart is especially conscious of the sins journalists commit. In "Voice," he lampoons the pompous ways we sometimes structure sentences. ("The administration is known to believe that the time is fast approaching when a decision about a military option must be considered.") He includes a glossary of journalese and a "Cliché Watch" that stretches to seven pages. I would dispute very little in this book—in fact, only one sentence, in the acknowledgments: "Nobody's more obnoxious than somebody who corrects your English." Nonsense.

Most of these books are available cheaper and faster online or as e-books.

ONLINE RESOURCES

When Yuxin Gao from China was preparing to enroll at CUNY, she was concerned about her listening and speaking skills, since she'd have to do a lot of interviewing in New York. I suggested that she find a native-speaker teacher in Beijing for the summer and helped her locate one through a former colleague. "How did it go?" I asked after their first meeting. Not well: he turned out to have a very British accent, which is not what she needed. For her purposes, a Chinese teacher would have been better than nothing; a British native speaker would have been even better; but an American accent was best. So, instead of private lessons in Beijing, she met with me weekly on Skype. (I also suggested she try to meet some native speakers through the China Culture Center in Beijing, which caters to expatriates and offers many programs in English.)

Gao is far from the first student to polish her English online. More and more English teachers are experimenting with teaching online; all you need is a reliable Internet connection (by no means guaranteed in many parts of the world), an account on a conferencing website like Skype or Google Hangout, and an easy way to make international payments, like Paypal. In addition, many websites offer English lessons. Some are free like Learn English Online (http://www.learn-english-online.org) and LiveMocha (http://livemocha.com/pages/languages/learn-english); others are for-profit companies like Bertelsmann's Learnship (https://www.learnship.com). The widely advertised Rosetta Stone (rosettastone.com)—available online, on CD-ROM or by download—is not cheap, but it offers both American and British options. It also has the advantage of comparing your speech to a composite of native speakers', providing instant evaluation of pronunciation and accent. If you're interested in following a full, structured course in English, start Googling and choose the program that seems right for you.

In addition, hundreds of websites on ESL (English as a second language) or EFL (English as a foreign language) offer instruction, exercises and interactive quizzes—all free. Among the ones I consult most often are Dave's ESL Café (http://www.eslcafe.com) and Activities for ESL Students (http://a4esl.org). For help with your own problem areas, simply search for keywords. If you're having trouble with, say, prepositions, you can Google *ESL prepositions*; to narrow the search, add search terms like *exercises* or *quiz*. Interactive quizzes are especially useful because they provide instant feedback. One of my favorites is a4esl's 67-question quiz on phrasal verbs (http://a4esl. org/q/j/ck/fb-phrasalverbs.html); I encourage students to do it as fast as they can to see what they know without having to think, then repeat the questions they missed until they score 100 percent. You can set similar goals for yourself on other quizzes.

The Internet also supplies a wealth of listening comprehension exercises in the form of YouTube and podcasts, covering almost any subject; they introduce listeners to a wide range of American voices and accents. Among the most popular are "This American Life," from Chicago Public Media (thisamericanlife.org) and several from National Public Radio, including "Fresh Air," "StoryCorps" and "How to Do Everything." Barbara Marcolini, CUNY class of 2016, recommends "Serial," "Radiolab" and "Invisibilia"; she calls them "interesting stories, great narrative and different from everything we have in Brazil." Many podcasts are available free and by subscription directly from NPR (http://www.npr.org/podcasts) or on iTunes. When studying via podcast, listen not only for overall comprehension of content, but also for pronunciation, vocabulary, idiom and rhythm.

Finally, it's the rare (and foolish) English-language newspaper or news service these days that doesn't have a well-developed website. So read international publications or the English-language sites of your local ones. Read for vocabulary, story structure, style and tone as well as for content. The most advanced websites supplement their articles with video, audio and interactive features, providing a complete package that can help refine your reading and listening comprehension, as well as show you how news is reported and presented in English-speaking cultures. In addition, some organizations like the British Council present short English lessons in advertisements.

MOBILES, TABLETS AND RECORDERS

Those addictive handheld devices—which you may already use as reporting tools (see Chapter 5)—offer access not only to Internet resources but also to a growing number of English-teaching apps. At least two students in CUNY's entrepreneurial journalism program—one from Japan, one from Colombia—have worked to develop apps using newspaper articles as language-teaching tools, so *stay tuned*. (That's an idiom from American televison meaning to keep watching or paying attention.) As with web-based instruction, shop around for the apps that work best for you, and take advantage of any free trials. Like online dictionaries, dictionary apps offer audio for pronunciation.

On a digital voice recorder, you can listen to yourself reading aloud from your own writing or other texts to get a feel for how you sound in English—your pronunciation, your rhythm, your intonations. That will indicate what you still need to work on. Or record yourself speaking a passage from a movie, TV show or podcast; then compare it to the original. If you're working with a native English-speaker, play the recording and ask for feedback. Or ask your teacher to record words and sounds you find difficult—for example, commonly mispronounced words like *tired* and *iron*—so you can practice, record yourself and compare. The possibilities are limited only by your imagination.

FILMS AND TELEVISION

Good news for journalists whose brains are tired after a long day's work: it's OK to watch TV! Movies, too. Watching English-language media on DVDs, streaming services like Netflix and Hulu, or old-fashioned broadcast TV is an excellent way to relax while still improving your English.

Most people watch strictly for entertainment, but you can learn from even the silliest movies if you watch strategically. Movies test listening comprehension and expose non-native speakers to different accents, new vocabulary, idioms and slang. The rewind button makes it possible to go back and listen again to passages you didn't understand the first time, over and over if necessary. Subtitles on DVDs or streaming spell out the words you're hearing, improving your reading comprehension in the process. (Going out to the cinema gives you less control over your learning process. Movies may be dubbed into your language; the only subtitles will be in the local language; and there is no rewind button.)

Match subtitles to your level and comfort in English. Just starting out? Watch the film in English with subtitles in your native language to understand the content and see how accurately you hear. Feeling a little braver? Switch to the English subtitles, again to test your listening but also to see how what you hear is written (as I do when I go to the movies in countries where I know just a little of the language). Feeling really brave? Skip the subtitles entirely, or turn them on only to check what you are hearing if you are unsure or simply don't understand. (I frequently turn on the subtitles when watching TV with accents I find difficult—for example, certain British regional or class accents that are all but impenetrable to Americans. As a woman tells her TV-watching husband in a *New Yorker* cartoon by Zachary Kanin: "At some point, there's only so high you can raise the volume before you admit you're never gonna understand what British detectives are saying." (http://www .condenaststore.com/-sp/At-some-point-there-s-only-so-high-you-can-raise-the-volume-before-you-a-New-Yorker-Cartoon-Prints_ i12908022_.htm)

Movies and TV have one other major advantage: what you hear is the way people really talk. Textbook English is very different from street English, and good screenwriters make their characters sound realistic and appropriate to their environments. Watching the finished product will give you a feel for the crucial rhythms, the accents and the ways people express themselves in everyday English.

Movies and television shows set in the media world will expose you to professional English—and situations. Historically (though with notable exceptions) Western films have portrayed journalists as adventurous, idealistic truth-seekers, as we like to think of ourselves. Here is a suggested viewing list that will introduce images of media figures in American, British and Australian film, and how they have evolved through the 20th century and into the 21st. (Films are listed roughly in chronological order of their plot settings, not necessarily their release dates.) While storytelling conventions like workplace romances often cloud the professional picture, these films will give you an idea of what Western journalists do, should do and, often, shouldn't.

Citizen Kane (1941). Orson Welles's masterpiece, considered by many film scholars to be the greatest film ever made. The rise and fall of an early-20th-century newspaper mogul, loosely based on the American publisher William Randolph Hearst. Required viewing. For background: **Hearst vs. Pulitzer,** an episode of National Geographic's American Genius series (2015).

Newsies (1992). A Disney musical based on the newsboys' strike during the 1899 newspaper wars in New York, chronicled in **Hearst vs. Pulitzer**. Watch it with the kids.

The Front Page (1931, 1973). Ben Hecht and Charles McArthur's classic 1920s stage comedy about a crusty managing editor's desperate attempts to keep his star reporter from defecting to a respectable job while a major news story is breaking. In the 1940 adaptation **His Girl Friday**, the reporter is the editor's ex-wife.

Woman of the Year (1942). A romantic comedy and cautionary tale, all in one. A sportswriter and a foreign affairs columnist fall in love, only to learn how difficult a two-career relationship can be when both careers are in journalism.

Newsfront (1978). A newsreel team in post–World War II Australia clings to its medium as it confronts the beginning of the television era.

Deadline USA (1952). A managing editor crusades against organized crime just as his family-owned newspaper is in danger of being sold and closed. With the corporatization of news rampant today, this film is as fresh as it was 60-plus years ago.

Good Night, and Good Luck (2010). A fictionalized portrait of CBS News, its star reporter Edward R. Murrow and its journalistic principles during the McCarthy era of anti-communist witchhunts in the early 1950s.

The Hour (2011–2012). A British miniseries reminiscent of "Broadcast News" (see below), but set in a London TV newsroom in the 1950s. The romance is there, but a comedy it's not.

All the President's Men (1976). How two young *Washington Post* reporters' investigation of a "third-rate burglary" led them to the White House and brought down the presidency of Richard M. Nixon. A case study in investigative reporting, adapted from Carl Bernstein and Robert Woodward's own memoir.

Network (1976). A surrealistic portrait of a national TV network that exploits a news anchorman's breakdown for ratings. Like **Deadline USA**, it remains as fresh as the day it was released.

Lou Grant (1977-1982). When *The Mary Tyler Moore Show*, a hit 1970s sitcom set at a Minneapolis TV station, came to an end, Mary's crusty boss, Lou Grant (Ed Asner), found new life as city editor of a daily newspaper in Los Angeles. In an unusual transition from comedy to drama, this spinoff series thoughtfully examined real social and journalistic issues.

Broadcast News (1987). A romantic comedy about a driven TV news producer, the empty-headed anchorman she loves and the less photogenic news writer who loves her. A product of its time, right down to the videocassettes and shoulder pads on women, but it gives a sense of the people and processes shaping a network newscast.

Absence of Malice (1981). A Miami reporter is tricked into publishing false information that damages a businessman's reputation and life, leading to an examination of journalists' sometimes conflicting responsibilities.

The Killing Fields (1984). The true-life story of a *New York Times* reporter, Sydney Schanberg, and his efforts to rescue his Cambodian colleague, Dith Pran, left behind during the brutal Pol Pot regime in the 1970s. (Spoiler alert: Dith Pran survived and went on to a long and happy career as a *Times* photographer in New York.)

The Paper (1994). A day in the life of a New York City tabloid, specifically an editor considering a leap to the most prestigious paper in town. An exhausting depiction of a print newsroom of its time. Someone even yells, "Stop the presses!"

Spotlight (2015). The Oscar-winning account of how the *Boston Globe* Spotlight Team pursued its investigation of sexual abuse by Roman Catholic clergy, leading to a cardinal's downfall and repercussions in the church worldwide.

Whiskey Tango Foxtrot (2016). Tina Fey puts a fish-out-of-water spin on Kim Barker's book *The Taliban Shuffle,* a memoir of her days reporting from Afghanistan in the early 2000s. Fey's character leaves her comfort zone as a cable news producer to test herself as a reporter embedded within a U.S. military unit.

Shattered Glass (2003). An ambitious young magazine reporter finds the easiest way to success is to fabricate his stories. Based on a true story, as is **A Fragile Trust: Plagiarism, Power and Jayson Blair at *The New York Times*** (2013), an Independent Lens documentary on the similar 2003 case that brought down two top editors and began a round of soul-searching in a newsroom usually considered above reproach.

Truth (2015). A case study of the CBS News report on George W. Bush's military service whose weakness in sourcing toppled Dan Rather (Robert Redford) from the anchor desk in 2005.

The Devil Wears Prada (2006). A thinly disguised look at the inner workings of America's top fashion magazine, *Vogue,* as seen through the eyes of an entry-level assistant. For a documentary look at the real-life Vogue: ***The September Issue*** (2009).

State of Play (2009). A veteran print reporter bumps up against new media as he competes with a blogger in investigating the death of a Congressional aide. This American feature film was adapted from the 2003 British miniseries of the same name; both are worth watching.

The Social Network (2010). The (fictionalized) story of Facebook, from its origins in a Harvard University dormitory to worldwide domination.

Page One (2011). A documentary about the inner workings of *The New York Times*, focusing on David Carr, the revered media writer who collapsed in the newsroom and died in 2015. A lighter look inside *The Times*: **Bill Cunningham New York** (2010), on the paper's roving fashion photographer.

The Newsroom (2012–2014). Life and love in the struggling fourth-place 21st-century network. Like **The Hour**, Aaron Sorkin's three-season series tackles serious issues, but there are plenty of romantic distractions in this workplace comedy/drama.

The Interview (2014). Warning: not for all cultures. A lightweight TV talk show host and his producer try to reinvent themselves as serious journalists when Kim Jong-un, Supreme Leader of North Korea, grants them an interview. But then the CIA asks them to assassinate Kim. Conceived as a light comedy, this film provoked an international firestorm—and that's the polite word—after threats from Kim. It was withdrawn from theatrical release and caused its Hollywood studio head to lose her job.

That is everything I know about the subject of American English for the media—until the next CUNY journalism student comes in for coaching. He or she will bring up a new point I've yet to consider, as has happened any number of times during the writing of this book. Then there'll be a new addition—maybe even, someday, a new edition.

For now, as Walter Cronkite of CBS News would say: And that's the way it is.

As his colleague Edward R. Murrow would say: Good night, and good luck.

And as generations of journalists—up to and including Ken Aragaki, CUNY class of 2015—would say:

—30—

ACKNOWLEDGMENTS

This book would not exist without any and all of the international students at the CUNY Graduate School of Journalism, classes of 2012 to 2016. Many are represented, some by name, with permission. (If you're one of those who said, "OK, but no names!" bask in your anonymity.) Special thanks to the regulars who rarely missed a week of coaching and frequently contributed to the English for Journalists blog, among them Qingqing Chen, Yuxin Gao, Sophie Gauthier, Camilo Gomez, Miyuki Inoue, Michiko Kuriyama, Natalia V. Osipova, Cariba Party, Emilie Pons, Elena Popina and Maria Sanchez Diez.

Thanks to the J-school leadership, who let me invent the job of ESL coach, left me alone to do it, always helps it run smoothly and seems open to anything; to Deb Stead, whose initial phone call ("Can you come down? We need someone like you!") woke me from a nap and changed my direction entirely; to Steve Dougherty and others who sat around a conference table circa 2013 and said, "You should write a book for us." (My response: "Yeah, right.") One of them was Tim Harper, the editor of the CUNY Journalism Press; thanks to Tim for teaching me Book Publishing 101, and to his student publishing associates, Victoria Edwards and Tola Brennan, for their work on getting the book into print.

Thanks to Courtney Andujar for the cover design, and to the designers, production staff, and marketing and distribution people from

OR Books who provide the backshop support for CUNY Journalism Press, including John Oakes, Colin Robinson, Emily Freyer, Emma Ingrisani, Jen Overstreet, Justin Humphries and Natascha Uhlmann.

Special thanks to Amanda Bartlett for meticulous proofreading.

Thanks again to all the professors and coaches who sat for interviews: Dean Sarah Bartlett, Carrie Brown, Greg David, Tim Harper, Lonnie Isabel, Margot Mifflin, Deb Stead, Wayne Svoboda and Judy Watson.

To Jane Bornemeier and Ellen Walterscheid, for doing my job while I spent a semester teaching in China and then giving it back when I returned.

To Hana Cervinkova and especially Ula Kłobuszewka at the University of Lower Silesia in Wroclaw, Poland, my academic home away from home for nearly a decade now. They gave me the freedom to experiment with an English for the Media course in 2013 and let me do it again as a Fulbright senior specialist in 2016.

To all my private students in New York, Poland and China, especially the very patient Paulina Sielska, Justyna Mokrzecka and Kamila Stepnik.

To Janice Florey, educator extraordinaire, my tireless cheerleader since the first day of sixth grade and first reader of most of this book; Philip Radcliffe, without whom there very likely would have been no "international" in my career or my life; and Leslie Kandell, who has done her best to distract me for 21 years and counting, and who lent her home (where these words were written) as emergency lodging when mine was occupied by a CUNY journalism student. (Thank you, Roberto Capocelli.)

Finally, to Caitlin Morgan and everyone in the New School's English language teaching program, where my own midlife career transition began. If any readers are thinking about teaching English to speakers of other languages and attending an ELT open house at the New School, be careful. It can change your life.

Diane Nottle
New York City, May 2016

INDEX

editors, value of   62, 63
elegant variations   205
elision   111, 113
Elle   171
embed   276
emphasis   207, 261, 262
engagement editor   276
English language, differing with other languages   70, 72
English language, origin of   14
English originals vs. translations   47, 61
English, British vs. American   15, 158, 252, 265
English, teaching   16
English, thinking in   49
Entertainment Weekly   171
entrepreneurial journalism   13, 23, 26
er, sounds   146
estimate / expect / predict   254
euphemisms   15
evening plans   177
every day / everyday   255
exclamation   140, 141
eyebrow   35

Facebook   280
fall on (ones's) sword   179
false names   104
features   27, 60
feed   276
few and far between   300
fewer / less   255
file   34
films and television   306-311
First Amendment, American Constitution   23

Flack   289
flowery   43
flush left / ragged right   35
follow-up questions   76-79
Fortune   43
forum   277
fragments   206
Freedom of expression   23

garbled grammar   17
gender and pronouns   208
gerunds and infinitives   210-212
get   256
get the picture   180
GIF   277
go with the flow   77
gonna   112
good writing / communication   43, 65, 81, 105, 127, 171, 187, 243, 285
graf   34
grammar   22, 45, 62, 70, 89, 110, 173, 195, 225, 227, 245, 287
grammar points, troublesome, solving   191
grammatical errors   45, 47, 191
graphics   277

H & J   35
h, sounds   147
Hack   289
handheld devices   305, 306
hard news   31, 33
Harper, Tim   81
hashtag   277
Headlines, writing   11
herding cats   180
historic / historical   256

trilingual 164
tu and *du* combination   150
turn in   179
TV, as learning tool, 132, 133
Twitter / tweet / retweet   270, 280, 282, 283
twls   32
typo   39

uh, weak vowel sound   136
unique user / visitor   283
URL   278
usage   15, 38, 62, 89, 90, 110, 117, 142, 300
used to, pronounciation with different meanings   150

Vanity Fair   73
verb   20
verb morphing   160
verb suffixes   167
verb tenses   218
vertical   283
video   283
video reporting, ethical challenges in   127
visual imagery   129
vocabulary, new   271
vocabulary-building   154, 160, 177
vocal cords   135
voice pitch   70, 79, 136-138, 140

voice—active and passive   192, 244
voiced and unvoiced sounds   135, 149
voiceover   283
vowels   134, 135
walk-up   172
wanna   112, 116
warts and all   92
watchdog   24
Watson, Judith   65
wearing too many hats   176
wearing two hats   153
web-scraping   274, 283
who and whom   238-240
who's / whose   268
widget   284
word choice   158, 161
word cloud   284
word families, building   168
wordiness   240
Wordpress   280
words, value of   154-156
writing ways, cultural differences   48
writing,   58
writing, long-form   81, 82
writing—differences in, print vs. broadcast vs. online   128

Zenger, John Peter   24